ART EDUCATION 11–18

2nd Edition

Related titles

Teaching Art and Design – Roy Prentice (ed.)

Getting the Buggers to Draw – Barbara Ward

Art Education 11–18
Meaning, Purpose and Direction

2nd Edition

Edited by
Richard Hickman

continuum

LEEDS TRINITY UNIVERSITY
SM

Continuum International Publishing Group

The Tower Building   80 Maiden Lane
11 York Road   Suite 704
London   New York
SE1 7NX   NY 10038

First published 2000
This edition published 2004. Reprinted 2005, 2006, 2008 (twice), 2009, 2011

British Library Cataloguing-in-Publication Data
A catalogue record for this book is available from the British Library.

ISBN 978-0-8264-7200-7 (hardback) 978-0-8264-7201-4 (paperback)

Typeset by YHT Ltd, London

Contents

Acknowledgements

I am indebted to all of the contributors, who have readily given of their time and expertise to share their thoughts on art education with other professionals, and to the teachers and students who have given so much inspiration.

Richard Hickman
Cambridge, August 2003

Contributors

Nicholas Addison teaches on the PGCE and MA courses at the University of London Institute of Education. He taught for sixteen years at secondary and sixth-form level prior to his higher education work. His educational research centres on the integration of critical and contextual studies within studio-based learning. He is Chair of the Association of Art Historians Schools Group.

Andy Ash is co-director of the PGCE course at the University of London Institute of Education. He also contributes to the training of graduate art teachers at the University of Reading and at Homerton College, Cambridge. His previous teaching experience includes secondary and further education. He has a particular interest in sculpture and in the use of ICT, and has collaborated on a research project with the Tate Gallery, London.

Lesley Burgess is course leader for the PGCE course at the University of London Institute of Education and Co-Director of the Artists in Schools training programme. Before moving to the Institute in 1990 she taught for fifteen years in London comprehensive schools. She is a former chair of the Teacher Education Board for the National Society for Education in Art & Design (NSEAD). Her research focuses on contemporary art and artists in education.

Paul Duncum is Associate Professor of Art Education, School of Art and Design, University of Illinois at Urbana-Champaign. He was previously a lecturer in Visual Art Curriculum at the University of Tasmania, Australia. He has published regularly in international journals and has made a significant contribution to the development of Visual Culture Art Education. He co-edited (with Ted Bracey) a series of essays entitled *On Knowing – Art and Visual Culture*.

Colin Grigg was the Visual Arts Education Officer at the Art Council of Great Britain from 1988 to 1993, where he founded the National Association for Gallery Education (ENGAGE). In 1993 he became Head of Schools and Community Programmes at the Tate Gallery, London, where he established the Gallery's first community services. Since April 1999 he has been co-ordinator of a major art and literacy project involving a partnership between the Tate Gallery and the University of London Institute of Education, entitled Visual Paths: Teaching Literacies in the Gallery.

James Hall is Principal Lecturer in Art Education at University of Surrey Roehampton. He co-ordinates the Art Teaching Studies Area in the Faculty of Education and teaches on undergraduate and postgraduate programmes. His research interests include the education, training and professional development of teachers of art and design, and artists' prints. He is currently researching the development of the professional knowledge and expertise of teachers of art and design in secondary schools. As a practising printmaker, he is a regular contributor to artists' bookworks.

Richard Hickman is Director of Studies for Art History at Homerton College, Cambridge and course leader for the art component of the University of Cambridge Post Graduate Certificate in Education (PGCE). His teaching experience includes thirteen years as a teacher of art and design. He has been a lecturer in art education since 1985, and has published in a number of books and journals on art education. He has also presented papers at several international conferences. He has worked as a senior examiner for national examinations in art and design and as an inspector for art and design and technology. He has had five solo exhibitions and has exhibited in England, France, Singapore and Australia.

Howard Hollands is Principal Lecturer in Art and Design Education in the School of Lifelong Learning and Education at Middlesex University, where he jointly co-ordinates the PGCE Art and Design Programme. He is also responsible for the art and design modules for the BA (Ed.). He was formerly Head of Art at Holland Park School, London. He is Honorary Editor of *The Art Book* and a member of the editorial boards of the *Journal of Art and Design Education* and *Engage*, the Journal of the National Association for Gallery Education. His research interests are in critical studies and the relationship between art, education and visual culture.

Rachel Mason is Professor of Art Education at University of Surrey Roehampton, where she is Head of the Centre for Art Education and International Research. She has taught art and art education in England, Australia and the USA and is well known for her research and publications on multicultural, cross-cultural and international art education. She is a former president of the British National Society for Education in Art and Design (NSEAD) and a vice-president of the International Society for Education through Art (InSEA). A second edition of her book *Art Education and Multiculturalism* was published by NSEAD in 1996. *Beyond Multicultural Art Education: International Perspectives* (co-edited with Doug Boughton) was published in 1999.

Darren Newbury is currently research co-ordinator for visual communication at Birmingham Institute of Art and Design, University of Central England. He completed his PhD on the theory and practice of photographic education in 1995, and has published in the areas of photographic education, research education and training, and visual research. His professional experience includes appointments as researcher for Styles and Sites of Photographic Education (funded by the Arts Council), co-ordinator of the Research Training Initiative and co-director for Digital Visual Imagery Encountered, Used and Produced by Young People Outside the School Environment (also funded by the Arts Council). His research interests are in photography and visual education, visual research methods and art and design.

Michele Tallack originally trained as a painter and went on to lecture and tutor in the Department of History of Art, University of Cambridge. Currently she lectures in art history at Anglia Polytechnic University and is Director of the Eastern Arts and Essex Local Education Authority Artists in Schools initiative, training artists and teachers to work together on artists' residencies. From 1990 to 1995, she was Director of the Anglia Polytechnic University and Cambridgeshire Local Education Authority Critical Studies Project, working with primary- and secondary-school teachers of various subjects on using artists and artefacts in their teaching. Her special interest in educational philosophy is reflected in recent publications on issues related to multicultural art education.

Foreword

Contributors to this anthology prove themselves well equipped to capture the tensions, paradoxes and ironies within which art education operates today. Never has art education been more complex or more conflicted, and never have the challenges it faces been greater.

Once upon a time, art teachers didn't need to know much about art. Knowing nothing about art was actually a virtue. In their classrooms, teachers were meant merely to hover about, waiting for their young charges to find their own, unique means of expression. Then, sometime in the last 40 or so years – it depends upon whether we are thinking in terms of proposals by academics, curriculum guidelines, state-mandated standards, or classroom practice – teachers found that they not only needed to teach studio skills but also art history and art criticism, and that in order to lead discussions about the nature of art and its social significance, they needed acquaintance with philosophical aesthetics. If teachers once didn't need to know much at all about art, they now needed to master quite substantial bodies of core knowledge.

The anxieties produced by these vastly increased demands were, however, at least partly assuaged by the idea that there existed a more or less stable art world from which to derive curricula. For example, there existed the grand narrative of the ascent of Western art, which, according to most textbooks, was only minimally complicated by the art of other cultures. Everyone knew, pretty much, what art was and where to find it and, consequently, what there was to teach. There were long-established disciplines of art, bodies of agreed knowledge among experts, and therein lay some security. The disciplines were never actually as uniform as educators sometimes liked to believe – some may not even be disciplines at all – but curriculum designers used strands like studio, history and criticism 'knowledge and understanding' that ostensibly referred to the professional artworld of galleries, art journals and the art sections of libraries around the world. This anthology rightly reflects the ongoing concerns of this approach to art education, which, after all, is that which currently informs most government-initiated curriculum documents.

But now, as the twenty-first century has opened before us, there is clearly a need to acknowledge that art education cannot be divorced from the plethora of image production and consumption that operates beyond the confines of the professional artworld. The professional artworld has acknowledged this itself. The once seemingly solid wall between fine and popular visual art has significantly been broken down, and we now talk of artworlds in the plural. And instead of *art* there is talk of *visual culture* as a way to include all visual imagery, fine and popular, past and present. The first edition of this anthology recognized this shift in art education from art to visual culture, but in this second edition the transition is addressed more explicitly.

To address the visual culture of the vast and ever-expanding entertainment industry some knowledge of sociology is required, including feminist theory, critical theory, media education and theories of globalization. Dealing with television, the Internet, tourist sites and souvenirs, advertising in all its forms, video games and so on, let alone all the cross fertilization between these and other forms, requires different kinds of knowledge than, for example, dealing with how to critique a Picasso painting. It requires a different mindset. As the authors of this second edition argue, it requires that we rethink our relationship to our subject of visual art and to our students, and even that we begin rethinking the purposes of education. If students come to school with substantial intuitive knowledge of visual culture, how does that change the role of teachers? Are schools to be less places of received knowledge and more safe havens in which students can work to understand and respond to issues presented by the communication networks of global capital?

In a postmodern period, art educators are acknowledging that there is no single historical narrative, and rather see virtue in the art of diverse cultures. Now, art educators are accommodating their practices to what has been called a 'society of the spectacle'. The visual culture of global capitalism, once an anathema to art educators, is now seen as grist to their mill. If much of art education remains built on the foundations of the professional artworld, it also now increasingly attempts to negotiate a position in relation to the vast, baroque plethora of images that circulate daily through international communication networks. Much of art education can still be likened to looking at a painting where everything can be grasped as a gestalt, but increasingly it is more like looking at an Islamic wall mosaic where, being so complex and interconnected, it is only possible to focus on limited parts at any one time.

However, as if negotiating visual culture was not enough for teachers to deal with, teachers now must also, in an utterly paradoxical way, attempt to negotiate the micro management of schools by governments. At the same time that art education is beginning to take on the complex challenges of contemporary visual culture, it is being pressured by government mandates to teach according to highly detailed standards. Teachers have usually had no say in constructing these standards, which, moreover, seem to deny the complex and idiosyncratic nature of their subject. While art education is attempting to deal with the unprecedented complexity of visual production and consumption in the contemporary world, teachers are being forced to conform in unprecedented, mind-numbing detail to bureaucratic dictates. While attempting to deal with the society of the spectacle, art education has to deal with the fact that ours is increasingly a society of surveillance. Where visual culture fans out in all directions, governments, in pursuit of rational order and economic survival, now more than ever require teachers to conform to top-down, 'cookie-cutter' standards.

It is a difficult time for art educators, one full of fundamental conflicts, confusions and increased demands. The authors of this anthology provide theoretical frameworks within which to conceptualize these many issues. Additionally, through discussions and descriptions of exemplary practice, they offer navigational skills with which we can all work our way through the minefield of current societal pressures. Their hope is that thereby our lives as art educators, and the lives of our students, are made not only bearable, but a joy.

Paul Duncum
Associate Professor of Art Education, School of Art and Design,
University of Illinois at Urbana-Champaign.

Introduction

RICHARD HICKMAN

Much of the writing for the first edition of this publication was completed in the closing years of the twentieth century. Certainly, the authors were mindful of the ongoing changes in society and how such changes impinge upon art, education, and art education. In this second edition, the authors have reflected upon their original texts in the light of developments over what might be termed the 'Pan-Millennial' period, and each has added a postscript. In addition, there is a concluding chapter which examines the changing nature of art education, with reference to the move away from 'canonical' notions of art towards the more inclusive concept of visual culture, focusing in particular upon the role of studio practice in the post-modern era.

This book alerts readers to possibilities. It asks questions; fundamental questions such as: What kind of art do we want school students to produce? What kind of art do we want school students to engage with? and, more fundamentally, Why do we bother in the first place? While being eclectic and diverse there is a common thread throughout concerned with the nature, meaning and purpose of art in education. The postmodern world is pluralistic, with no single meaning, purpose or direction for art education; indeed there are many. In this context it is necessary to look closely at the frameworks upon which much current practice in art education is built, and to re-examine some fundamental principles. If we really believe that art is of value to young people we should note carefully the messages given here by the various authors. In order to make art more relevant, exciting and meaningful to students in school we need to draw upon the incredible resources at our disposal and the intellectual dynamism, creativity and imagination of our time.

The sometimes precarious nature of art in the secondary-school curriculum ensures that art educators, more so than many of their colleagues, are wont to justify their existence, or, more accurately, to give considered rationales for the allocation of time to their subject. One positive aspect of this is that there is no shortage of informed and well-argued rationales for art education as an integral part of an adolescent's education. While art education is for the present firmly in place in many developed countries, it remains for some an unaffordable 'luxury'. Advocates of the value of an education in art have long espoused its *central* place in a child's education.

As I write this particular section, I am a day's walk away from the Albanian border at a time when thousands of refugees from another Balkan conflict are living in misery. I am reminded of a personal statement from an applicant to an art education course who had done voluntary work as an art teacher with children in Eastern Europe. She stated that initially she felt that this was in some ways not addressing their real problems, but found also that art in their lives, in the form of the opportunity to express their feelings in a personal way, was just what they needed. Such needs were identified by Herbert Read as he sought to come to terms with the destructive power of the Second World War: ' ... the secret of our collective ills is to be traced to the suppression of spontaneous creative ability in the individual'.[1]

The first chapter deals with the essence of the book, looking at some of the rationales which have been put forward for art education. In particular the chapter examines the legacy of Herbert Read, looking at the relevance of his ideas for contemporary international art education. The subsequent four chapters focus on the relationship between school art and the visual culture of the wider world. Lesley Burgess and Nick Addison give a thoughtful and thought-provoking analysis of the role of contemporary art practice in schools. Colin Grigg and Howard Hollands both challenge accepted canons of art; Grigg looks at the influence of museums and galleries while Hollands focuses on the part played by publishers. Darren Newbury argues the case for a broad approach to the art curriculum, based on the notion of visual literacy.

The remaining four chapters look at specific aspects of art education in more detail. Andy Ash considers the impact of new technologies upon teaching and learning art, examining the potential of the World Wide Web. As with other contributors, Ash provides a resource for research in the form of a useful list of references and websites. All of the contributors to this book are concerned fundamentally with values associated with the teaching of art. Michele Tallack, James Hall and Rachel Mason each examine some of the values upon which the subject is based. Tallack argues for critical studies to be at the centre of the art curriculum, rather than as a 'servant' to studio practice, putting forward a model for art education which is values-driven. Rachel Mason draws upon her research into craft education to look at different perspectives on the role of craft in schools, comparing Japanese and English practices and exploring the different values which inform the two perspectives. Hall examines the much-neglected area of spirituality in relation to art teaching and puts forward a convincing case for there to be a spiritual dimension to art in schools.

Each chapter has implications for classroom practice, and this is made explicit in many places. In general, such practice would include challenging established canons of art, valuing students' personal individual experiences, promoting co-operative working and contextualizing students' art work with reference to a range of cultural and historical contexts. While many artists and art educators have been working with ideas which challenge not only the tenets of modernism but have been developing concepts and practice evolved from *post*modernism, some classroom practice is rooted in *pre*modernist thinking. Implicit in this book is the notion that students in schools, who are twenty-first-century citizens, should no longer be on the receiving end of concepts and processes rooted in the nineteenth century.

This publication can be seen to be part of a transition in art education, marking a point between postmodernism and that which is to come – 'neo-eclecticism' perhaps (although we have probably had enough of '-isms'). We look forward to a pluralistic and coherent vision of art, and art in education, which is underpinned by not one but many philosophies; one which is not constrained by federal- and state-imposed curricula, and which gives teachers and students the freedom to explore, to take risks and to make mistakes.

Note

1.   Read, H. (1943) *Education Through Art*. London: Faber & Faber, p. 202.

Chapter 1

Meaning, Purpose and Direction

RICHARD HICKMAN

It has been my privilege to see thousands of lessons in over 100 different schools. Most have been characterized by teachers' commitment to and love of their subject, and their remaining passionate and convinced of the intrinsic value of their job in the face of, in some cases, poor resources and administrative indifference. Some of the most inspired and inspiring teaching I have ever witnessed has been in art lessons, with students being intrigued, enchanted, delighted and full of a sense of real achievement. I can also say with some confidence that the most meaningless, purposeless and mis-educational activities I have seen have also been in those lessons designated 'art'.

So what is it that makes one art lesson meaningful and worthwhile and another meaningless and worthless? First, we must ask, 'Meaningful to whom?' and the answer has to be, 'To the students'. That does not mean that we throw out 'high art' in favour of the current animated cartoon series on television as a focus for our critical attention, nor that we eschew paint and pencil in favour of scanning in and manipulating images through a computer; but it does mean that we examine our established practices in the light of contemporary art practice, contemporary commentary on visual culture and current technologies. Of central importance is valuing students' personal responses to looking at and making art, and using their initial affective responses to art works (including their own activities) as our starting point. It is doing our students a gross disservice if we assume that their aesthetic interests are confined to what many would consider to be the novel and the shallow. However, if an activity is to be deemed worthwhile it needs to be worthwhile to those engaged in it. It may be true that a particularly gifted teacher can inspire the most recalcitrant of students with the most unpromising material, but we are not all especially gifted, and some students are reluctant learners. It is up to the art teacher to stimulate, motivate and induct students into the world of art, craft and design. We can go some way towards making our lessons relevant and interesting by examining why we are engaged in teaching art in the first place.

RATIONALES FOR ART EDUCATION – MEANING AND PURPOSE

This section looks in more detail at the various rationales that have been put forward since the Second World War, looking in particular at the relevance of Herbert Read's ideas to contemporary art education. Read gave form and direction for the development of art in modern education and did much to advance its cause by his passionate and lucid advocacy.[1] His writing was underpinned by a belief in the civilizing influence of art. Efland sums up Read's philosophy by quoting the following passage:

> The gigantic catastrophes that threaten us are not elemental happenings of a physical or biological kind, but are psychic events. We are threatened in a fearful way by wars and revolutions that are nothing else but psychic epidemics ... The secret of all our collective ills is to be traced to the suppression of spontaneous creative ability in the individual ... *Destructiveness is the outcome of unlived life!*[2]

However, while this passage clearly illustrates Read's indebtedness to the then relatively new discipline of psychology, it is not entirely Read.[3] The true Readian philosophy is encapsulated in the following extract:

> The lack of spontaneity in education and in social organisation is due to that disintegration of the personality which has been the total result of economic, industrial and cultural developments since the Renaissance.[4]

This passage shows Read's concern with social, economic, cultural and psychological factors and reveals a hint of what the late David Thistlewood referred to as 'philosophical anarchism', describing Read's output as giving a 'sociocultural dimension to art education'.[5] Read put forward five areas which encapsulate the purpose of 'aesthetic education':

i) the preservation of the natural intensity of all modes of perception and sensation;
ii) the co-ordination of the various modes of perception and sensation with one another and in relation to the environment;
iii) the expression of feeling in communicable form;
iv) the expression in communicable form of modes of mental experience which would otherwise remain partially or wholly unconscious;
v) the expression of thought in required form.[6]

These five areas focus on the idea that aesthetic experience is concerned primarily with expression and the refinement of the senses, and such concerns are only made meaningful through the process of communication. It is worth noting that Read felt that in order to achieve success in these five areas, the single most important requirement was the fostering of a 'sympathetic atmosphere' by the teacher: ' ... to create an atmosphere of spontaneity, of happy childish industry, is the main and perhaps only secret of successful teaching'.[7] The five aspects of aesthetic education cited above were seen as giving universal meaning to aesthetic activities. Read asserted that aesthetic education is fundamental to general education in fostering 'growth of what is individual in each human being'.[8] The concept of creative growth was taken further by Read's contemporary Viktor Lowenfeld a few years later[9] and has had an enormous influence upon generations of art teachers and their students in the English-speaking world.

In 1982, art teachers in the UK saw the arrival of two publications which in their modest ways have contributed to the shaping of art teachers' perceptions about the nature of the art curriculum: Maurice Barrett's *Art Education* and the first edition of the *Journal of Art and Design Education (JADE)*.[10] Barrett lists 21 'worthwhile outcomes' for art education which relate variously to self-expression, problem-solving and perceptual development. Eight of the 21 are concerned with the 'manipulation of visual form' through experimentation with materials and visual elements (such as the ability to represent in two dimensions what has been seen 'as objectively as possible').[10] Following the Readian tradition, the overall message is concerned with students finding their identity through self-expression and personal response to the social world, and developing self-reliance and independence. There is an implicit case made for the role of art education in students' socialization.

The first issue of *JADE* contained at least three important articles relating to the nature of art education: Edmund Feldman's 'Varieties of Art Curriculum', Paul Edmonston's 'A Rationale for a Curriculum in the Visual Arts' and Brian Allison's 'Identifying the Core in Art and Design'.[11] Feldman stresses that art in education is essentially a moral enterprise and is therefore different from, for example, art in commerce or art in psychiatry. In particular he asserts that art in schools should not be confused with the 'bizarre antics of gallery artists'. Moreover:

> We can always hire educational technicians to advise us about when to teach transparent watercolour technique, or to how best to study the art of mosaic-making. Right now, however, because the situation is so urgent, we should worry about art and human decency. (p. 44)

Feldman raises more questions than he answers, but at least he asks highly pertinent questions:

> So it behoves us – teachers and curriculum makers – to consider every artistic act seriously: What does it mean? What modes of thinking does it extol? Where does it seek joy? Where sorrow? What feelings does it praise? What delights does it celebrate? What behaviour does it enjoin? (p. 44)

These questions relate to the work of practising artists, but could just as easily refer to art lessons. Feldman appears to be saying that if we must draw upon the work of contemporary artists to inform our work in schools, we should do so with caution. This appeal to teachers' conservatism appears to do little to advance the notion of making contemporary visual arts relevant to young people, but if we shift the focus from teachers and curriculum makers to students, then we have the opportunity to encourage meaningful debate and help students to engage in direct and personal ways with the art of their generation.

Paul Edmonston's article revolves around the role of art within the aims of general education, in particular its 'humanizing' role. He cites five 'components' which he argues should form the basis for an art curriculum:

- sensory and perceptual;
- knowledge of art history;
- positive and informed attitudes towards art;
- use of tools and media; and
- aesthetic understanding.

These 'components' are very similar to Allison's 'domains' which appear in the same edition:

- expressive/productive;
- perceptual;
- analytical/critical; and
- historical/cultural.

Allison reminds us not to confuse curriculum content with curriculum purpose, and that it is the purpose which determines the content. This is, to some extent, self-evident, but we should bear in mind that much purpose can *emerge* from content. In any case, in the day-to-day rush of classroom life, it is easy to forget *why* certain activities are done. Most art teachers, I assume, have a tacit, perhaps subconscious, understanding that a particular activity is intrinsically worthwhile. The problem arises, however, when such activities occur simply because they have always occurred, or they form part of a safe and successful repertoire. They then become embedded into the school art orthodoxy; at one time the Van Gogh pastiche, the squashed cola-can drawing and the green-pepper ceramic form were exciting, interesting and innovative.

The individual art teacher remains the essential driving force for imaginative, creative and challenging art education in schools. Classroom teachers are not simply vehicles for the delivery of state-sponsored curricula; they each have their individual strengths, will all subscribe to a theory (or more often a *melange* of theories) of art and will operate within particular world views. Little research has been done on the influence of teachers' personalities, attitudes and values on the kind of artwork produced in schools, but based on anecdotal evidence I would suggest that the single most important factor in determining the nature of schools' art activities is the personal belief system of individual art teachers, notwithstanding the imposition of guidelines and directions from 'above'. Fraser Smith, in discussing art teachers' values, categorized art teachers into the following: high priests (subdivided into magicians and mystics); technocrats (subdivided into engineers and designers); social workers; pedagogues; and, lastly, anomics.[12] Each of these types has a set of values associated with it, and these values form the basis for a certain approach to the teaching of art. For example, the high priest, according to Smith, is concerned largely with providing opportunities for individual personal expression, whereas the technocrat is more concerned with presenting art as a problem-solving activity, encouraging inventiveness and giving opportunities for exploration and understanding of materials. The social workers on the other hand will wish to encourage growth of imaginative ideas and provide opportunity for developing social awareness. The pedagogue's concern is more wide-ranging, and is allied to the humanities rather than other practical subjects, with a focus on developing the aesthetic responses of students. Smith's other identifiable group, the anomic, has an approach to art teaching which is a mish-mash of all the above, underpinned by a general hostility and fundamental conservatism. An emergent type, predicted by Smith, is the semiologist. It is this group of art teachers which is likely to carry forward the banner of 'visual literacy'.[13]

Given that art is not one subject but many, and that each of its constituent disciplines (such as ceramics, textiles and fine art) has a range of approaches and philosophies, it is not surprising that practice is so varied. This is to be celebrated, but it does leave us with a complex, perhaps insurmountable task in formulating an all-embracing philosophy of art education. It is clear that a more appropriate starting point comes by asking the question 'Why do we teach art at all?'

Richard Siegesmund, in an article entitled 'Why Do We Teach Art Today',[14] tackles the issue head on, and following Efland's lead,[15] examines three distinct philosophies of art education: expressionistic, reconstructivist and scientific-rationalist. Expressionistic approaches have informed the teaching of many art educators for perhaps half a century; they are bound up with notions of creativity, imagination and, of course, self-expression. The reconstructivists' philosophy of art education is fundamentally different from, and in many ways in conflict with, that of the expressionists; instead of 'art for art's sake' they espouse 'art as a means to an end', the end being social change.[16] It is at the interface between these conflicting rationales that obfuscation of the issues arises, where teachers individually and collectively give conflicting signals to their students with regard to the nature of art and approaches to learning in art. Perhaps by looking back to Herbert Read we can see a way forward that resolves the apparent conflict between the two positions. Read's emphasis, as exemplified in the five areas cited earlier in this chapter, is clearly on feeling and expression, but he saw the overall purpose of art education as having more universal value, and it being concerned with making society more civil by fostering 'the organic unit of society, the *citizen*'.[17] Thus it can be seen that Read's view of the purpose of art education goes beyond a desire for a vehicle for self-expression and beyond valuing art for its own sake. The true inheritors of Herbert Read's philosophy of art education are not the expressionists but the reconstructivists.

Scientific rationalism is a term sometimes used to describe the approach taken by those art educators who claim that art offers a particular way of knowing; that it is a discipline with its own methods of inquiry. This approach has lent an air of academic respectability to art education in that it offers a certain epistemological status, both psychologically and philosophically. The very existence of academic journals such as *Studies in Art Education* reinforces this. Elliot Eisner has for many years advocated an epistemological basis for art education, rooted in the notion that art is a way of knowing with its own characteristics, and which provides a route to latent cognitive processes.[18] A useful contribution has been made to advances in art education, based on principles of scientific rationalism, by developmental psychologists such as those associated with Harvard Project Zero.[19] Project Zero was founded, as an interdisciplinary collaborative enterprise, in 1967 by Nelson Goodman who provided the philosophical basis for the work. Goodman was among the first to propose that visual images as well as words can operate as symbol systems, and that being literate means being visually literate, in terms of being able to decode certain symbol systems, in addition to being able to read and write. This means that art can be seen as a form of enquiry.[20]

Scientific rationalism is a convincing doctrine, but one which tends to eschew any concern for making and appreciating art for its own sake – a concern that is not to be found solely within the expressionist camp – and there is the potential for a distinct lack of joy to be associated with it.

The assertion has surfaced in recent years that learning in art facilitates learning in other subjects. My immediate response to this notion echoes that of Elliot Eisner: should we not be asking whether learning in, for example, mathematics supports learning in art?[21] While the idea of transference of learning between art and other subjects might well be justified (and there *might* be evidence to support it), as a justification for the inclusion of art in the school curriculum it is potentially pernicious in that it detracts from the intrinsic value of art education, reducing it to a prop to service other areas of the curriculum. This effect is amplified if art is seen as 'the arts', in which case music, dance, drama and poetry are seen as a single entity and are reduced to support status (in this case the whole being significantly less than the sum of its parts).

Siegesmund, with a leaning to scientific rationalism, conceives a rationale for art education which aims to bring together an eclectic mix of rationales for, and approaches to, art in education under the term 'reasoned perception'. This rationale sees art as being part of the mainstream of disciplined inquiry, not as a form of knowing outside of rationality, nor as a 'neutral instrument for creating social awareness'. From the perspective of reasoned perception, art is seen as a 'realm of feeling, sensory concepts, and exquisitely varied forms of human representation' that help us understand and give meaning to our environment. This sounds eminently reasonable if, as Siegesmund contends, the 'normative goals of school [are] to build cognitive skills'.[22] However, if we accept that schools are, or should be, concerned with broader goals, such as the development of social skills, then the rationale of reasoned perception seems inadequate, even arid.

Since the nineteenth century, an education in art had been seen by many to be a skills-based enterprise designed to equip students for the labour market. It would be wrong to ignore or dismiss the vocational aspect of learning in art;

something as basic as improving hand–eye co-ordination takes on a greater significance if we are teaching potential dental surgeons, but specific vocational considerations must come fairly low down in our priorities, even with older students who are about to enter the world of work. Employers, if reference requests are anything to go by, are looking for ability to work as part of a team, a sense of humour, effective time management, and commitment. Art education has its role to play in all of these, but its distinctive contribution to students' learning lies in its concern for understanding and appreciating the visual world, both through making art and through interaction with the work of others; 'interaction' meaning more than simply looking; it implies engaging with, analysing and reflecting upon the artwork of peers and that of professional artists and art makers.

The introduction of Discipline Based Art Education (DBAE) in American schools has had an enormous impact upon the way art is taught and this has rippled out to other countries.[23] However, as noted above, it is the purpose which normally determines the content and DBAE is basically a way of organizing curriculum content, not a complete and self-contained philosophy of art education. Critical studies, seen by some as the British equivalent of DBAE, has tended to develop in a less rigid and more holistic manner. John Swift notes that the use of artists' residencies in particular 'has allowed the physical excitement, personal obsession, hard work and critical engagement to be manifest'.[24] However, he warned in 1996 of the development of certain orthodoxies arising from an uncritical use of established canons, which have since become widespread, such as pastiches of post-impressionist paintings.

DIRECTION

Clearly, art education has to be concerned with learning *about* art as well as *making* art, but some would also argue that learning *through* art draws upon students' abilities to produce art as their critical engagement with art objects. The questions remain: What kind of art making? Which art objects?

I do not intend to advocate any specific approach, nor to propose a specific rationale for the teaching of art, but I will present a few thoughts which might contribute to developing a way forward. To put the role of art education into a much broader context, it is worth asking 'What do students need in the postmodern age?' One answer, in view of the growing trend for 'cyber-relationships' and the much publicized breakdown of the family unit, could well be 'contact with their own selves', which takes us back to the idea of art-making as a vehicle for self-expression and for exploring one's essence. Herbert Read viewed this aspect of art education as being the key to emotional growth and essential for psychological health.

The world has changed a great deal since Read was writing *Education Through Art*. Some might argue that human beings have changed also, not least in their perception of the world and their place in it. We are much more aware of different cultures and we have become part of a global economy in a way which could not have been envisaged before the arrival of today's electronic communication systems. With so many everyday needs being met by mass commerce, citizens of industrially and commercially developed countries are in danger of denying what many would see as a basic human need, that of the need to create and, associated with this, the development of practical skills. In our desire to focus on the importance of process, we should not forget that the end-product is valued enormously by students who have little knowledge of the debate about process and product, as reflected in the many artworks produced in school which are taken home and cherished. The value of making is something of which we should not lose sight in our quest for an aesthetically evolved and culturally aware population.

Such a quest needs to be part of a multiple vision, incorporating Read's view of art education as an essentially civilizing activity, intrinsically linked with a tolerance of difference.[25] John Swift and John Steers[26] identify a number of problems associated with what is known in England as the statutory Orders for Art[27] and suggest ways by which these might be addressed. Their manifesto is underpinned by a rationale for art in education which in turn is based upon three fundamental principles: difference, plurality and independent thought. These principles are embodied in their promotion of risk-taking, personal enquiry and the challenging of established orthodoxies, especially those associated with cultural hierarchies.

Multicultural approaches to art education have been advocated for many years, but all too often the use of visual material derived from other cultures is seen out of context and is devalued by focusing attention on purely formal elements. At worst, some approaches perpetuate stereotypes, and close minds rather than open them.[28] If an education in art is to have meaning in the postmodern world it should draw upon a pan-cultural range of signs, symbols and images. The knowledge base for this is vast and beyond the grasp of any one individual, but the way forward for art teachers must be to provide students with the research skills and tools of criticism necessary to interpret the range of visual material available. Research skills in this context include the experimentation and exploration associated with studio practice, as well as more traditional modes of enquiry such as observation schedules. It also means attaching more value to students as active participants in a dialogue between teacher and learner.

Stuart Macdonald in his examination of postmodernism in relation to art education asserts that change in art education should reflect the 'pluralism and internationalism of contemporary art, design and architecture itself'.[29] This means adopting a much broader world view, which goes beyond kicking against centrally imposed guidelines and the apparent constraints of examination requirements, to seeing the possibilities inherent in curriculum frameworks which at first appear narrow.

The cultural relativism promulgated by other art educators, such as Graeme Chalmers, is not without its dangers, as Chalmers himself acknowledges,[30] but in his advocacy of an anthropological approach to art criticism (in the DBAE framework) he has found a useful theoretical base. In this way, art in education makes a strength out of what is often perceived as its weakness: the lack of a strong theoretical base derived from an established discipline. The dynamic nature of the subject ensures vitality, but only if we are willing to move on and draw upon a wide range of disciplines.

IMPLICATIONS FOR THE CLASSROOM

The objectives model as a basis for teaching and learning in art has already been thoroughly critiqued,[31] and its appropriateness questioned many times; but it remains, I suspect, a favoured one among many teacher educators. My principal objection to the use of specific learning objectives in art is that they encourage concern for trivia, and in the case of behavioural objectives, ignore the very things which give art its strength – tacit and intuitive understanding. Moreover, most art teachers around the world do not, in my experience, naturally think in this way. It is far more common for a teacher to think of an activity or a theme which seems to be rich in potential for learning than to start with a learning objective and think of ways to achieve it, notwithstanding the imposition of prescribed curricula.

As the art teacher is usually in the position of being older, more knowledgeable and more aware of possibilities than most students, it does not seem unreasonable to rely on that person for determining the nature of the art work (and other stimulus material) to which students are exposed. However, it makes sense for students to be involved actively in choosing artists and artefacts for critical study. This could be enhanced and greatly enriched by collaborative work with other professionals and, more excitingly, with school students from other countries and cultures via, for example, the internet. Students' research skills are enhanced through the guided and structured use of new technologies, such as the World Wide Web to search for images and information about artists and cultural artefacts. But a more enriching use of such technologies is the dynamic interchange of ideas made possible by interacting with people around the world.

Group work and the use of computer technology generates many questions about the nature of art and the art-making process. For example, the ephemeral nature and potential for instantaneous multiple distribution of work done on computers goes against traditional notions of the longevity and uniqueness of the art object, while collaborative work does not fit into the western, Romantic view of art as an activity pursued by the lone genius. It is important therefore to reconsider our assumptions about what art is, who produces it and by what means. Such considerations have a direct impact upon the kind of work we ask of our students in our schools. We do, however, need to be wary of 'aesthetic relativism'. An artwork can mean what you want it to mean, but it also means a lot more. In giving our students a focus for their critical attention, in terms of examining cultural context, there is little hierarchical difference between a Renaissance painting and a 1950s comic book. Judging the intrinsic value of each is another matter. Art teachers are in an excellent position to promote a particular kind of lifelong learning: to provide students with the skills and perceptual tools to appreciate their environment and to interact aesthetically with their surroundings, as well as with phenomena classed as 'art'.

School students need guidance and structure, particularly those who do not experience stability in their everyday life. This does not mean prescriptive teaching, nor does it imply an authoritarian teaching style, but it does mean creating an environment for learning within which the teacher and the students can operate happily and effectively. The art teacher facilitates learning through a considered use of exciting and relevant visual material, but, more than this, *the teacher must also teach*; it is not enough simply to provide opportunities for heuristic learning. Students need to understand their own role when engaging with artworks (as maker as well as viewer) in the making of meanings. The teacher has the responsibility to take the student forward, but from a place where both feel secure.

It is important to create opportunities for reflection and contemplation in our classrooms. This is difficult to achieve but worthwhile. Creating the right atmosphere is perhaps the key to facilitating reflection. The visiting artist, or artist-in-residence, has a part to play in this; the art classroom operating as a working studio can facilitate students' learning in and through art in a subtle yet effective way by creating an atmosphere of purposeful enquiry, creative experimentation, risk-taking and contemplation. In such an environment, the three fundamental principles, difference, plurality and independence of thought, put forward by Swift and Steers can thrive.

A crucial aspect of Read's philosophy as encapsulated in *Education Through Art* is the emphasis on education rather than art. Stated more bluntly, art as a means to an end, not an end in itself. There is of course room for both, recognizing the intrinsic value of art and valuing the process of art-making as a form of enquiry. One of the most exciting and productive aspects of engaging in art activities is the potential for genuine enquiry, making connections which cross traditional subject boundaries. There are opportunities for collaborative work which extend well beyond the customary association with other arts subjects and also beyond activities associated with design and technology (there appears to be a tacit understanding among English art teachers that the 'design' in art and design is somehow different from the 'design' in design and technology). While personal, individual expression lies very near to the heart of much teaching in art, there are many opportunities for collaborative work of a cross-curricular nature. Although I am loath to suggest specific activities (as citing examples tends to narrow the range of possibilities, and exemplar material often becomes dated very quickly) there is much to be gained from working with geography colleagues on projects which use land artists as a starting point, or with mathematics colleagues exploring the numerical values of Islamic designs.[32]

Student teachers of art are encouraged to reflect upon their teaching as a matter of course; they are usually actively involved in self-appraisal and lesson evaluation. Unfortunately, these kinds of activities tend to be squeezed out by the pressures associated with day-to-day classroom teaching to a full timetable. It is nevertheless essential for the wellbeing of art education, and ultimately for the aesthetic health of the population, for teachers to continually appraise what they are offering their students in the light of contemporary practice and current developments in media and equipment. This can take the form of simple questions: Am I teaching my students something worthwhile? What is its purpose? Is it relevant to their needs? Does it build upon previous learning? And most importantly, does it make them more human? As with most things in life, in art education we cannot have clear direction unless we have clear and meaningful purpose, but sometimes the purpose only becomes apparent after the event.

POSTSCRIPT

Since 1999, when this introductory chapter was first written, there has inevitably been events of significance – wars and large-scale attacks on civilians for a variety of spurious reasons – as well as technological developments. How do these things impinge upon what we consider to be art and art education? With regard to conflict, it is surely a major aim of education to understand ourselves and others as human beings, and also to know and understand other people's cultures and acknowledge, even celebrate, diversity and difference. Art education has a central role to play in this, but in order to do so, there is a need to broaden our understanding of what constitutes 'art'. The concept of art has been wrestled with by many intelligent and informed people for many years; fine art in the western tradition has come to be associated in some quarters with such things as racism, sexism and class distinction. The move toward the notion of 'visual culture', which is a wider and more inclusive concept, is to be welcomed. In particular, if we are to value our students as individuals, then we need to value their views and help them understand their visual world. Even those with impaired vision can have a personal world of visual imagery with its own associations and significance: the art teacher can help guide students to discover, respond to and appreciate their sensory environment in creative and imaginative ways. Giving students opportunities to explore their inner world of feelings and emotions can help them acquire greater self-knowledge and, I believe, help develop empathy. When this is coupled with learning about the visual culture of people from other places and times, there must surely be a positive outcome in terms of reducing conflict.

Advances in technology, such as digital photography and the ability to capture, modify and send images across the world, have an enormous impact upon the way we see the nature of craft and studio skills. The digital revolution means that we now have a far greater range of media available. Moreover, the appeal of our subject is broader, and student self-esteem is not confined to those who 'can draw'.

I advocate a curriculum which both values students' visual culture and which introduces them to a wide range of visual forms as a focus for engagement. In addition to learning skills of criticism and acquiring knowledge of visual form, students need to be taught skills through which they can generate their own images, explore their inner world, respond to their environment in a meaningful way and manipulate and experiment with media and materials to help develop problem-solving skills. To do less would be to do a disservice to young people and deprive them of a whole dimension of understanding. Whether such a curriculum can be delivered within the confines of art education as it is generally understood is another matter.

Notes

1. For example, Read, H. (1943) *Education Through Art*. London: Faber & Faber.
2. Efland, A.D. (1990). *A History of Art Education: Intellectual and Social Currents in Teaching the Visual Arts*. New York: Teachers College Press.
3. This paragraph, cited by Efland and ascribed to Read is a collection of three different writers. The writers, quoted by Read in the Efland extract, are: (lines 1–4) Jung, C.G. (1940) *The Integration of Personality*, trans. Stanley M. Dell. London, pp. 293–4; (lines 4–5) Read, *op. cit.*, p. 202; (line 6) Fromm, E. (1942) *The Fear of Freedom*. London, p. 158.
4. Read, *op. cit.*, p. 202.
5. Thistlewood, D. (1993) 'Herbert Read: an appreciation'. *Journal of Art and Design Education*, **12**(2), 144.
6. Read, *op. cit.*, pp. 8–9.
7. *Idem.*
8. *Idem.*, p. 8.
9. Lowenfeld, V. (1947) *Creative and Mental Growth*. New York: Macmillan.
10. Barrett, M. (1979) *Art Education: A Strategy for Course Design*. London: Heinemann; McDonald, Stuart (ed.) (1982) *The Journal of Art and Design Education*, **1**(1).
11. Feldman, E. (1982) 'Varieties of art curriculum', 21–45, originally published in J. Hausman and M. Engel (eds) (1981) *Fourth Yearbook on Research in Arts and Aesthetic Education: Curriculum and Instruction*. St Louis, Missouri: CEMREL; Edmonston, P. (1982) 'A rationale for a curriculum in the visual arts', 47– 57; Allison, B. (1982) 'Identifying the core in art and design', 59–66.
12. Smith, I.F. (1980) 'Art', in R. Straughan and J. Wrigley (eds) *Values and Evaluation in Education*. London: Harper & Row.
13. See Raney, K. (1999) 'Visual literacy and the art curriculum'. *Journal of Art and Design Education*, **18**(1), 41–7 for an in-depth examination of this term.
14. Siegesmund, R. (1998) 'Why do we teach art today? Conceptions of art education and their justification. *Studies in Art Education*, **39**(3), 197–214.
15. Efland, *op. cit.*
16. Amongst examples of articles by 'reconstructivist' art educators, I would include, *inter alia*, Duncum, P. (1997) 'Art education for new times', in *Studies in Art Education*, **38**(2), 69–79; jagodzinski, j. [sic] (1997) 'The nostalgia of art education: reinscribing the master's narrative', in *Studies in Art Education*, **38**(2), 80–95; and Blandy, D., Congdon, K. and Krug, D. (1998) 'Art, ecological restoration and art

education', in *Studies in Art Education*, **39**(3), 240–43. For a useful account of how reconstructionist ideas in art education can be translated into classroom practice see Clark, R. (1998) 'Doors and mirrors in art education: constructing the postmodernist classroom', in *Art Education*, **51**(6), 6–11.

17. Read, *op. cit.*, p. 221.
18. Eisner, E. (1994) (2nd edn) *Cognition and Curriculum Reconsidered*. New York: Teachers College Press.
19. Howard Gardner is the Project Director and David Perkins is the Co-director; both have written extensively on developmental psychology relating to art education. See, for example, Gardner, H. (1990) *Art Education and Human Development*, and Perkins, D. (1995) *The Intelligent Eye: Learning to Think by Looking at Art*, both published by the Getty Centre. The website for Project Zero is: http//www.pzweb.harvard.edu
20. Goodman, N. (1978) *Ways of Worldmaking*. Indianapolis: Hackett.
21. See for example Eisner, E. (1998) 'Does experience in the arts boost academic achievement?' *Journal of Art and Design Education*, **17**(1), 51–60.
22. Siegesmund, *op. cit.*, p. 212.
23. The four constituent disciplines of DBAE are: art history, aesthetics, art criticism and studio practice. See Smith, R. (1989) (ed.) *Discipline Based Art Education: Origins, Meaning and Development*. Illinois: University of Illinois Press. An example of its international influence can be seen in Ua-Anant, M.S. (1987) 'A system for analysing and evaluating Thai art curriculum content'. *Journal of Multi-Cultural and Cross-Cultural Research in Art Education*, **5**(1), where the author advocates a DBAE approach for Thai schools.
24. Swift, J. (1996) 'Critical studies: A Trojan Horse for an alternative cultural agenda?' In L. Dawtry, T. Jackson, M. Masterton and M. Meecham (1996) (eds) *Critical Studies and Modern Art*. New Haven and London: Yale University Press.
25. The concept of 'multiple visions' for art education was originally put forward by Burton and co-workers in response to the Getty-sponsored Discipline Based Art Education initiative in America (Burton, J., Lederman, A. and London, P. (eds) (1988) *Beyond DBAE: The Case for Multiple Visions of Art Education*. North Dartmouth: Southeastern Massachusetts University.
26. Swift, J. and Steers, J. (1999) 'A manifesto for art in schools'. *Journal of Art and Design Education*, **18**(1), 7–13.
27. The original Orders for art revolved around two attainment targets: investigating and making, and knowledge and understanding; the new (as of 2000) Orders for art are little changed in essence but conflate the two attainment targets into one, with four strands: skills knowledge and understanding; experimenting with and using media; reviewing and adapting work as it progresses; and investigating others' work and applying knowledge and understanding. The 'National' Curriculum in this form applies only to England rather than to the UK as a whole.
28. For a fuller examination of this issue see Hickman, R. (1999) 'Representational art and Islam: a case for further investigation', in R. Mason and D. Boughton (eds) *Beyond Multi-Cultural Art Education: International Perspectives*. Waxmann.
29. Chalmers, F.G. (1996) *Celebrating Pluralism: Art, Education and Cultural Diversity*. Los Angeles: Getty, p. 12.
30. Macdonald, S. (1998) 'Post-it culture: postmodernism and art and design education'. *Journal of Art and Design Education*, **17**(3), 234; see also Macdonald, S. (1999) 'The trouble with post-modernism'. *Journal of Art and Design Education*, **18**(1), 15–21.

31. See Ch. 6 ('Educational aims, objectives, and other aspirations') in E. Eisner (1985, 2nd edn) *The Educational Imagination*. New York: Macmillan.

32. For an interesting example of how mathematics and visual art can be combined in a collaborative project, see Cossentino, J. and Shaffer, D.W. (1999) 'The math studio: harnessing the power of the arts to teach across disciplines'. *Journal of Aesthetic Education*, **33**(2), 99–109. The project was inspired by the work of M.C. Escher and aims to create 'a learning environment that combines serious mathematics with genuine artistic thinking'.

Chapter 2

Contemporary Art in Schools: Why Bother?

LESLEY BURGESS AND NICHOLAS ADDISON

> Look, there are politics in every conversation we have, every deal we
> make, every face we kiss. There is always an exchange of power, an
> exchange of position – it happens every minute. I make art about power,
> love, life and death.[1]

> The whole modernist cult of the child in which the child was seen as this
> innocent figure of pure, unsocialized creativity ... is a crock of shit and
> is part of the problem.[2]

INTRODUCTION

Contemporary art, especially in its most recent manifestations, has become a
popular topic for reportage in the UK. Along with the Turner Prize, which
receives an annual rebuke from the media, the type of work that attracts most
coverage is the very work schools find most problematic; that which engages
the social, political and transgressive. Similarly, artists who use unexpected or
radical materials, means of production and dissemination are liable to offend
traditionalist propriety. The media are often sensationalist, focusing on a
perceived propensity for blasphemy, pornography and other such 'modern
crimes', as Julie Burchill insists:

> There has never been a better time to be a child molester. In the old
> days, you would have to lurk around the playground in a shabby mac,
> with only a few sherbet lemons or a fictional puppy in your pocket with
> which to tempt your prey. Now ... you can take the object of your desire
> to gaze upon ... the works of the ageing, dirty-minded children such as
> Damien, Dinos and all the boys and girls at the Saatchi Nursery for
> Way-ward Youth.[3]

Burchill believes that this type of art serves only to 'blind society with spectacle'
so that it becomes desensitized, anaesthetized or corrupted by the degenerate

and deviant imaginations of the guardians of taste and their favoured artists. She, along with similar journalists, is herself responsible for this interpretative profile. Regularly in the London *Evening Standard* Brian Sewell attacks contemporary art, revelling in his ability to provide graphically explicit descriptions of its most abject and subversive aspects. Increasingly, it is through the mediation of this type of media coverage that public perceptions of what constitutes contemporary art are formed and reinforced. Students and teachers are not immune to this:

> In such ill-fated interchanges, the audience has often believed that artists were being unnecessarily obscure or confrontational at the same time that artists have felt misunderstood and unappreciated. The result has been mutual disappointment and hostility.[4]

It is assumed that such hostility is reflected in responses by young people, as if outrage were a natural rather than learned response. Schools are also responsible for shaping students' attitudes to contemporary art. While the media trivialize it through sensationalism or ridicule, schools dismiss it as problematic and inappropriate. The way contemporary art is decontextualized and marginalized uproots it from its dialectical relationship to those institutions that seek to control public discourse, and denies it the role it might have in educating students to challenge hegemonic structures. Indeed, contemporary art can be seen as a challenge to the bourgeois values of traditional educational institutions. However, Willis reminds us that common cultural forms, supposedly antithetical to contemporary art, are also a challenge to those same structures of power.[5] These common cultural forms are often produced by young people in contradistinction to institutional codes of decorum, and accompany them into the classroom. For many students they are a more profound influence on their sense of identity than the formal curriculum. There is an antithesis between an elite contemporary practice on the one hand and a base common culture on the other. Both are at odds with mainstream education, and both are subject to denigration. Such assumptions are countered by Lacy,[6] Paley,[7] Dixon[8] and Robinson,[9] who promote routes of convergence; an alliance between the two cultural forms in contexts located outside the school. We contend that this partnership needs to include schools.

DEFINING THE FIELD

Changes in art education at secondary level?

> As we move towards the Millennium, we are still delivering art curricula in our schools predicated largely upon procedures and practices which reach back to the nineteenth century – processes and practices which cling to a comfortable and uncontentious view of art and its purposes. As a result, secondary Art & Design education ... is, in general, static, safe and predictable ... A hybrid, divorced from contemporary ideas in the spheres of art practice, critical theory, art history or museology.[10]

The late Arthur Hughes, from whose paper the above quotation is taken, was one amongst many educationalists, including Abbs,[11] Willis,[12] Binch and Robertson,[13] Meecham[14] and Dalton,[15] who have despaired at the perceived unwillingness of teachers to question the status quo, a conservatism that belies the reflective practice that has been central to teacher education for a generation.[16] Teachers have not been completely static when responding to the changing field of visual and material culture; remember the reliance on secondary sources in the form of the ubiquitous transcription or collaging of reproductions from the Sunday supplements in the 1960s and 1970s, and the 'U-turn' in favour of primary resources evidenced in the spectacular still-life installations of the 1980s, which were somehow meant to answer the requirement for 'neutral stimuli'!

Practice has continually shifted since the promotion of critical approaches to the art curriculum first advocated in the 1970s by Field[17] and Eisner.[18] Since then there has been a plethora of initiatives promoting curriculum development in the UK, but although some were generously funded at the start they were not effectively sustained.

There has also been an attempt to accommodate the principles of equal opportunities through strategies of visibility, both multicultural and gendered, and, more significantly, anti-racist and anti-sexist initiatives. However, before these could be consolidated the requirement to address the critical and contextual components of the National Curriculum Art Order (NC) (1992) diverted attention to the canonic in relation to 'our' cultural heritage. However, the NC directive for students to respond to the 'work of others' engendered a liaison between schools and gallery/museum education departments which, depending on the venue, engaged students with contemporary practice. Occasionally this recognition may have been pragmatic or only token – visibility and celebrationist tactics taking the place of a critical investigation of difference. Educational practice may not have been radical, but it was never static.

Table 2.1 categorizes approaches to the typical art curriculum (ages 11–18) of today. The categories are not exclusive, indicating approaches that can be combined. For example, genre-based outcomes can be managed through formalist, perceptualist or expressive means: although in some schools a single approach dominates. However, there are two which are no longer evident: basic design, a cogent programme in the 1960s and 1970s, lost because its workshop-based strategies, if not its holistic philosophy, were subsumed by technology; anti-racist art education, promoted in the 1970s and 1980s, lost because it was no longer perceived as urgent in a post-apartheid era. However, with the publication of the Macpherson Report (1999) on the death of Stephen Lawrence, this was, with hindsight, premature. Notwithstanding, the situation is less severe than Hughes claims. A number of categories are open to contemporary critical practice, although, by and large, they belong to modernist paradigms questioned by Cunliffe[19] and Atkinson.[20]

Table 2.1 Approaches to the art curriculum

Perceptualist	Mimetic procedures, a search for the 'absolute copy' reduction to appearances[21]
Formalist	A reduction to the visual elements, exercise-driven, representational and/or abstract[22]
Expressive	Intuitive making through affective and/or material exploration: privileging the essential and individual[23]
Genre-based	Preconceived types perpetuated by teacher expertise and the imitation of exemplars, the successful work of past students, e.g. still life, lifedrawing, landscape, CD covers, ceramic figures
Pastiche	The imitation of canonic exemplars, occasionally assimilating the postmodern practice of parody[24]
Technical	The development of a succession of discrete technical skills: drawing followed by printmaking, followed by batik, etc.
Object-based	A response to common – sometimes themed, often spectacular – artefacts in the form of a big still life/ installation, e.g. natural and made forms; a multicultural potpourri[25]
Critical and contextual	An investigation of art as a means of social and cultural production privileging cognitive and analytical procedures[26]
Issue-based	An integration of the personal with the social, political and moral through responses to current and contentious issues[27]
Postmodern	Promoting plural perspectives and approaches and embracing the new technologies[28], [29]

Contemporary practice in art

Any attempt to define the expanding field of contemporary art is bound to be reductive if it hopes to contain what is a characteristically fluid phenomenon, subject to, or perhaps productive of, change. This section looks at what is most visible, that is work promoted by the institutions responsible for disseminating contemporary art and whose artists are often in critical dialogue with those same institutions.

As early as 1936, Benjamin predicted that in the age of mechanical reproduction the 'auratic' would be marginalized. By auratic he meant those seemingly authentic acts of creation that are in fact dependent on ritual; art in the service of religion, art *as* religion and so on:

> the instant the criterion of authenticity ceases to be applicable to artistic production, the total function of art is reversed. Instead of being based on ritual, it begins to be based on another practice – politics.[30]

Contemporary art can usefully be defined as belonging to two contested critical spaces, the late modern and the postmodern. Advocates of the late modern tend to subscribe to the notion of art as ineffable; a 'high' cultural phenomenon which, although socially and culturally specific, is never reducible to its contexts. This perpetuates art as an auratic, even transcendental, practice, contributing to, but not indicative of, social discourse. The postmodern is theorized as a more plural, more inclusive range of practices, accommodating difference; and the late modern as critical, ephemeral, marginal, popular, reproducible, as well as historical returns of neo-this and -that. It is inextricably bound to the day-to-day events of mass social discourse, public or private, profound or banal, whether from a celebratory or critical position. If the former is characterized by the unique object assessed in terms of quality, the latter is characterized by the photograph and, more recently, the website accessed in terms of interest and desire. The implications that the interested browser may have on the motivation to learn cannot yet be tested; only once access to the internet and digital technologies is comprehensively available in schools will this be quantifiable. However, it is increasingly clear that more and more artists and students are utilizing new technologies to produce and disseminate their work.

When arguing for the political significance of contemporary art, Foster[31] sidelines the all-embracing category 'postmodern' in favour of the term 'neo-avant-garde', a term he coins to define and defend those artists who retroactively reclaim the critical practice of the historical avant-garde. He suggests that their re-engagement does not take the form of repetition (reinventing Duchamp's bicycle wheel) but critical reconstruction, a return to and redefinition of a lost model whose radical function was to test boundaries and displace customary practice. Teachers, by focusing on this practice, which is always in a dialectical relationship to dominant and hegemonic modes of visual and material culture, can select work to engage students in debates that have shaped the post-industrial, post-colonial world and assist them in understanding the institutions which determine their lives:

> if this model of *retroaction* can contribute any symbolic resistance to the work of *retroversion* so pervasive in culture and politics today – that is, the reactionary undoing of the progressive transformations of the century – so much the better.[32]

Seen from this perspective, the type of radical practice advocated, the counter-project so frightening to the emerging neo-conservative consensus, is in fact a return, a very real instance of cultural heritage.

Table 2.2 indicates some of the characteristics of two parallel tendencies in twentieth-century art. The avant-garde (historic and neo) designates those artists and groups who have continuously questioned the universalizing agendas of an official modernism. If this is true, then it could be said that progressive postmodernism largely entails a continuation of the counter-project instigated at the turn of the twentieth century. To avoid associations with periodization, the term postmodernism, with its implication of an end to modernism, is not used. Although acknowledging historical specificity, this table recognizes continuities as well as discontinuities, allegiances as well as oppositions, commonalities as well as difference. It also suggests that the characteristics of the neo-avant-garde may now be seen as the characteristics of an 'official' contemporary practice; that is practice designated as significant by the institutions of art.

Practice in schools rarely explores these characteristics. It neither addresses creativity nor critical inquiry, although it often attempts to accommodate students' self-expression: the 'innocent figure of pure, unsocialized creativity';[33] and occasionally involves them in identity politics: 'an exchange of power, an exchange of position'.[34] School art is essentially concerned with cultural reproduction, the perpetuation of 'traditional' skills. However, these discrete representational and craft skills are increasingly perceived as marginal to the core skills of statutory education with its demands for transferability. How can an engagement with contemporary art reconceptualize the art and design curriculum? Why bother?

We believe that contemporary art, or at least the critical counter-project, engages with issues and practices which are central to the principles of the revised National Curriculum, namely, that students

> engage critically with a rapidly changing visual [and material] culture, acknowledging difference, and evaluate the use of traditional and new materials and technologies ... explore meanings and interpretations of works of art, craft and design and evaluate their role and impact in contemporary life. They learn how to become actively involved in shaping environments ... [35]

Although contemporary art often refuses classification, it is useful strategically to align artists who engage with bodies of knowledge that many schools find problematic (Table 2.3). In this way teachers can resource issues and practices for critical discussion and investigation. For reasons of accessibility artists have been selected because of the availability of their work in reproduction and as the focus of critical texts in English. It is evident that most of them could belong to more than one of the categories.

MODELS FOR A POSTMODERN CURRICULUM

A Manifesto for art in schools

In January 1998, cognizant of the review of the English National Curriculum planned for 2000, the National Society for Education in Art and Design

Table 2.2 Characteristics of two parallel tendencies in twentieth century art

Official modern	*Neo-avant-garde*
creativity: innovation	critical inquiry: redefinition
aesthetic refinement: autonomy	aesthetic play: border-crossing
passive viewer: immanent and transcendental meaning; aesthetic literacy	active viewer: constructing meaning; visual literacy
aura, originality, autonomy	reproduction, repetition
quality, disinterestedness	interest, desire
spatial: presence, 'sublime instantaneousness'	temporal: flux
optical	performance: theatre, spectacle
conviction	doubt, deconstruction
universal, essential	relative, conditional, strategic
exclusive	inclusive
ineffable	textual, site-specific
literal, serious, utopian	allegoric, ludic, fallen
eternal, immutable	ephemeral, fugitive
progressive, teleological	progressive, contingent
political, institutional	political, personal agency
self-expression	self-consciousness

(NSEAD), funded by the Arts Council of England, convened a focus group of art educators across all phases. Its remit was to 'produce a radical discussion paper', partly in response to the spread of 'school art' orthodoxies. Rather than be content with superficial amendments to existing tired formulae, it set out to try to create a vision of art and design education for the next decade, examining

Table 2.3 Strategic classifications

Installation, site-specific work and performance	The dominant modes of contemporary practice,[36, 37] e.g. Cornelia Parker, Richard Wilson, Gillian Wearing
New technologies	Practitioners who utilize, sometimes critically, digital technologies, e.g. Marina Abramovic, Jenny Holzer, Bill Viola[38, 39]
Political critique	Overtly political in intention; identifying, investigating and exposing institutional power, networks of control, systems of abuse, e.g. Hans Haacke,[40] Susan Hiller,[41] Guerrilla Girls,[42] Group Material.[43] Towards the close of the twentieth century a significant alliance has been formed between artists associated with class, gender and post-colonial politics as a result of ideological and demographic change.
a) Gender	Exploring gender as a construct
(i) feminist	Judy Chicago, Susan Hiller, Barbara Kruger, Mary Kelly, Cathy de Monchaux, Cindy Sherman, Hannah Wilke[44, 45]
(ii) queer politics	Robert Gober, Catherine Opie,[46] Millie Wilson[47, 48]
b) Diasporic	Examining representations of 'otherness' in the context of the post-colonial; promoting diverse cultural perspectives: Keith Piper, Yinka Shonabare, Chris Ofili, Zarina Bhinji, Bracha Lichtenberg Ettinger, Adrian Piper[49, 50]
c) Art for social action	Issue-based production that moves beyond the institutions of art to work with and in the community: Tim Rollins, Mierle Laderman Ukeles, Susan Lacy, Richard Layzell, Rachel Whiteread[51, 52]
Boundary-crossing a) Practitioners who test the conventions of discrete practices	Michael Brennand-Wood, Caroline Broadhead, Tracy Emin, Faith Ringgold, Helen Storey[53, 54]
b) Practitioners who test the conventions of acceptable form and content	Sophie Calle, Helen Chadwick, Chapman brothers, Gilbert and George, Damien Hirst, Mike Kelly, Tania Kovats, Carolee Schneeman[55, 56]

its future from first principles. The resulting manifesto calls for a 'postmodern solution for a postmodern situation'. As Hickman notes above (see Ch. 1), the manifesto proposes a rationale based on three fundamental principles: difference, plurality and independent thought, outlining the need for teachers to replace orthodoxy with innovative and imaginative approaches, and espousing the need to encourage qualities such as empathy, playfulness, surprise, ingenuity, risk-taking, curiosity and individuality. It identifies the problems currently plaguing art education and offers possible solutions. In its conclusion it calls for

> more opportunities for learners to understand art as something that does actually matter in their lives ... offer more choice, autonomy and empowerment through the development of a more critical, enquiring, reflexive and creative mindset, and to assist self-generated and self-aware learning.

It identifies a need to

> broaden the range of choice and type of study available across all art forms without any implied hierarchy. Offer opportunity for different types of study and a range of media planned to raise consciousness of current personal and social issues, their representation in past and present art forms, and through different cultures ... [and] reconsider the values implicit in current evaluation, assessment and evaluation practices, to whom the results of such practices are addressed and for what purpose, and their respective usefulness.[57]

To a large extent the dissatisfaction expressed in England about school art orthodoxies is mirrored in the USA. The introduction of Discipline Based Art Education (DBAE) resulted in a revision of the curriculum in the 1980s, but in its application this often proved to be a dislocated approach in which the 'disciplines' of aesthetics, art history and art criticism were segregated from the studio. In the main, pedagogic practices were predicated on 'modernist conceptions of art which placed a high premium on self expression and originality', and formalism, 'the persistence of the practice of teaching art by introducing elements and principles of design as a basis for studio production and art criticism'.[58] Little or no attention was paid to contemporary practice or its discourses.

Efland *et al.*[59] promote a curriculum in which the boundaries separating art, craft, design and critical practice are questioned. They identify the following postmodern principles to inform pedagogic practice and alter the modernist curriculum:

Little narratives

a) from universal to pluralist tendencies
b) from scholarly disciplined knowledge to local informants and knowledge

c)   from elitist to democratic, receptive of non-western art, that of minorities, women and popular culture

d)   a melding of local content and regional interests with national interests

Power–knowledge link

a)   impact of social forces (institutional) in validating and/or marginalizing the arts and education

b)   exemplified in professional discourses, e.g. architectural decisions, art history and criticism

c)   conflicts between dominant and less dominant social groups in validating knowledge

d)   language as a tool of power

Deconstruction

a)   a method critiquing the elucidation of fixed meanings

b)   from authorial interpretation to reception

c)   emphasis on collage, montage, pastiche, using lens-based and digital technologies

d)   computer interactivity altering the artist/viewer separation

Double-coding

a)   the postmodern recognizes multiple codes and messages questioning the modern curriculum

The Canadian Roger Clark similarly advocates a shift from the status quo towards postmodernism. He suggests that there are two alternatives for curriculum change. The first is 'reformist', the second 'reconstructionist'. Whilst the first identifies ways of adapting existing curricula to the postmodernist art world, using modernist formalism as a foundation for more interpretative studies, the second completely rejects the notion that traditional modes can be adapted to 'accommodate the social activist principles of post-modern scholarship'.[60] The implication of this latter position is that a *tabula rasa* is required before reconstruction can take place. We hope to suggest a less traumatic solution building on Raymond Williams's notion of changing social structures through a process of 'long revolution':

> The nature of the process indicates a perhaps unusual revolutionary activity: open discussion, extending relationships, the practical shaping of institutions. But it indicates also a necessary strength: against arbitrary power whether of arms or money, against all conscious confusion and weakening of this long and difficult human effort, and for and with the people who in many different ways are keeping the revolution going.[61]

TENSIONS BETWEEN CONTEMPORARY ART AND (ART) EDUCATION

Resistance

> Education is particularly resistant to the 'post-modern message'. Education theory and practice is founded on the discourse of modernity ... Postmodernism's emphasis on the inscribed subject constructed by language, discourses, desire and the unconscious, seems to contradict the very purpose of education and the basis of educational activity.[62]

We have noted that art teaching has been subject to a series of successive shifts in practice, some dictated by government directives, others promoted by art educationalists. However, it is important to subject these changes to scrutiny in order to identify whether, as both Hughes[63] and Efland[64] suggest, they amount to little more than 'tinkering on the edges'. While it may be true that art teachers have always been allowed, even encouraged, to be idiosyncratic, they have never had the opportunity to be independent. The 'given' curriculum, defined by government agencies and examination boards can be seen to frame and thus delimit their practice.

It is tempting to forgive teachers for their apparent lack of ambition and reluctance to take risks, acknowledging that they are victims of circumstance, trapped by tradition, timetables, examinations and restricted and restricting resources. The popularity of the subject in schools and the high rate of examination success also militate against change. We must recognize that teachers, despite the tinkering, are constrained by their own education, their highly charged belief in modernist utopianism and their vicarious pleasure in the 'success' of their students.

Certainly, if we are to believe Usher and Edwards, postmodernism appears to have bypassed the entire edifice of institutional education. Sociology and media studies are perhaps the exceptions to this rule. These subject fields are not held back by the weight of 'heritage' in quite the same way as subjects whose genealogy is rooted in the classical liberal arts. What can happen is that a tradition formed over time is perceived as natural and fixed rather than cultural and subject to change. In fact, media studies is invading and populating areas of the curriculum that dare to engage with contemporary visual and material culture, those areas art and design teachers are reluctant to explore: 'The value of being located in the post-modern is the greater possibility for disruption of the 'given'; and in education there are far too many 'givens in need of disruption'.[65]

Modernism and art education

Most of the theories which underpin the practices of art education in schools today can be traced back to the first half of this century. Art education has continued to expand and develop but without much disturbance of its knowledge base which is rooted in the values and ideas of an official modernism. If the official modernist institutions of western culture are characterized by their adherence to a liberal belief in progress empowered through formalist experiment, either by means of individual development or the progress of society through good design, then universal education, and particularly art education, upholds its tenets. The former model holds dear the self-actualization of each student, evidenced in the unique creative object. What this privileges is the 'expressive subject', an individual whose singular understanding of experience can be communicated directly, as it were unmediated. This is very different to the 'inscribed subject' proposed by Usher and Edwards; one who is aware that what they produce is a representation, a construct, not an emanation. Alternatively there are voices calling for the abandonment of modernist practice in favour of a return to the western humanist tradition exemplified by academic art.[66] This is no more than a construction of a national heritage, an ideological site for renewing a conservative vision of the past within the confines of an authoritarian present. Although postmodern critical practice in no way perpetuates canonic tradition, it is at least in dialogue with past codes and conventions unlike those modernist practices that sought to deny tradition.

Peter Abbs, perhaps one of the most widely read commentators on arts education today, suggests there is a false dichotomy between the past and the present. He believes that progress in the arts depends on a sense of tradition which can be translated into a modern idiom. He bemoans the fact that teachers have undervalued the place of the cultural continuum. He identifies two dynamic views of cultural time – the conservative and the postmodern – and asserts that they are oppositional. One is the 'kind of piety to ancestors', the other is 'a turbulent iconoclastic spirit, indefinitely restless, infinitely searching, infinitely dissatisfied'. Abbs believes we need both. He claims:

> We need to be able to submit ourselves to the intrinsic qualities of great works of art across time, but we need to preserve, simultaneously, the freedom to change, to subvert, to tell again with a different outcome ... In the first view the cultural continuum offers us work which challenges us, educates us, expands us ... in the second it offers us material to be endlessly refashioned, raided, rectified, reformulated.

> In re-appropriating a culture we discover, with elation, those metaphors which illuminate and extend, but we also, inevitably, encounter metaphors which restrict, which cage, which damage; and these need to be cast again in the human imagination according to our own sense of truth, however precarious.[67]

What is needed in order to avoid a reduction to a simple notion of chronology or a negation of the past, is a broad, diverse approach which rejects traditional, diachronic and fixed classifications in favour of synchronic and flexible framing. Any organization of knowledge which involves an attempt to reduce the holding strength of classification involves a constant reappropriation of the past in relation to a constantly changing present.

Problems and possibilities

'For god's sake leave theory alone; teachers, never mind students, can't make any sense of it.'[68]

There is a very real danger that if teachers attempt to 'dumb down' the complex theoretical issues and methodologies of critical practice for use by students, the resulting inquiry will be a disjointed and distorted caricature of academic procedures. Brandon Taylor cautioned influentially against the use of modern art in teaching art to the young:

a seriously wrong understanding is worse than no understanding at all. [I would] counsel extreme caution generally in making assumptions about the relevance of early twentieth century avant-garde art images to the life and developing interest of the younger child.[69]

He describes the adverse psychological effect of 'distortion' (here related to Cubism) on their developing analytical minds; a sort of threat to their sense of bodily integrity. This debatable argument is countered by Maureen Price:

An *Art History and Critical Studies* programme needs to establish the conditions in which the principle of pluralism in visual representation can be recognised and valued. This objective can be pursued by placing increased emphasis on those areas of cultural production traditionally regarded as marginal to European cultural history, thereby destabilising to some extent the dominant notion of the 'norm' ... where intellectual structures are particularly complex, as in Brandon Taylor's example of modern culture, the material needs to be subjected to continuous reappraisal with a positive view to discovering possible points of access for the pupil.[70]

Taylor's caution is pessimistic and timid. As Price asserts, it is up to the teacher to find ways to access art that they find problematic. Students in school are surprisingly adept at forming and substantiating opinions if provided with, indeed inculcated into, a culture of enquiry. Andrew Brighton claims: 'the underdeveloped discursive culture of art in English art schools culturally disempowers students'.[71] It is these disempowered students who in turn become disempowered teachers. Although art and design teachers may be seen as 'experts' because they provide 'answers', bel hooks claims that they do not have the pedagogic skills to transform the culture of the classroom into one that is discursive and engaged, one that invites multiple perspectives and reciprocal learning.[72] This can lead to a situation where young people are prevented from participation by a culture of dependency. Their opinion is not sought, is undervalued and/or dismissed. This is not to promote a culture in which students' opinions are accepted uncritically, assenting to particular readings and personal connotations as if they were generalizable, a promiscuous descent into the nether-regions of pure reception theory. Nor does it privilege the methods of deconstruction in which binary oppositions are pitted one against the other so that the dominant discourse is challenged and negated, ultimately leading to the convergence and collapse of conventional signs.

John Sturrock engages with the slippery nature of signs:

> Whatever thoughts we may have as readers, whether they are expressed to others or not, form a continuum with the text itself (including images). They are, in Peirce's term, its interpretants, the signs evoked by the signs on the page. There are infinitely many possibilities and levels of such evocation according to the interests, the intelligence, the knowledge, the temperament of the reader ... The role of the poststructuralist reader is not, however, merely to register as many readings and ambiguities as he or she can; a semantic head-count for its own sake would not do. The aim rather is to appreciate where and how the text under consideration falls apart.[73]

Given this propensity – the human as a meaning-making being,[74] students relish the opportunity to interpret visual and material culture. Teachers tend to rely on historical art as a focus for pastiche and interpretation. However familiar, it could be argued that these exemplars are more difficult to understand than contemporary art because the contexts that once conditioned their production are less evident than the conditions and motivations stimulating contemporary practice. Students and contemporary artists have a similar field of experience; an experience in and with difference. In addition, the languages used by artists are not necessarily at odds with those used by students: the fact that artists are involved in the counter-project does not mean that they all engage in the linguistic niceties of academic discourse. Some of the art cited in section 1 of the strategic classifications, is highly visceral and affective; some is ironic, amusingly appropriating familiar objects from the urban and domestic landscape, some employs the double-coding students know from advertising, while at the same time criticizing this means of production.

MANAGING A PLURALIST CURRICULUM

As we have seen, many reformists have advocated the reconceptualization or reconstruction of the art curriculum. Some have suggested that the term 'art' should be dropped and replaced by 'cultural production' or 'visual and material culture'. Others bemoan the neglect of design; the loss of 'visual production' to technology. The wholesale abandonment of the specificity of art in favour of the inclusion of the entire field of visual and artefactual production is, in pragmatic terms, an impossibility. It cannot be managed within the time allocated to art and design in secondary schools. If we consider the parallel position of the 'logocentric curriculum' for students aged between 11 and 16, particularly the dominance of language within that curriculum, it comprises approximately two-thirds of available time, one third being specifically linguistic. The visual, as a discrete area of study, is given about one twenty-fifth. Literacy is perceived as central to learning, despite the recognized shift from verbal to visual means of communication.[75] Literacy is exalted as the most effective and transparent symbolic means for assimilating, understanding and communicating knowledge. The subjects of the school curriculum privileging this symbolic tool include English (language and literature) and the humanities (history and religious education). If 'cultural production' or 'visual and material culture' are to be seriously studied, similar time and cross-curricular recognition are necessary to forge a viable curriculum, i.e. the grammar of visual and material culture; production and reception; art, craft and design histories; perceptual psychology; aesthetics; interdisciplinary investigation.

Such a situation is unlikely to materialize. However, contemporary art in the form of the counter-project and intercultural pluralism is a site where these interests converge. In addressing contemporary art, the art and design teacher needs to consider not only its content but how it might inform practice in the classroom. In addition teachers must reflect on their own pedagogy and identify the methods and strategies they can employ to ensure a level of congruence between teaching and contemporary practice. To assist us in realizing a model for a critical and progressive pedagogy we refer to terms identified by Grossberg: 'hierarchical', 'dialogic', 'praxical' and 'affective'.[76]

In the hierarchical model teachers conserve their role as a figure of authority while addressing 'problematic bodies of knowledge'. This ensures that they determine the frames of reference by which an issue can be discussed: 'it is the teacher who draws the line between the good the bad and the ugly, between the politically correct and the politically incorrect'.[77] This is a traditional model where the teacher as expert and moral guardian determines what is right. It is a role that teachers are loath to give up and which they are encouraged to sustain by convention. This model evidently falls apart when teachers are representing art from a culture in which they are not immersed but in which some of their students may be. Take for instance Richard Billingham's photographic record of his family, an insider's raw view of what, to an outsider, might appear hopelessly 'dysfunctional', quite beyond the decorum of the kitchen-sink realism with which it has been associated.[78] The dialogic, however, invites students' contributions.

The dialogic model questions the balance of power inherent in the hierarchical model. The teacher invites students to participate by presenting and discussing their own perceptions, thereby acknowledging different subject positions. The authority of the teacher is thus questioned and everyone is encouraged to reflect on their assumptions, beliefs and values. The dialogic model acknowledges differences, past and present. It is similar to classical debate but differs in that it refuses to defer to representatives or canonical exemplars. Merely reappropriating a past culture, be it Socratic or otherwise, cannot work unless current contexts and intervening developments are part of the equation:

> Simultaneously honour and reformulate experiences associated with the historical without being trapped in either it or its objectification ... don't position history as an absolute to be memorised and consumed in the

manner of formal educational exercises, but as a point of 'mediation'
that requires continuous sustained rereading, reworking and
reconstruction.[79]

Judy Chicago's *Dinner Party* (1979), a collaborative installation, addresses the
dialogic on a number of counts, rereading, reworking and reconstructing
women's contribution to history. Not only does it answer patriarchy's nega-
tions and insistence on unique authorship; it also engages in a dialogue between
craft and conceptual practice.[80]

At its best the exchanges and transformations of meaning that characterize
the dialogic model accommodate the play of reception theory tested against the
objectivity of analytical methods. However, it falls down unless students are
empowered with critical and discursive skills.

The praxical recognizes the dialogic but is not content to leave it there.
Opinions are not only raised and discussed; areas of difference and consensus
require action; action that may question and challenge institutional power. On
an immediate level this might relate to the curriculum and its mode of delivery
so that teaching and learning are negotiated. When a student identifies his/her
own interests and jointly plans, with the teacher, an individual learning path, to
some extent the praxical model is adopted. However, the praxical promotes
working collaboratively for social change. In contrast, conventional practice
usually privileges individualism. Social change can only be effected by forming
alliances with the wider emancipatory community and joining in their political
struggle. This model becomes problematic if change merely establishes a new
orthodoxy. Unless the process is continuous it can easily revert to a hierarchical model. For example, we might anticipate that Richard Long's solitary
walks, being site-specific, temporal works, refute commodification in a gallery.
But through the photographic record they re-enter that terrain and take on the
values of the market. Tim Rollins's experiments with KOS, in which 'dis-
affected adolescents' from the USA participated in collective visual
interpretations of literary works, produced an engaged dialogue with the past.
There is a danger that the impact of such challenging practices can be diluted in
the principles of bourgeois inclusivity; difference is accommodated before it can
pose any substantial threat.

The affective pedagogy marks a subtle shift. It brings together the discursive
practice of the dialogic and the political idealism of the praxical while
acknowledging that the expanding field of visual cultural requires people to
make connections between diverse domains, discourses and practices. Grossberg defines this synthesis as an

> affective pedagogy, a pedagogy of possibility (but every possibility has to
> risk failure) and of agency. It refuses to assume that even theory or
> politics, theoretical or political correctness, can be known in advance. It
> is a pedagogy which aims not to pre-define its outcome (even in terms of
> some imagined value of emancipation or democracy) but to empower its
> students to begin to reconstruct their world in new ways and to

re-articulate their future in unimagined and perhaps even unimaginable ways.[81]

This might seem to abandon all conventions, all authorial control. Ellsworth suggests that it is all well and good in theory but that it 'has developed along a highly abstract and utopian line which does not necessarily sustain the daily workings of the education its supporters advocate'.[82] In fact affective pedagogy does not seek to save the world but rather to raise consciousness and the capacity of students to take some responsibility for their own learning, recognizing the possibility of change through critical engagement. This notion of an affective pedagogy corresponds to hooks's 'engaged pedagogy'; one of continuous flexibility and flux. She insists that 'engaged pedagogy' does not offer a blueprint; rather it 'recognises each classroom as different, that strategies must constantly be changed, invented, reconceptualised to address each new teaching experience'.[83]

How, as art and design teachers, can we make sense of this rhetoric so that contemporary art has some impact in the classroom? We offer a series of strategies for critical pedagogy:

Interventions

Griselda Pollock asserts:

> The structural sexism of most academic disciplines contributes actively to the production and perpetuation of a gender hierarchy. What we learn about the world and its peoples is ideologically patterned in conformity with the social order within which it is produced.[84]

Strategies of visibility and intervention have raised an awareness of gender as a social and cultural construct. This awareness impacts on other areas of difference, for example those of class, race, ability, age and sexuality. In addition to external resources – institutional, human etc. – teachers can invite the contribution of students. Their (sub)cultures can act as interventions into the official curriculum; what Shohat and Stam refer to as 'affective investments'.[85]

The work of Adrian Piper is an example of multiple intervention. Her video art, a medium that is in itself a technical intervention within the traditional art and design curriculum, confronts viewers with issues that raise repressed questions of identity: race, sex, class:

> One of Adrian Piper's videos ... informs the 'White' spectator that he/ she is in all probability part Black, since after 400 years 'there are no genetically distinguishable White people in this country'. And 'now that you know you're Black', she asks provocatively, 'aren't you eager to enjoy the benefits that blackness brings?' And 'if racism isn't just "our" problem, but equally "yours", how are we going to solve it?'[86]

Clearly such issues can be problematic; the classroom may become a site of challenging interaction. It is therefore essential that teachers develop a safe environment so that they can direct the classroom dynamic using dialogic systems such as paired, small-group and whole-class discussion, brainstorming and concept-mapping, student reviews, critiques, presentations and curated exhibitions, including catalogues.

External interventions are equally vital. Through partnerships, such as artists' placements, practice in schools can be challenged, extended and developed. The contemporary artist is 'the intruder that struggles to articulate what's missing, what's absent, what's hidden – when everything seems so readily apparent ... the unheard voice, the different gaze'.[87]

Mediations

As educators it is vital that we also enable students to move outside their immediate frames of reference. Without context, cultural production is thrown into isolation; it appears to be self-contained and self-serving. In order to do justice to the diversity of contemporary practice and to take on its methods the classroom must be developed into a place for investigation and enquiry, not only for debate and discussion. We have seen how the dialogic model is able to develop a relationship with the past:

> The radical educator deals with tradition like anything else. It must be engaged and not simply received. Traditions are important. They contain great insights, both for understanding what we want to be and what we don't want to be. The question is: in what context do we want to judge tradition? Around what sense of purpose? We need a referent to do that. If we don't have a referent then we have no context to make sense of tradition.[88]

The difficulty in art and design is to manage the wealth of traditions afforded by gallery and museum culture. It is not always possible to facilitate interventions where the subjects speak for themselves. At times teachers and students must take responsibility for representing others. As a strategy, we suggest that in extending cultural knowledge they focus on points of interaction; the intercultural curriculum. Pluralism is not a new phenomenon; cultures are rarely discrete and autonomous; rather they are fluid and dynamic, mediated through continuous interaction, whether confrontational or consensual. Yinka Shonibare explores the legacy of colonial interaction, conflating the signs and customs of colonizers – whether that of the Victorians or today's global markets – with indigenous peoples, producing witty but provocative visions of hybridity.

Many artists have drawn on the techniques of ethnography, embracing and deploying strategies of scrutiny while simultaneously critiquing such practice. One of Sophie Calle's installations records her covert action as she takes on the role of a chambermaid in order to record photographically the personal items and habits of hotel guests, from the contents of their suitcases and bathroom detritus to their intimate conversations and pages from secret diaries. Likewise students could represent the sixth-form common-room, the tobacco-stained corners, the insults and flatteries or the exchanges of hope and desire.

Transformations

> ... border pedagogy necessitates combining the modernist emphasis on the capacity of individuals to use critical reason to address the issue of public life, with the post-modern concern with how we might experience agency in a world constituted in differences.[89]

Critical reason may seem at odds with the unpredictability, the doubts and absolute certainties of difference. How can we disentangle critical reason from its positivist and materialist orthodoxy so that we come to recognize difference as legitimate? Symbolic and physical lines of demarcation are the means to construct, contain and conserve identities; to reinforce difference through rituals of purity and pollution. However, the collapse of borders is indicative of post-industrial, post-colonial culture; the diasporic reality of a transforming pluralist society. The critical analysis of systems of demarcation enables us to understand how such systems are constructed and given value without necessarily destroying belief in them: it enables us to realize that, given different circumstances, our own beliefs would be different. It allows us to imagine ourselves as other.

> There are times in life when the question of knowing if one can think differently than one thinks and perceive differently than one sees is absolutely necessary if one is to go on looking and reflecting at all ... But what then is philosophy today – philosophical activity, I mean – if not the critical labour of thought upon itself? And if it does not consist, in place of legitimating what one already knows, in undertaking to know how, and up to what limit, it would be possible to think differently?[90]

Traditionally, crossing borders is to transgress, whether those borders are borders of class, gender, race, age, sexuality or ability. Traditionally, the school is a place of almost schizophrenic imperatives; it demands that students conform to rigid codes in terms of social behaviour while advocating a spirit of disinterested, independent inquiry in their work. If the students cross this border, if they inquire into the validity of the social codes, they are invariably sanctioned. In contrast, border pedagogy asks that the whole learning community examines existing structures and demarcations; for example, that teachers consider themselves as learners, and students realize their potential as knowledge providers; that both have agency.

Border pedagogy asks that learners move into unfamiliar territory, whether of practice, place or time; it de-centres as it re-maps. Like contemporary art it encourages risky practice. However, risk is not possible without first establishing a safe but critical learning environment. Where others have suggested conversive transformation[91] we suggest the less traumatic process of incremental transformation; one that, having built a safe environment, develops the dialogic and discursive, invites interventions and broadens knowledge in partnership with external agencies, particularly contemporary galleries and artists, challenging students to go beyond what is already known. While conversive transformation encourages the grand gesture and spectacle, incremental transformation is more grounded in critical inquiry. It encourages more subtle, less oppositional practices; rather than soap-box oratory and confrontation, it uses humour and irony; rather than force the certainties of passion, it acknowledges the contingencies of desire. We believe it is *worth* bothering.

POSTSCRIPT

In the four years since writing this chapter, there has been noticeable change in some schools and colleges in the UK, especially post-16. We suspect that it is in those schools and colleges, where teachers have developed partnerships with contemporary art galleries and artists, that contemporary practices are being seen as viable, in terms both of fulfilling examination criteria and the Examination Boards' moderation process, and of students' personal engagement with the expanding field of visual culture. As the practice of artists diversifies, it is increasingly important to work with individuals and institutions outside mainstream education. It is by means of such partnerships that it is possible to challenge emerging educational practices and, at the local level, to prevent practice becoming formulaic or turning into a new orthodoxy.

However, it is not only external partnerships that are supporting change, but also the way in which the initial and continuing education of art and design teachers is being reconceptualized. For example, the artist/teacher scheme initiated by the National Society for Education in Art and Design (NSEAD) in collaboration with institutions of higher education enables teachers to re-engage with their practice in such a way that they work in dialogue with contemporary practice and critical theory. This militates against the modernist procedures that may have previously limited their practice in schools. For many, this dialogue is not entirely new: but for others, especially those who are initially reluctant and/or resistant, suspicion gives way to recognition as they come to see both the strengths of diversity and their own potential as agents of change.

The dialogic model is not without its critics. Burbules, for example, in the context of multicultural education, is suspicious of the asymmetrical power relations between those instigating dialogue and those who are invited to contribute 'freely'.[92] Somekh highlights the skewed power relations developing in the context of schools that work in partnership with external agencies. Here, although there may be a declared equality, in practice teachers' knowledge, located in the experiential and pragmatic, can be subsumed by the theoretical and institutional rhetorics of action research.[93] Nonetheless, we believe partnerships, however bothersome, are a significant catalyst for curriculum development. Initiatives between contemporary art galleries and new courses in initial teacher education are making possible meaningful collaborations in the development of subject knowledge and pedagogy, as are interventions by student teachers within historical sites.[94] It must be remembered that art and design students entering the teaching profession are themselves contemporary artists; as Robins articulates, many will have already gone through one cleansing rite as they leave school to enter higher education,[95] and the challenge is to prevent this process from being repeated. The challenge is a very real one.

Notes

1. Kruger, B. (1996), in L. Weintraub *Art on the Edge*. New York: Art Insights Inc., p. 194.
2. Kelly, M., in *ibid.*, p. 228.
3. Burchill, J. (1997) 'Death of innocence' *Guardian G2*, 12 November.
4. Becker, C. (1996) 'The education of young artists and the issue of audience', in L. Dawtrey *et al.* (eds) *Critical Studies and Modern Art*. Milton Keynes: Open University, p. 176.
5. Willis, P. (1990) *Moving Culture*. London: Calouste and Gulbenkian Foundation.
6. Lacy, S. (ed.) (1995) *Mapping the Terrain: New Genre Public Art*. Seattle: Bay Press.
7. Paley, N. (1995) *Finding Art's Place*. New York and London: Routledge.
8. Dixon, M. (1995) *Art With People*. Sunderland: Artists' Newsletter Publications.
9. Robinson, K. (Chairman of National Advisory Committee on Creative and Cultural Education) (1999) *All Our Futures: Creativity, Culture and Education*. London: DfEE.
10. Hughes, A. (1998) 'Reconceptualising the art curriculum'. *Journal of Art and Design Education*, **17**(1), p. 41. (The paper was originally presented as a presidential address by Arthur Hughes at the NSEAD national conference in Glasgow, 1997.)
11. Abbs, P. (ed.) (1987) *Living Powers*. London: Falmer Press.
12. Willis, P., *op. cit.*
13. Binch, N. and Robertson, L. (1994) *Resourcing and Assessing Art, Craft and Design: Critical Studies in Art at Key Stage 4*. Corsham: NSEAD.
14. Meecham, P. (1996) 'What's in a National Curriculum?'. In Dawtrey *et al.*, *op. cit.*
15. Dalton, P. (1996) 'Modernism, art education and sexual difference', in K. Deepwell (ed.) *New Feminist Art Criticism*. Manchester: Manchester University Press, pp. 44–51.
16. Schon, D. (1987) *Educating the Reflective Practitioner*. San Francisco: Jossey Bass.
17. Field, R. (1970) *Change in Art Education*. New York: Routledge & Kegan Paul.
18. Eisner, E. (1972) *Educating Artistic Vision*. New York: Macmillan.
19. Cunliffe, L. (1996) 'Art and world view: escaping the formalist labyrinth'. *Journal of Art and Design Education*, **15**(3), 309–26.
20. Atkinson, D. (1999) 'A critical reading of the National Curriculum for art in the light of contemporary theories of subjectivity'. *Journal of Art and Design Education*, **18**(1), 107–13.
21. Clement, R. (1993) *The Art Teacher's Handbook*. Cheltenham: Stanley Thornes.
22. Palmer, F. (1989) *Visual Elements of Art and Design*. Harlow: Longman.
23. Witkin, R. (1974) *The Intelligence of Feeling*. London: Heinemann.
24. SCAA (1996) *Consistency in Teachers' Assessment: Exemplification of Standards KS3*. London: SCAA.
25. Taylor, R. and Taylor, D. (1990) *Approaching Art and Design*. Harlow: Longman.

26. Taylor, R. (1986) *Educating for Art: Critical Responses and Development.* Harlow: Longman.
27. Kennedy, M. (1995) 'Issue-based work at KS4: Crofton School: a case study'. *Journal of Art and Design Education,* **14**(1), 7–20.
28. Efland, A., Freedman, K. and Stuhr, P. (1996) *Post-modern Art Education.* Virginia: The National Art Education Association.
29. Swift, J. and Steers, J. (1999) 'A manifesto for art in schools'. *Journal of Art and Design Education,* **18**(1), 7–13.
30. Benjamin, W. (1936) 'The work of art in the age of mechanical reproduction', reprinted in F. Frascina and J. Harris (eds) (1992) *Art in Modern Culture: An Anthology of Critical Texts.* London: Phaidon, p. 301.
31. Foster, H. (1996) *The Return of the Real.* Cambridge, MA and London: MIT Press.
32. *Ibid.*
33. Kelly, M., *op. cit.*
34. Kruger, B., *op. cit.*
35. QCA (1999) *The Secretary of State's Proposals for a Revised National Curriculum.* London: QCA.
36. Archer, M. (1996) *Installation Art.* London: Thames & Hudson.
37. Farrell, A. (ed.) (1997) *Blurring the Boundaries: Installation Art 1969–1996.* San Diego, CA: Museum of Contemporary Art.
38. Art and Design Profile no. 31 (1993) *World Wide Video.* London: *Art and Design* magazine.
39. Morgan, S. and Morris, F. (1995) *Rites of Passage: Art for the End of the Century.* London: Tate Gallery.
40. Bourdieu, P. and Haacke, H. (1995) *Free Exchange.* Cambridge: Polity Press.
41. Hiller, S. (1996) *Thinking About Art: Conversations with Susan Hiller.* Manchester: Manchester University Press.
42. Guerilla Girls (1995) *Confessions of Guerilla Girls.* London: Pandora.
43. Lacy, S., *op. cit.*
44. Women's Art Library [www.womensart.org.uk] *make.* WAL quarterly magazine.
45. Broude, N. and Garrard, M.D. (eds) (1994) *The Power of Feminist Art.* New York: Abrams.
46. Bright, D. (1998) *The Passionate Camera: Photography and Bodies of Desire.* London and New York: Routledge.
47. www.womenslibrary.org.uk
48. www.queer@art.org.uk
49. InIVA [www.iniva.org.uk]
50. *Third Text* (quarterly journal presenting perspectives on contemporary art from the 'third world').
51. Paley, N., *op. cit.*
52. Lacey, S., *op. cit.*
53. Addison, N. and Burgess, L. (in press) *Teaching Art and Design in the Secondary School.* London: Routledge.
54. Jeffries, J. (1995) 'Weaving across borderlines', in K. Deepwell, *op. cit.*
55. Frayling, C. *et al.* (1999) *Vision: 50 Years of British Creativity.* London: Thames & Hudson.
56. Shelton, A. (1995) *Fetishism: Visualising Power and Desire.* London: Lund Humphries.
57. Swift, J. and Steers, J., *op. cit.,* 12–13.

58. Efland, A. (1987) 'Curriculum antecedents of discipline-based art education'. *Journal of Aesthetic Education*, **21**(2), 89.
59. Efland, A. *et al.*, *op. cit.*, pp. 91–113.
60. Clark, R. (1997) 'Purposeful uncertainty', in R. Irwin and K. Grauer (eds) *Readings in Canadian Art Teacher Education*. Ontario: The Canadian Society for Education through Art, p. 9.
61. Williams, R. (1961) (1965 edn) *The Long Revolution*. Harmondsworth: Penguin.
62. Usher, R. and Edwards, R. (1994) *Post-modernism in Education*. London: Routledge, p. 3.
63. Hughes, A. (1998) 'A further reconceptualisation of the art curriculum', in *Broadside 1*. Birmingham, University of Central England: ARTicle Press.
64. Efland, A. *et al.* (eds), *op. cit.*, p. 47.
65. Usher, R. and Edwards, R., *op. cit.*, p. 31.
66. Tate, N. (1996) *Curriculum, Culture and Society*. London: SCAA (Schools' Curriculum and Assessment Authority).
67. Abbs, P. (1993) 'Backwards forward'. *TES*, 30 April.
68. Anon. (1998) Overheard statement by a professor of art history.
69. Taylor, B. (1989) 'Art history in the classroom: a plea for caution', in D. Thistlewood (ed.) *Critical Studies in Art and Design Education*. Harlow: Longman, p. 108.
70. Price, M. (1989) 'Art history and critical studies in schools: an inclusive approach', in D. Thistlewood (ed.) *Critical Studies in Art and Design Education*. Harlow: Longman, pp. 120–1.
71. Brighton, A. (1994) *Talking Art*. London: ICA, p. 38.
72. hooks, b. (1994) *Teaching to Transgress*. New York and London: Routledge.
73. Sturrock, J. (1993) *Structuralism*. London: Fontana, p. 151.
74. Bal, M. and Bryson, N. (1991) 'Semiotics and art history: a discussion of context and senders', in D. Preziosi (1989) *Rethinking Art History*. New Haven, CT and London: Yale University Press.
75. Kress, G. and Leeuwen, T. (1996) *Reading Images: A Grammar of Visual Design*. London: Routledge.
76. Grossberg, L. (1994) 'Introduction: bringin' it all back home: pedagogy and cultural studies', in H. Giroux and P. MacLaren (eds) *Between Borders*. New York and London: Routledge, pp. 16–21.
77. *Ibid.*, p. 16.
78. *Sensations* exhibition catalogue (1997). London: Royal Academy of Arts, pp. 52–7.
79. Paley, N., *op. cit.*, p. 178.
80. Jones, A. (ed.) (1996) *Sexual Politics: Judy Chicago's Dinner Party and Feminist Art History*. Los Angeles: University of California Press.
81. Grossberg, *op. cit.*, p. 18.
82. Ellsworth, E. (1989) 'Why doesn't this feel empowering? Working through the repressive myths of critical pedagogy'. *Harvard Educational Review*, **59**(3), 297.
83. hooks, b., *op. cit.*, p. 10.
84. Pollock, G. (1988) *Vision and Difference*. London: Routledge.
85. Shohat, E. and Stam, R. (1998) 'Narrativising visual culture: towards a polycentric aesthetic', in N. Mirzoeff (ed.) *Visual Culture Reader*. London: Routledge.
86. Shohat, E. and Stam, R. (1995) 'The politics of multiculturalism in the postmodern age', in *Art and Cultural Difference: Hybrids and Clusters*. Art and Design Magazine no. 43, 14.
87. Paley, N., *op. cit.*, p. 183.
88. Giroux, H. (1992) *Border Crossing*. New York and London: Routledge, pp. 17–18.

89. *Ibid.*, p. 29.
90. Foucault, M. (1954) 'Dream, imagination and existence', quoted in J. Miller (1993) *The Passion of Michel Foucault*. London: Flamingo, p. 36.
91. Taylor, R. (1992) *The Visual Arts in Education: Completing the Circle*. Lewes: Falmer Press; Hargreaves, D.H. (1983) 'The teaching of art and the art of teaching: towards an alternative view of aesthetic learning', in M. Hammersley and A. Hargreaves (eds) *Curriculum Practice: Some Sociological Case Studies*. Lewes: Falmer Press.
92. Burbules, N.C. (2000) 'The limits of dialogue as a critical pedagogy', in P. Trifonas (ed.) *Revolutionary Pedagogies*. New York, London: Routledge/Falmer.
93. O'Hanlon, C. (ed.) (1996) *Professional Development through Action Research in Educational Settings*. London: Falmer.
94. Schofield, K. (2003) 'Temporary residencies: student interventions in the gallery', in N. Addison and L. Burgess (eds) *Issues in Art and Design Teaching*. London: Routledge/Falmer.
95. Robins, C. (2003) 'In and out of place: cleansing rites in art education', in N. Addison and L. Burgess, *op. cit.*

Chapter 3

Art Education and the Art Museum

COLIN GRIGG

BACKGROUND

> If art contributes to, among other things, the way we view the world and
> shape social relations then it does matter whose image of the world it
> promotes and whose interest it serves.[1]

Art is fundamentally a complex form of visual language that is socially constructed and historically specific, be it a child's drawing or the work of a
professional artist. Children, in order to understand and participate in our
increasingly visual culture, need to engage directly with significant works of art
as well as acquire technical skills. This chapter is written to assist art teachers in
expanding their educational use of galleries in various ways:

- to make visible the history and forces that have shaped public art galleries
  which preserve what a previous government spokesman described as 'our
  national heritage', and to help form cultural values;
- to consider the way visitors, especially teachers, use the Tate Gallery and
  how this relates to the canon of art; and
- to explore certain critical studies and contemporary art history strategies
  used by the Tate Gallery Education Department to reframe students'
  engagement and understanding of the Gallery and the works of art displayed.

The Tate Gallery is among the world's foremost art museums, housing the
National Gallery of British Art and the National Gallery of International
Modern Art. The historic British collection includes outstanding paintings by
Hogarth, Gainsborough, Constable, William Blake, Turner and the Pre-
Raphaelites. The Modern collection contains important works by Kandinsky,
Mondrian, Picasso, Matisse, Brancusi, Henry Moore, Francis Bacon, Rothko
and Andy Warhol. The Gallery continues to acquire works by living artists
such as Anthony Caro, Paula Rego, Bill Viola and Damien Hirst. The col-
lection currently comprises some 60,000 artworks: over 4000 paintings, 1500

sculptures, 8000 unique works on paper, around 10,000 prints and over 35,000 works in the Turner bequest.

Each year the Turner Prize, awarded to an outstanding contemporary British artist, is accompanied by a chorus of 'yes, but is it art?' be it a cow and calf cut in half (*Mother and Child* by Damien Hirst) or suspended charred fragments of a burnt church (*Mass* by Cornelia Parker). Such a chorus of disapproval stems from an assumption that there exists a stable, universal definition of what is and is not art and, more particularly, that there is a set of empirical criteria for judging what is 'good' or 'great' art. Until the late nineteenth/early twentieth century, the bedrock of artistic judgements was the traditional western canon.

The Labour Party manifesto of 1945 stated: 'We desire to ensure to our people full access to the great heritage of the culture in this nation'; the National Gallery and Tate Gallery were seen as flagships of this cultural policy. Cultural history is inevitably a selective reading of the past from a present perspective, and after the war there was reassurance in seeing the great national collections as 'our cultural heritage', as maps to guide the way in an uncertain future. Today, such terms as 'our people', 'great heritage', 'culture' and 'nation' are all contested. However, in 1945 there still appeared to be a generally accepted canon of art, and the main issue of concern was one of access.

Cultural access was seen by the social visionaries of the postwar Labour government as not only a matter of physical entry but, most importantly, as also an issue of educational opportunity. For the privileged classes who provided the cultural leaders and administrators of the art establishment, the canon served as a fixed reference point. Kenneth Clark, in his autobiography, reflects: 'At the age of nine or ten I said with perfect confidence, "this is a good picture, that is a bad one ... " This almost insane self-confidence lasted till a few years ago.'[2]

DECODING THE TATE

This section explores the Gallery building, the nature of the collections and the exhibition programme, the curatorial approaches and the social values implicit in certain key individual works in the collection.

In the nineteenth century, the National Gallery had limited space and displayed an allegiance to the traditional canon, showing few British works in its new Trafalgar Square premises. So when pressure mounted to found a British collection, they looked for another site. When the National Gallery of British Art, the Tate, opened it was as an annexe to the National Gallery in Trafalgar Square and only achieved independent status in 1955.

A visitor's first impression of the Tate Gallery will be the imposing neoclassic facade, with its steeply raked, broad stone steps leading upward to a high portico of soaring Corinthian pillars that dwarf the visitor. Built in 1897 at the height of the British Empire, it conveys the imperial grandeur of Rome rather than the classical elegance of Greece. Sydney Smith, the architect, designed it 'to signify tradition, learning and authority'. The Gallery stands on the site of an early nineteenth-century penitentiary that ended its life as the holding jail for prisoners awaiting deportation to Botany Bay in Australia. When they cleared the site, it was large enough to not only build the gallery but, in time, a military hospital and housing for the poor also appeared. This reflected the changing attitude of the establishment from one of harsh social control in the early nineteenth century, so well captured in the novels of Dickens, to an attitude of social reform through massive programmes of public building that included houses, schools, hospitals, libraries and public museums and art galleries in the latter decades of the century.

Until recently the British have been suspicious of things continental and as if to contradict the homage to Rome displayed in the facade, Smith placed at the very pinnacle of the pediment a statue of Boadicea in her armour, the ancient British queen who expelled the invading Romans in the battle for Londinium. Today there are other, more characteristically modern, fixtures on the gallery roof: surveillance cameras. These indicate the high value now placed on works of art and the need for maximum security. The allusion to the old Millbank jail, the largest in Europe when first built, is continued inside with a network of closed-circuit television cameras and uniformed warders on patrol twenty-four hours a day.

The original gallery, opened by the Prince of Wales on 21 July 1897, was less than a quarter of its current size. The interior was dominated by the domed hall ringed with Doric columns, at the centre of which was a fountain surrounded by potted ferns. The general effect of the interior was a mixture of classical temple and grand country house. This induced in working-class visitors both a hushed reverence and a sense of how the rich lived.

There are four Tate sites: London Millbank, Liverpool, St Ives in Cornwall and a fourth, at Bankside London, opened in May in 2000. Tate Millbank and Tate St Ives are purpose-built galleries; one an expression of high neoclassicism, the other a postmodern building, all white stone and large windows, overlooking a sandy beach. Tate Liverpool and the new Tate Gallery of Modern Art at Bankside are conversions; one a James Stirling renovation of a nineteenth-century warehouse on the Albert Dock by the Mersey, the other a postwar power station opposite St Pauls on the Thames, redesigned by Herzog and de Meuron.

The Tate collections are shared between all these sites, so it is quite possible, over a period, that the same works will be displayed at all four galleries. An interesting project is to attempt to define the particular character of each site and to conjecture how each environment will shape and alter how one reads the same work of art.

To the casual visitor a national collection may appear to tell a seamless, comprehensive story. Nothing could be further from the truth. Collections such as those owned by the Tate are the outcome of accident, opportunity and the personal foibles of key individuals down the ages, as much as the realization of any grand art-historical design.

Henry Tate, the son of a Unitarian minister, began his working life as a grocer. By 1859 he owned six shops and took a share in a sugar refinery in

Liverpool. Around 1874 he set up his second sugar refinery in London, at Silvertown, in an old shipyard on the Thames. Tate's great innovation was producing sugar in cubes. This made him very wealthy. With his new wealth Tate began collecting contemporary British art, especially the Pre-Raphaelites. This is the equivalent to Charles Saatchi today, who collects young British artists such as Damien Hirst, though Tate's taste was somewhat more conservative. At this time, Victorian England had little in the way of state welfare provision and there developed a tradition of philanthropy. Henry Tate donated, over many years, funds to build hospitals and schools, and he decided, around 1890, to present his art collection to the nation. He gave 65 works, including Millais's *Ophelia* and Waterhouse's *The Lady of Shalott*.

When the Gallery first opened, Henry Tate's gift, which included money to build the gallery, was augmented by works from the Vernon and Chantrey bequests as well as British pictures in the National Gallery collection. It was this strange patchwork of artworks displayed on red, green and purple-brown walls that formed the founding collection. The government did not provide funds for acquisitions until 1946, so for the first 50 years the Tate depended on gifts and bequests.

The Chantry bequest provided funds for the purchase of works of art produced in Britain, but the fund was controlled by the Royal Academy Council. So at a time when Impressionism was the dynamic new force in European art, the Chantry bequest was still acquiring traditional Victorian academic works for the Tate Gallery.

The Tate has an international reputation for modern art from Europe and America, but its founding mission was to be a national collection of British art. We owe the Tate's great collection of modern art to a First World War German submarine. Sir Hugh Lane, a visionary collector, had agreed to leave certain major foreign artworks to the National Gallery on condition that a gallery be created for them. In 1913 he became Director of the National Gallery in Dublin and drew up a codicil to change his will and leave the paintings to Dublin. Lane, who was about to take a trip to America, came to the Tate and learned of plans to build a gallery there to house his gift. He had not settled the matter when he sailed for America on the liner *Lusitania* in 1915. Somewhere off the English coast the *Lusitania* was sunk by a German U-boat resulting in the loss of all on board. Dublin sought to claim the works but it was found the codicil had never been witnessed. The National Gallery, never enthusiastic about modern art, was eager, however, not to lose such a prize and intervened swiftly. It is by such accidents of history that great public collections are built. Ironically, by 1955 when the Tate achieved independence from the National Gallery, many of the major modern works were commandeered by the National for their collection.

When the artist J.M.W. Turner died in 1851 he left his own collection of works to the nation. With additions since then, this forms the great Turner Collection, comprising some 300 oil paintings and over 30,000 watercolours and drawings, a selection of which is housed in the Clore Gallery, designed by James Stirling, which opened in 1986. British modern art owes a particular debt to Turner; he became the major artist of his time, yet most of his works were landscapes with few figures and he increasingly rejected academic subjects and the high finish advocated by the traditional canon. His use of fields of colour and atmospheric effects was admired by the Impressionists and also inspired American abstract painters such as Rothko, who donated the Seagram murals so that they might be displayed near the Turners. The Turner Gallery enables students to study first-hand a major artist in considerable depth. Here you find thumbnail sketches made on a boat or train, watercolour sketches and large-scale oils enabling the viewer to follow the artist's whole creative process.

Apart from Whistler and Sargent, the Gallery owns virtually no pre-1940 American art. From the founding of the modern foreign galleries in 1926 with works from the Lane bequest and a fund set up by Samuel Courtauld, modern artists seemed, again and again, to be producing work that challenged directly the ideology of the traditional canon on which the national collections were based. The deliberate absurdities of Dadaism and Surrealism in particular made nonsense of Sir Joshua Reynolds' principles of 'high' art. Yet somehow public galleries, rather like cultural zoos, came to accommodate and tame those wild new ideologies. During this time American art was seen as a poor copy of European art and not to be taken seriously. But following the Second World War America emerged as the most powerful nation on earth and its artists reflected this new energy and confidence in large, brash works that not only challenged the old canon but equally confronted the new dogmas of European modern art. Even so, it was not until 1960 that the Tate began acquiring American modern art.

To understand more directly the competing ideologies that underlay the Tate's collections, consider three popular works: *The Lady of Shalott* (1888) by John William Waterhouse, Pablo Picasso's *The Three Dancers* (1925) and Jackson Pollock's *Summertime* (1948).

The Lady of Shalott was part of Henry Tate's original gift. What does it tell us about Victorian patrician values? The painting is based on a contemporary poem of the same name by Sir Alfred Lord Tennyson. It tells the story of a young woman imprisoned in a tower. Not only is she forbidden to leave the tower, she cannot even look directly out of the window but must observe the world through the reflection in a mirror. If she disobeys a curse will bring about her death. She spends her submissive days embroidering what she views in the circular mirror on a piece of cloth (shown in the boat). One day she sees the reflection of Sir Lancelot in his armour. Forgetting the curse she runs down stairs and jumps into a boat to pursue him to Camelot. The painting shows the moment when the curse takes its toll; she will be dead when the boat drifts into Camelot. The poem and painting were hugely popular in Victorian times, reflecting, perhaps, the patriarchal society that believed fathers or husbands owned their women and that a woman's role was to suffer and die for her man. We might regard such blatantly male-chauvinist ideals to be unacceptable to today's visitors, but this doomed lady, along with her sister in suicide, *Ophelia* (by Millais), remain hugely popular, especially among women visitors. A potentially fruitful and interesting gallery activity involves analysing carefully the complex symbolism of the painting and poem and then constructing an equivalent to reflect present-day values.

It is impossible for a single work to represent the extraordinary diversity of modern European art but *The Three Dancers*, an acclaimed masterpiece by Picasso does embody many of the qualities people associate with avant-garde art. *The Three Dancers* eloquently dramatizes the continuity and fracture between traditional art and the new spirit that informed culture in the early twentieth century. Picasso based the figure composition on a classical statue, *The Three Graces*. Whilst Waterhouse had designed his painting as a representation of public values, Picasso typifies twentieth-century artists' preoccupation with personal experience. The painting began as a celebration of the Ballet Russe of Diaghilev in which Olga Koklova, Picasso's new wife, was a dancer. Picasso reworked dramatically the painting after the death of his friend Ramon Pichot. Germaine, an attractive artists' model, portrayed here as a sharp-toothed monster on the left of the painting, had jilted another friend of Picasso, Carlos Casagemas, who subsequently shot himself. Soon afterwards, Pichot married Germaine, and on his death Picasso attacked the canvas violently, putting Pichot's silhouette in the window on the right. Though the central figure retains female forms from *The Three Graces*, the pose and position suggests this might represent a crucified Casagemas.

Picasso has taken a classical theme and painted a large-scale work in the tradition of the academic canon, but the harsh abstract shapes and colours, and violent handling, became characteristics of the new avant-garde canon in which artists expressed personal attitudes that sought to challenge social and artistic conventions. The work was acquired in the 1960s directly from Picasso through an intermediary, his friend, the English artist Roland Penrose. A rewarding exercise for students is to select a traditional composition and redesign it to embody ideas and experiences from their own lives.

Jackson Pollock was to art what James Dean was to acting – part of a new generation that appeared to owe little to its predecessors – rising from obscurity to world celebrity in a few years. Like Dean, Pollock lived life in the fast lane and died in a car crash in 1956 after drinking heavily. Postwar American art, such as *Summertime*, was large-scale and brashly abstract, shocking European, especially British, aesthetic sensibility. A retrospective of Pollock's work at the Tate in 1999 found this modern master was still seen in Britain as a dangerous investment (the Gallery had great difficulty in finding a major sponsor for the exhibition).

We have seen that, far from being a seamless, unified story, the Tate collections and individual works represent a diversity of ideologies. This diversity across 400 years, from Nicholas Hilliard's portrait of Queen Elizabeth I to Warhol's *Marilyn* diptych, allows for rich comparisons and contrasts; both of these works, for example, are concerned with the burdens of celebrity and the notion of female icons.

In 2000, the Tate Gallery in London formed two new galleries – the Tate Gallery of British Art and the Tate Gallery of Modern Art. This new development takes place against a very different background to that which accompanied the opening of the original Tate in 1897. We live now in a culturally diverse society whose plurality of voices legitimately challenge notions of Britishness and modernism.

> Things which are plural in the post modern world cannot be arranged in an evolutionary time-sequence, seen as each other's inferior or superior stages, neither can they be classified 'right' or 'wrong' solutions to common problems.[3]

Perhaps because of the very relativity of the present social/cultural environment, contesting traditional cultural values has become a particular focus for art historians and is now seen as an essential foundation of young people's cultural education. In this new agenda for art education, understanding how galleries contribute to 'the way we view the world' becomes as important as the study of the actual works they contain.

WHO FIRES THE CANON?

The canon of art is formulated and disseminated by a variety of agencies including schools, universities, publishers, mass media, galleries and art museums. Books have been especially influential in redefining the canon for a general audience. As a teenager, just after the war, my perceptions of art were kindled and shaped by Phaidon art books. I recall heated debates with a friend over the relative merits of Michelangelo versus Leonardo da Vinci, based entirely on grainy black-and-white plates in Phaidon books. Of all the books Phaidon produced, Gombrich's *The Story of Art*, published in 1950, has proved the most influential and enduring; for many teachers it has been the bible of art history for half a century. Reflecting on the ideas behind that book, Gombrich wrote:

> In my book *The Story of Art*, I had sketched the development of representation from the conceptual methods of the primitives and the Egyptians, who relied on 'what they knew', to the achievements of the Impressionists, who succeeded in recording 'what they saw'.[4]

In the 1960s, Thames & Hudson introduced the World of Art series, making art accessible to a wider public through affordable paperbacks. More recently, Taschen have published large-format, fully coloured paperbacks which have become popular in high-street bookshops. The necessity of publishers to package books for the international, especially American, market has resulted in the British public becoming familiar with many foreign artists who are rarely, if ever, on display in UK galleries. Artists such as Georgia O'Keeffe and Frida Kahlo are now commonly studied in UK schools whose teachers, let alone the students, have never seen the artists' actual work. In such situations teacher and student are actually studying a colour print, often only a few square inches in size.

The media's role in promoting and challenging the canon is complex and influential. In the UK, critics such as Brian Sewell see their task as defending the traditional canon and challenging innovation. Waldemar Januszczak, by contrast, champions the postmodern avant-garde, recently declaring the death of painting (didn't someone else do that a century ago?). Television series, with related books, such as Kenneth Clark's *Civilisation* (1969), John Berger's *Ways of Seeing* (1972) and Robert Hughes's *The Shock of the New* (1980) have had a profound impact on how art teachers approached the canon.

In the UK the Open University's programmes and courses, on modern art in particular, have also had a major effect on art education, and more recent series such as *Relative Values* have made millions aware of the whole machinery of the art world. For all the influence that education, books and the media have had, it is perhaps the role of art museums that remains central to the evolution and maintenance of the canon of art. Hans Haacke has gone as far as to suggest that museums 'are in the business of moulding and channelling consciousness'.[5]

Tom Gretton, the art historian, recently suggested that we owe the concept of a 'canon' to the Christian synod that convened between 340 and 348 AD.[6] The synod reviewed all existing religious texts and agreed on those that henceforth would be defined as the authentic word of God, the New Testament (St John's Revelation was the only later addition). Texts not selected were immediately condemned as not the word of God. The terms canon and canonical derive from the Greek word, *kanne*, a reed used as a measure or yardstick. It has now become a term for exemplary works, by which all others are to be measured. The Christian elders, validated these chosen texts, and the texts in turn validated the authority of the Christian elders, forming a circle of mutual empowerment.

The application of these terms to art is in the form of a metaphor and should not imply an incontestable right to be considered as models. However, like the Christian elders, the art experts who successfully champion particular artists or art are themselves associated with and validated by their advocacy of the same. The existence of a canon of art predates the use of the term and is bound up with another word, 'museum'. This word derives from 'mouseion', the classical Greek temple of the Muses, a place of contemplation and philosophical reflection. Geoffrey Lewis reflects that

> in classical Greece many collections of works of art were formed in temples from votive offerings to the deity concerned, housed in treasuries where they could be viewed by visitors on payment of a small charge.[7]

Such visitors, even then, included cultural tourists. When the Romans conquered the Greek empire in the second century BC they carried away many classical works of art to adorn their own temples or to feature in a patrician's private collection. Classical Greek civilization has been considered by European society as the highest achievement of human culture for over 2000 years. By the second century AD, Pausanias had written the first tourist guidebook to the classical sites of Greece, and this remained the essential companion for the

Lords, merchants and scholars who undertook the Grand Tour right up to the late eighteenth century. These Grand Tourists not only visited but also acquired, en route, antiquities, works of art and an extraordinary array of curiosities. These were, at first, kept in a piece of furniture known as a cabinet of curiosities but later they were housed in specially designed rooms in grand houses. These rooms, known as galleries, mixed family-commissioned portraits and artworks with masterpieces of eminent artists past and present.

One of the earliest 'galleries' to house such a collection was the bizarre assortment of objects and art acquired by the Medici family in Florence in the fifteenth century. At that time the work of artists, though achieving a new prominence, was still considered of far less consequence than a rare curiosity. Speaking of the Medici collection, Lewis states:

> The fact that Jan Van Eyck's *St Jerome* was purchased for thirty florins and 'the horn of a unicorn' for 6000 florins gives insight into the relative value of the pieces in the Medici collection.[8]

These great aristocratic collections became features of the Grand Tour. Education was one of the qualities the travellers from all over Europe had in common. Wealthy families hired tutors, often clergy who, amongst other things, taught Latin, Greek and the classics, ensuring each new generation of influential families was steeped in classical ideals.

In Zoffany's painting *The Tribuna of the Uffizi* (1772–8), commissioned by George III, we see a gathering of British connoisseurs in the Medici Palace. The Tribuna, however, is no temple of hushed contemplation, but rather a forum for lively debate. Already a clear canon of art has emerged with every serious tourist making the pilgrimage to see the *Venus de Medici* and Titian's *Venus of Urbino* and other Renaissance masterpieces.

The term 'masterpiece' harkens back to the medieval guilds. A young apprentice undertook many years of training before producing a piece of work to be judged by elder craftsmen. This work, if successful, was called the 'masterpiece' and the craftsman could now be known as a master in his own right (note the masculine term); the continuation of the term after the Renaissance carried with it the approval of the Academy.

Giorgio Vasari established the first Academy of art in Florence, under Medici patronage, in 1563, with Michelangelo as its first president. The Academy took its name from Plato's place of learning and signified that art had intellectual content that distinguished it from the purely artisan skills of the craftsmen. Policed by the academies of art that spread across Europe, a hierarchy of art genres developed that lasted until the twentieth century.

History painting was the most prestigious genre, often reflected in large-size canvases. Portraiture came next, which, in turn, was seen as more elevated than 'genre' painting, and landscape and still life considered of least merit. These distinctions were reflected in the scale, finish and quality of materials used, with leading artists generally focusing on history and portrait painting. Such academic criteria inevitably came to dictate the contents of private collections. In time many of these collections formed the basis of leading public art museums, one of the first being the Medici Collection in the Uffizi. It was bequeathed to the state by the last of the family, Anna Maria, in 1743, on these terms: 'That these things being for the ornament of the State, for the benefit of the people and for an inducement to the curiosity of foreigners.'[9]

From the mid-nineteenth century many intellectuals felt a crisis of religious faith. At the same time increasing democracy and social unrest left many patricians uneasy about the 'masses'. Matthew Arnold, in *Culture and Anarchy*, published in 1867, put into words what many were feeling at this time: 'Through culture seems to lie our way not only to perfection but even to safety.'[10] The Reverend Barnett, following Arnold's advice, founded the Whitechapel Art Exhibitions in 1881 to bring art to working-class people. Lord Rosebery opening the 1901 exhibition, said:

> If you offer this civilising agency, these rooms, this gallery, as a place where a rough fellow who has nothing else to do can spend his time . . . it cannot fail to have the favourable results.[11]

The notion of art as an agent for social reform survived up to 1967 when Lord Goodman, then Chairman of the Arts Council said, in the House of Lords:

> Young people lack values, lack certainties, lack guidance . . . I believe that once young people are captured for the Arts, they are redeemed from any of the dangers which confront them at the moment.[12]

THE HANGING DEBATE

The great private collections, such as we see in Zoffany's painting, were frequently arranged in a decorative design that revolved around a centrally placed, large, highly finished history painting or portrait, balanced by rows of smaller works, usually presented in matching ornate gilt frames. Many public galleries founded in the nineteenth century inherited these private collections and, along with them, retained the picturesque hang. Giles Waterfield comments:

> The Picturesque Hang, and the associated idea of the Tribuna or Greek Gallery, rests on the assumption that works of art of certain schools and periods form an accepted canon.[13]

In 1800 the canon included Renaissance to late seventeenth-century works in which artists such as Rubens or Van Dyck held pride of place. But a collection was primarily judged on the strength of its classical sculpture and Italian painting. The order of merit in regard to accepted artists was made evident by the prominence a work was given within the picturesque hang. During the nineteenth century many public galleries changed from this purely aesthetic hang to one that reflected an art-historical logic. This approach to classifying and ordering art works owes its inspiration to the extraordinary rich expertise of eighteenth- and nineteenth-century German scholars.

In his typically exaggerated manner, Waldemar Januszczak states:

> The German mind looked out at the chaos of culture at the end of the eighteenth century and arrogantly decided to impose some order on it. Winckelman invented the Greeks, Jakob Burckhardt invented the Renaissance, Goethe invented enlightenment.[14]

What these and other German thinkers such as Hegel and Kant brought to the study of art was a theory of cultural progression with distinct criteria for defining works. Johann Joachim Winckelman published his *History of Ancient Art* in 1764. This book had a formative impact on visual connoisseurship, and, through this, on the collection of works of art. Other German writers such as Karl Friedrich Rumohr and Gustav Friedrich Waagen developed the earlier theories into the historic survey text, an interconnected historical-cultural chain leading from pre-Greek to modern day, each stage leading to ever greater perfection. Interestingly, Ernst Gombrich when Director of the Warburg Institute was also Professor of the History of the Classical Tradition at the University of London, from 1959 to 1976.

Karl Friedrich Schinkel, a German architect and painter, was a member of the first international association of archaeologists to undertake a systematic study of ancient Greek sites. Schinkel went on to design the Altes (old) Museum in 1830 in Berlin, one of the first purpose-built public museums in Europe. Schinkel's design set a trend for other public museums being built across Europe and America. It is a neoclassical temple for art, the portico held aloft by a phalanx of eighteen Ionic columns. Inside is a great rotunda modelled on the Pantheon in Rome, housing Roman copies of Greek sculptures. The Altes Museum was conceived by Rumohr and Waagen, and Waagen became its first director. The Museum realized, in the layout of its collection, the historic-survey model developed in their writings which, in turn, became the model for most of the world's great museums. The Metropolitan Museum in New York, founded in 1870 by a consortium of clergymen, philanthropists and unionist politicians, was established on the Altes Museum historical-survey model, all housed within an imposing neoclassical building. Philippe de Montebello, the current director (at 1999), still believes in the museum as a temple:

> I like to be able to walk up the grand staircase to a museum. I think art should be displayed in an environment that is suited as much as possible to it and gives a sense of grandeur. Art is on a high plane. Art is man expressing himself at the highest point of his consciousness and you don't want to step off the street into something that is ordinary.[15]

If the Metropolitan represents the apogee of the traditional European art-history museum, then another New York museum, the Museum of Modern Art (MOMA), founded in 1929, established the canon for modern art.

THE CANON OF MODERN ART

Mary Quin Sullivan, Lee P. Bliss and Abby Aldridge Rockefeller were rich New York society wives, with a passion for modern art, who decided to create their own museum. They chose the 27-year-old Alfred Barr Jnr as Director. MOMA began life in a rented apartment on Fifth Avenue, finally moving into a purpose-built gallery in 1939. In 1936, to accompany his exhibition of Cubist and Abstract art, Barr presented in the catalogue a schema that proposed a logical structure for modern art from Impressionism to abstraction. Kirk Varnedoe, Director of the Department of Painting and Sculpture of the present-day (at 1999) MOMA, concedes that the idea most associated with Barr and MOMA is of 'a grand irresistible lineage based primarily on formal values or stylistic values to the exclusion of other things'.[16] Since the 1930s MOMA has been the 'Kremlin' of modernism, and Barr's formalism, reducing the complexity of art to shape, form, line and colour, entered British art education as a largely unquestioned fundamentalism.

> A featureless gallery with white walls, with even track lighting. On the walls are canvases all of about the same size hung at eye level, frames never more than two inches thick. To the lower right of each canvas is a label, all the same size and set at the same distance from the canvas.[17]

This is Brian O'Doherty's description of the white cube of the modern-art gallery. Gone is the grandeur of a temple or a country house; the art is isolated like a fever patient in a hospital ward. Devoid of all social context, the curator has complete control over how the works should be experienced and interpreted. The gallery visitor must become sensitized to the curatorial 'voice' – the logic behind the selection and grouping of works that creates relationships which never existed in the minds of the artists themselves.

Public galleries are not only custodians of national heritage, concerned with researching and displaying their collections, but also, increasingly, depend on special-loan exhibitions. Exhibitions are a temporary drama among the permanence of the collection. For exhibition planners they provide an opportunity to feature new perspectives and fuller contextualization of familiar masterpieces. For major art museums the economic pressures for ever greater numbers of visitors has led to the mounting of more and more ambitious exhibitions. Thomas Hoving, Director of the Metropolitan in New York, 1966–77, developed the concept of the 'blockbuster' in America. The first blockbuster in Britain was the Tutankhamun exhibition held at the British Museum in 1972, which attracted over half-a-million visitors. With each mega-exhibition comes a weighty catalogue far too big to act as a guide during the exhibition visit. Its function is both as an *aide memoire* or souvenir and a definitive compendium of current scholarship. There is an increasing range of other exhibition souvenirs, from carrier bags and jigsaws to silk scarves and bone china. Blockbusters also attract considerable media coverage, often spawning special television programmes. The celebrity of blockbusters makes them attractive for corporate sponsors who, in turn, fund widespread advertising and large, full-colour posters. The Royal Academy in London, with no collection on display and no government grants, relies on major, glamorous exhibitions for its survival.

Nicholas Serota became Director of the Tate Gallery in 1988, before which he had established a reputation for curating exhibitions at the Whitechapel Art Gallery. Because of limited wall space, only a fraction of the collection can be displayed. Nicholas Serota decided to radically re-hang the gallery each year, using the collection to change new exhibitions. This came into being in 1990 as New Displays. Apart from ensuring different works get an airing each year, the novel arrangements deliberately challenge any notion of a single story of art. The same work may appear another year, but in an entirely new arrangement, engendering a new reading. There are a variety of hangs including chronological groupings, rooms covering certain art movements (such as Surrealism), works hung to a theme or concept (such as The City or portraiture), groupings of works by a particular artist (such as William Blake) and displays of certain donations or private collections. It can be informative to look at the way works are actually displayed. The Pre-Raphaelite room has red damask walls with paintings hung in several rows, some hung ten or more feet up and placed fairly close together, giving a picturesque, country-house look. Postwar art, by contrast, is usually displayed in a 'white box' with generous space between a single row of art works. Whatever the logic of a display, the placement of works follows a refined aesthetic design. Curators spend days working out where works will go and the exact height at which each painting should be hung.

For students to begin to understand how curators work, and how the placement of works of art influences how we experience and make meanings of what we see, they could be asked to select a number of reproductions (say six postcards) to make a display. When a student has designed a hang for his or her chosen works the rest of the group can try to work out the idea behind the selection and discuss how each work is experienced in relation to the others. As an example of how the context affects the way we see a work of art, consider the history of Jacob Epstein's monumental sculpture *Jacob and the Angel* (1940). This powerful work is now acclaimed as a masterpiece, but it was originally bought by a fairground manager and exhibited as a freak, alongside the bearded lady and two-headed goat.

TEACHERS AND THE CANON OF SCHOOL ART

> There is no greater obstacle to the enjoyment of great works of art than our unwillingness to discard habits and prejudices.[18]

Who are the most commonly used artists in schools and how is their work used? The UK Qualifications and Curriculum Authority recently undertook a national survey of primary and secondary schools[19] and found the most popular artists were Van Gogh, Picasso, Monet, Matisse and Lowry. Four of these artists are associated with Parisian modernism. Despite the majority of secondary-level art teachers having attended art college, the selection in no way reflects art of the last 50 years, indeed it equally shows little commitment to art prior to 1850. From the ages of five to fourteen, the Impressionists are a main focus, and in addition to the five artists already named, work by Mondrian, Hockney and Klee is used. In the seven-to-fourteen age range, Henry Moore, Andy Goldsworthy, Escher and Klimt make an appearance. Between the ages of eleven and fourteen, certain movements are considered. Listed in order of popularity these include Surrealism, Pop Art, Cubism, Op Art, Fauvism, Expressionism and Futurism. American artists account for only 4 per cent, with Warhol, O'Keefe and Lichenstein the most used. By far the most common reason for studying an artist's work was to assist the students in making their own artwork. The survey found that knowledge and understanding of the purpose and meaning of art, and how ideas develop and change, are given least attention across the whole age range. Major British artists such as Constable, Gainsborough, Stubbs, Hogarth, Blake, Turner, Bacon and Caro are little studied while Escher, Lowry, Arcimbaldo and Andy Goldsworthy, who are far less significant, *are* studied.

Many of the most popular artists are never encountered first-hand by the student, and this is perhaps a key to the selection. Sixty-two per cent of those surveyed said the choice of artists was due to source material in school. Does this mean art history education in Britain is dictated to by the availability of cheap colour reproductions? There are, of course, many enlightened teachers who do ensure their students acquire a balanced cultural history of the world in which they are growing, but for many it would appear there is a serious imbalance between making and meaning, with the typical school art canon bearing little relation to what is on display as 'our national heritage' in major public galleries. Nor does this typical school curriculum reflect the richness of insight offered by the new art history or the cultural diversity of our society.

Since 1993 the market research company MORI has carried out regular surveys of those who visits the Tate in London.[20] From these we have found that the Tate is popular among well-off under-35s from London and the south east of England. This ongoing survey has been backed up by occasional in-depth visitor research.[21] This revealed that half the visitors came 'to browse', and of the other half, who had a particular reason for visiting, most expected to see modern and contemporary art. This survey did not include teachers or schoolchildren. The bias towards seeing the Tate as a gallery of modern art is not, however, reflected in the sale of postcards. Postcards are a useful gauge of what visitors would like to remember of their experience in the gallery. What will your students purchase? What does this tell you about them and about their experience in the Tate? In 1998, the ten most popular works of art as reflected in postcard sales were as follows:

1.   Waterhouse: *The Lady of Shalott* (22,250)
2.   Millais: *Ophelia* (21,700)
3.   Matisse: *The Snail* (15,500)
4.   Rodin: *The Kiss* (13,600)

5. Rossetti: *Proserpine* (12,960)
6. Dali: *Lobster Telephone* (12,400)
7. Picasso: *Weeping Woman* (12,200)
8. Dali: *Metamorphosis of Narcissus* and Hughes: *April Love* (both 12,100)
9. Turner: *Norham Castle Sunrise* (11,900)
10. Sargent: *Carnation, Lily, Lily, Rose* (11,100)

Seven of the top ten were made in the 50 years from 1850 to 1900; four are Pre-Raphaelite in style; seven feature females; only two (Dali's *Lobster Telephone* and Rodin's *Kiss*) are sculptures. What is it about these works that appeals to visitors? Is it that most tell us a story, or is it a more sentimental attraction?

In the Tate, each gallery contains written information in the form of wall panels and labels; there are also catalogues and the audio-guide, TateInform. These are worth studying, along with newspaper critics' articles, to see what kinds of language and what forms of vocabulary are used. Our experience of works of art is, of course, initially visual and emotional, but almost immediately we try to explain to ourselves what our response is, and this will be in words. Using the text panels and labels in the gallery it would be useful to discuss how this information influences or enhances a viewer's understanding of art.

We can identify genres of writing like genres of art. The word 'style' is derived from the Roman 'stilus', a writing instrument. In the gallery there are technical descriptions: art-historical; historical; sociological; biographical; writing which can be augmented by art critics' writing containing analytical and emotive language. Focusing on a single work, or room, students can draft texts in each of the above genres of writing, noticing what each can offer or exclude. During the summer of 1998, Tate Millbank also put up poetry labels; some are already existing texts and some are made especially by visitors.

Another interesting project exploring the interaction of languages and art is for students to identify a work they particularly enjoy and then pretend to be the artist. Others are given roles such as an academic, a tabloid newspaper reporter, a television presenter or a retired major living in suburbia. They question the artist and he must answer in character. For example, if the student was Lichtenstein, then he must portray a modern American artist; if he chose William Blake, he must be an early nineteenth-century London visionary. As a variation on this approach, students can select their favourite among the Turner Prize shortlist and defend the choice in debate before the actual winner is announced.

PLANNING YOUR GALLERY VISIT

Here are a few suggestions when planning a visit to a gallery. First, have a clearly defined purpose, research what is on display and whether there are any existing resources produced by the gallery which can assist you. Encourage the use of sketchbooks and note-taking, not for students' imaginative compositions, but as a means of analysing and recording what they encounter. Focus upon a few works around a clearly articulated theme. Explore ideas through analysis and comparison, rather than trying to cover the hundreds of works on display in a single visit. Ask students to place the works you have selected in a broader context, both within the building and within a socio-historical setting. Consider how each work is displayed, to what works it is adjacent, the contents of the room as a whole and any wall panels and labels. Consider how the work was made, relating this to the particular content, values and meaning the artist sought to convey.

As an example of how you might apply this approach, let us consider four paintings that explore the experience of city life: *Landscape with Rainbow, Henley on Thames, c.*1690 by Jan Siberechts; John Constable's *The Opening of Waterloo Bridge*, 1832; L.S. Lowry's *Industrial Landscape*, 1955 and Anselm Kiefer's *Lilith*, 1987–89. It is interesting that none of these would fit the traditional canon of art.

Landscape with Rainbow, Henley on Thames

The majority of people reading this book will have been born and lived most of their life in a town or city. The environment profoundly affects how we perceive the world and our place in it. It is therefore an important theme for artists and art educators. Each of the four artists created their image of urban life in a specific social and historical context that has shaped the style and content of their paintings. The most important early landscape in the Tate Gallery shows town and country existing in harmony. A fertile nature serving a prosperous market town with symbols of God presiding over both rainbow and church tower. The painting would have been commissioned by a wealthy landowner or merchant to represent his interests.

The Opening of Waterloo Bridge

This is one of the great set pieces of Constable's mature style. He uses an historical event to represent the differing forces that were shaping nineteenth-century society. In the foreground the Prince Regent, representing the monarchy, leaves the mansion of the Prime Minister, his way lined by ceremonial troops; so parliamentary, monarchical and military power are shown as united. The prince sets out in an ornately carved and gilded boat on the River Thames, the great artery of London by which the ships of the world brought their provisions to England. The Waterloo Bridge links the newly industrialized South Bank with its belching chimneys and slums, to the prosperous North Bank with its banks, law courts, elegant townhouses and fashionable shops. Constable was born and bred a farmer's son and brings that outsider's observations to the clamourings of the city. The city is rendered in the same restless brushstrokes as his landscapes, so that the people are reduced to blurred shapes, and the human drama plays second fiddle to a vast, shifting sky, the tide of men's affairs distorted in the dark mirror of the river.

Industrial Landscape

Lowry was born, and lived all his life, in an industrial town in the north of England. For much of his life he was a rent collector and so had a direct awareness both of the region's buildings and the lives of working-class people, and these became the focus of his paintings. The painting represents a generalized impression of the industrial wasteland, dominated by tall smoking chimney-stacks, mill buildings, bridges and waste-tips. In the top left is the Stockport viaduct and in the foreground, dwarfed by the factories, is a blackened street of houses whose inhabitants move about like so many ants. The lasting appeal of Lowry's vision is that, for all the harshness of their lives, he brings also a celebration of the working-class spirit.

Lilith

This massive painting, with copper wire spewing out from its burnt surface, appears, close-to, as an abstract work, but seen from a distance, an apocalyptic cityscape emerges. The artist visited the city of Sao Paulo in Brazil, which has experienced uncontrolled growth over the past decade, while at the same time Brazil's economy has collapsed. Kiefer graphically depicts the city disintegrating into violent chaos, the great skyscrapers hardly recognizable as the whole surface is reduced to the colours and textures of earth and ashes.

The history of art education in Britain is one of eccentric, often arbitrary, choices, which until recently stemmed almost entirely from children making art. Everyone is a cultural consumer. Less than one per cent actually work in art and design and yet cultural education remains poorly understood and poorly taught in many schools. In recent years art history has become closely engaged with theory, involving philosophy, semiotics, sociology and psychoanalysis. These approaches have opened up new perspectives on the meanings and social context of art which could form a new focus for art education and, hopefully, go some way towards healing the rifts between theory, history and practice. This chapter has offered a number of pathways by which teachers and students can gain an insight into the role that public art galleries play in defining and promoting the way we view the world and construct a cultural canon of art.

POSTSCRIPT

> Man makes his environment
> Then the environment makes man
>   Karl Marx

Working with children from culturally diverse backgrounds recently has caused me to reflect on the conditioning role of environment and education in determining not only our language, but our very consciousness.

The original Tate gallery gave a sensation of entering a grand country mansion, reminding the public that it had been shaped by an aesthetic consciousness stemming from a public school and Grand Tour education only the wealthy could acquire. This was a form of art education that emphasized refined sensibility and cultural knowledge, with practical skills being seen as more suitable for ladies (or Bohemians) to pursue. The controlling voices of art museums today continue to be recruited largely from this tradition of public school, Oxbridge, and Courtauld.

If patrician connoisseurship remains the determining influence on many art museums, the other major strand of art education, which emerged in Victorian Britain, had the factory as its institutional goal. Prince Albert championed this approach in the Great Exhibition and through founding the Victoria and Albert Museum in Kensington. Along with the V & A, art schools were established across the country in order to train potters, textile printers, iron and wood workers. It was a curriculum that favoured basic literacy over literature, manual skills over critical skills, and an aesthetic of pastiche.

Dumb poetry and spoken painting

Despite talk of postmodern eclecticism, Victorian mentalities still inform cultural institutions and art education. The education system is constrained, both in maintaining nineteenth-century rigid subject divisions and in the narrow, school-based way many art teachers construe cultural education.

Over the past six years, I have focused on issues concerned with the interaction of literacy and art[22], and have been perturbed by the number of art teachers that confessed 'I don't read books.' QCA is currently investigating the teaching of literacy in art education, yet over 20 years ago (in 1982) the UNESCO 'Declaration on Media' stated:

> The school and the family share the responsibility of preparing the young person living in a world of powerful images, words and sounds. Children and adults need to be literate in all three of these symbolic systems, and it will require some reassessment of educational priorities. Such reassessment might well result in an integrated approach to the teaching of language and communication.

Art museums, if they are to be more than heritage sites, and art education, if it is to achieve more than minority status, need to address these fundamental concerns. Above all, we need to be aware that works of art, like literary texts, do not *contain* meaning, but rather meaning is *produced* by and in the consciousness of the observer.

> You are thinking about the painting, like you are just there in the painting. You look and maybe get fed up, but when you come back home you can't stop thinking about it ... Then I can write a book or something, it's just like that. You keep remembering and you get more ideas. (Pupil, aged 11)

Notes

1. Haacke, H. (1984) fifth Biennale, Sydney, quoted in S. Nairne (1987) *The State of the Art*. London: Chatto & Windus, p. 14.
2. Clark, K. (1972) *The Other Side of the Wood*. London: John Murray.
3. Bauman, Zygmunt (1990) quoted in R. Hewison *Future Tense*. London: Methuen, p. 176.
4. Gombrich, E. (1950) *The Story of Art* (preface). London: Phaidon.
5. Haacke, H. 'Museums: managers of consciousness', in S. Nairne, *op. cit.*
6. Gretton, T. (1998) Loaded Canons Conference, Tate Gallery, November.
7. Lewis, G. (1992) 'Museums and their precursors', in John M.A. Thompson (ed.) *Manual of Curatorship* (2nd edn). London: Butterworth and Heinemann, p. 6.
8. *Ibid.*, p. 8.
9. Medici, Anna Maria, quoted in G. Waterfield (1992) *Palaces of Art*. London: Dulwich Picture Gallery catalogue.
10. Arnold, M. (1867, reprinted 1963) *Culture and Anarchy*. Cambridge: Cambridge University Press, p. 6.
11. Lord Rosebery, quoted in Borzello, F. (1987) *Civilizing Caliban*. London: Routledge & Kegan Paul, p. 76.
12. Lord Goodman, *ibid.*, p. 133.
13. Waterfield, G. (1992) 'Picture hanging and gallery decoration', in G. Waterfield *op. cit.*, p. 49.
14. Januszczak, W. (1998) 'Art history is not all it's painted'. *Sunday Times*, 20 November.
15. de Montebello, P. (1991), speaking on *Relative Values*. BBC2 broadcast, autumn.
16. Varnedoe, K. (1993) speaking on *Modern Art Practices and Debates*. BBC2 Open University MOMA broadcast.
17. O'Doherty, B. (1991), speaking on *Relative Values*. BBC2 broadcast, autumn.
18. Gombrich, E., *op. cit.* (preface).
19. QCA (1998) 'Survey and analysis of the artists that teachers refer to and use in teaching teaching art 5–16'. London: Qualifications and Curriculum Authority.
20. Tate Gallery MORI poll (internal report), 1996.
21. Tate Gallery visitor audit (internal report), 1994.
22. Grigg, C. (2003) *Visual Paths to Literacy Handbook*. London: Tate Britain Education.

Chapter 4

Ways of Not Seeing: Education, Art and Visual Culture

HOWARD HOLLANDS

In 1999, no one really knows what art is any more, or what it ought to look like. Or what it is for. This causes anxiety for some, while others see it as a kind of freedom ... the definition, re-definition and de-definition of what it can and cannot achieve has been the major subject of the art of this century ... a story, largely, that has taken place in the cities of the western world.[1]

This chapter aims to locate some of the key critiques of art and design education as they relate to the role of published material about art aimed at both student and teacher. These materials play a key role in determining the environment in which teachers and students engage with art. 'Art' as a Western European construction and reconstruction, generating literally a wealth of historical baggage, reveals a dilemma for those of us involved in the teaching of the subject. What would we be doing and teaching if the word itself disappeared? At least we would no longer have to struggle constantly to justify our place in an overcrowded and competitive curriculum. As Searle suggests, it is the interaction with the word 'art' which has generated so much interest for the artist, critic and teacher. It is now the relationship between art and the increasingly familiar term 'visual culture' which provides the challenge for art education. In art education, we have to accept a radically broader definition of 'art' and 'education', one which reflects more of what now counts as art or as visual culture and which operates across different fields of knowledge and experience and, thereby, the curriculum.

Slipping back to 1974 for a moment, it is no accident that the significance of a work produced then by another art critic, John Berger, and his book and television series *Ways of Seeing*[2] is only now being recognized more widely within the field of art education. Berger was, even then, dealing with the troubled relationship between art and visual culture. Images of flared trousers, floral shirts and flower-power hairstyles in the publicity images throughout his book may be enjoying their second coming, culturally speaking, but the original concept of *Ways of Seeing* itself is as potent as ever. Why is this, and what is the concept? The innovative form of both the publication and the television series has, of course, influenced work that was to follow. It was essentially the self-questioning attitude adopted by Berger himself towards the medium of television and its relationship to content which was entirely missed by most of us in the school art education community. *Ways of Seeing* discussed its own *raison d'—etre* in a manner that was, and still is, outside the frame of reference for many art teachers. It is this process that remains its enduring strength, rather than any specific content, which has now to some extent been superseded. English and media education was the quickest to spot the significance of the book. However, *Ways of Seeing* strikes another chord with us now through the developing awareness of a cultural pedagogy. Books about art education have traditionally avoided discussing culture. This is not surprising given the absence of theory in art education then and since, in relation to what has been loosely called critical studies. School art education in the 1970s had not managed to move on from 1950 and, apart from a handful of exceptions, has been unable to accommodate or contribute to the postmodern world. As for critical studies, media education picked up the challenge abandoned by art education. Berger's book offered one model of how art and education might effectively work together. The attitude adopted by Berger showed a confidence in the reader/learner to continue, take forward or challenge the issues Berger himself was addressing. Drawing upon the work of Walter Benjamin,[3] his book concludes with a statement given an entire page of its own:

To be continued by the reader

This statement resonates in the empty space of the page in a way reminiscent of John Cage, and all those artists who were more interested in absence than presence. Recognizing the role of the spectator/reader/consumer in the process of production, the book draws attention to the relationship of text and image to the visual space of the page. It also recognizes the place of the book in the social space in which it is produced and received. This sense of the book as part of a continuum, of question and answer, is reinforced through the cover of the original edition, a cover which reproduces the same image and text of the first paragraphs to be found inside the book. This assists Berger's aim of producing a work which itself becomes part of the environment it is critiquing and which refuses to claim a particular kind of authority over art or visual culture. This was contrary to the other popular UK television series of the time, *Civilisation*, and the accompanying publication by Kenneth Clark.[4] *Civilisation* was presented as a given view of art and was not open to debate or question, echoing so much published art-historical material then, and since, aimed at schools. It seemed that as far as schools were concerned, neither art education nor art history could be questioned. This was in stark contrast to many of the debates raging amongst artists, critics and historians as well as those engaged in the newly emerging cultural studies. It also reflected the role of the market with the professional world of art publishing and art history promoting the canon, the status quo, in art and critical study in school. There was money in the monograph.

Widespread concern was being felt that art history in schools was not reflecting contemporary debates about the changing nature of the discipline. Higher education in the UK, with the notable exception of the University of Essex, showed little interest in school art history. Art books for schools have not questioned the art canon in the way that Berger did in his role as critic. The fault, however, was not one-sided; too many artists, historians and critics adopted an arrogant and ignorant stance towards pedagogy and what was going on in schools, and many still do. Art teachers were seen as second-class citizens peddling amateur art and art-historical practice. This attitude is reinforced through the tedious enquiry 'do you still find time to do your own work?' the assumption being that teaching is somehow 'not doing'. The recent, well-meaning project of National Awards for British teachers mimicking the Oscars, reveals a more contemporary, patronizing concept. An impossible situation for the teacher, as Geoff Cox suggests:

> The 'impossibility' inherent in all art education is that the value of the information supplied as well as the artistic competence it encourages is always discredited in advance. It might be simply reiterated that art education only serves to underwrite established values and expertise and that art produced within educational situations is always discredited as necessarily amateur practice. For access to art through art education is always subject to the relations of production of art in the service of, and affirming art's exclusivity. The function of art education is generally untenable as it generally fails to acknowledge its own function in hierarchies of knowledge, taste and 'distinction'.[5] And yet, how is value ascribed in these contexts and what useful connections might be drawn across these fields of art and education?[6]

Clearly, within the hierarchies of knowledge, taste and distinction to which Geoff Cox refers (and which draws heavily on the work of Bourdieu) the art teacher has to consider what art is, what a book or teaching-pack is, what a television programme and what a CD or website is. What role do these play in the formation of culture and the development of cultural concepts in the minds of young people? Art and art education publishing have emphatically avoided any consideration of their own role, or assumed authority, in this process. Berger was critiquing the new technologies of television and publicity. The current so-called digital revolution and information superhighway, now hitting schools in the UK, amidst heavily funded hype at both governmental and corporate level, is not posing the fundamental questions about the relationship of this technology to both art and education. In fact, quite the reverse; it is being used like other forms of publishing media to underwrite the authority of art, not to challenge it. Technology is seen as a panacea – something firmly rejected by Berger. In 1974, with hands stretched out, he fixed us in his gaze and implored us to question and challenge the medium he was using and what he was saying through that medium. Interestingly, the new technologies of art as they feature in education are adopting many outdated features of the traditional art lesson, instead of helping us to see them in a new light, turning Berger's siren warnings on their head.

The lack of questioning or a rationale for the digital revolution is revealed through the UK National Council for Education Technology (NCET) publication *Fusion*.[7] This booklet exemplifies so-called good practice by rerunning a formalist ideology through new technology. Ironically, the fact that it is such a new and fashionable technology actually serves to strengthen outmoded practice.[8] The self-critical has been an absent dimension of critical study in art and design throughout its development and this continues under the guise of new technology. In fact, it is more the absence of recognition of visual culture in the art rooms and the decline of media studies within the curriculum that has allowed the art curriculum to drift ever further from our visual world. The debate is with us now as a result of the current 're-conceptualising of the art curriculum'[9] as Arthur Hughes calls it, and the series of papers presented in *Directions*[10]; these papers are summarized in the Manifesto for Art Education produced by John Swift and John Steers,[11] and are referred to by Burgess and Addison in Chapter 2 of this book as a 'postmodern approach to the curriculum'. Many of the arguments in *Directions* challenge those pedagogies which deny any relationship between art and design education and visual culture. These pedagogies are all the more worrying in the pervasive regimes of measurement and accountability. Traditional, competitive subject definitions and divisions have helped to create a stagnant climate. Art is seen simply as an alternative, or a counterbalance, to other disciplines; this notion of counterbalance is at odds with both the way we learn, and how art operates in the wider community.

WHAT DO DRAGONS THINK ABOUT IN THEIR DARK LONELY CAVES?[12]

In 1995, Alison Bancroft struck a chord when analysing issues of inclusion and exclusion in seven new teaching-packs designed to support teachers in the implementation of the English National Curriculum. It was about this time that we began to see publishers showing a keen interest in art and design education conferences relating to the new curriculum for art. Here was a ready market needing some prescriptive materials for a prescriptive curriculum. They recognized that the Art National Curriculum was making demands on teachers for which they were neither prepared nor resourced. The publications which emerged seemed to be avoiding what was happening in the broader world of visual culture and the ideologies being transmitted through art in school. Schools were lapping up the new resources and, with them, the selected artists being promoted. A persistent problem has been the notion that resources are all that are required and the teacher will do the rest. There has been little debate around the meanings inherent in the way we select and use resources. The same artists began to show up with monotonous regularity in the work produced by students. As long as the references to artists were in evidence then the demands of the National Curriculum had been met.

Bancroft noted that

> The National Curriculum states that 'art' should be interpreted to mean art, craft and design. As categories these are value laden, culturally, historically, socially and politically defined constructs. I use them reluctantly, but broadly speaking the overwhelming majority of images in the packs can be placed in the traditional Western category of fine art: most of these are paintings.[13]

Arthur Hughes provides a context for this while contemplating the future of critical studies in art education and considers his own role in developing an awareness of the field:

> Gradually, in individual schools, a largely unplanned and uncoordinated process began to take hold. In terms of art history we were self-taught. Much of our background knowledge came from commercially produced film strips (and, in particular, the notes that went with them), together with a fairly superficial reading of an art history text written for young people of the age we were teaching: Ernst Gombrich's classic, *The Story of Art*. Most of us, of course, read this book uncritically. We knew nothing of different schools of or approaches to art history ... to us it was a simple linear, causally deterministic progression centred upon what Gombrich has called the 'making of good pictures' ... in this sense art history was evaluative.[14]

The Story of Art might be a good story, certainly, but it is only one story. There are many histories of art and perhaps we should be just as interested in the ones told by artists, critics and the youngsters themselves. Echoing Hughes,[15] Bancroft makes the point that the rapid expansion of so-called critical studies lacks any theoretical base, which is not surprising as the Art National Curriculum as a whole had no stated rationale. She too raises the question of conflicting terminologies to define similar practices. She describes her research intention as

> to consider the body of knowledge and approaches that are being defined through the publishing of educational materials, the practical physical expression and construction of the boundaries of Critical Studies through what is included and what is excluded, and to use these materials to map out some of the areas that need much more rigorous attention.[16]

Bancroft's selection of publications was made in relation to the English National Curriculum for Art. She pays close attention to the statement of the National Curriculum for Art as meaning art, craft and design which immediately presents us with assumptions in the publications about what constitutes these subjects. It is also interesting that the proposal for the latest revision to the National Curriculum is for a title of 'art and design'. Bancroft, in her paper, examines these value-laden categories; she quotes one example of a nineteenth-century 'Beaded Cloth Hat' from the Yoruba tribe with the following statement on the back of the card with the image: ' ... the astonishingly sophisticated works of art produced by the Yoruba have only been discovered in the 20th century.'[17]

By whom and for whom we might ask? Bancroft's point is that teaching packs using images to support critical studies immediately face problematic questions of curatorship, in the same way as a museum or gallery, or indeed the teacher putting up a display in the classroom.

Consider the following statements by Dorling Kindersley, one of the most successful international publishers of art books for youngsters, when describing their approach:

> We take all of our own photographs for our books, all shot on a white background for clarity, and for a 'museum or gallery like' feel.
>
> To DK, the association with a gallery lends authority to the title ... sometimes we gain the benefit of an author provided by the gallery.
>
> A beautifully produced book aimed at a world-wide market ensures publicity of the name and becomes a showcase for the content of the gallery.[18]

We can see how this publisher of very well produced books aims to create a certain authoritative notion of art in the context of a particular idea of the museum or gallery. Indeed, Dorling Kindersley enlist many of the major galleries of Western Europe and North America to underwrite the content of their publications as associate producers. Only the major players of the museum and gallery world can take part of course, reinforcing the concept of a mainstream culture which will tolerate only a little token 'other'. They provide a range of predetermined routes in relation to given artists in given contexts, and everything is presented within a corporate language and design.

Bancroft continues her argument with a discussion of three levels of knowledge and understanding. The first level is the knowledge gained by observation mediated by the student's own experience. The problem identified here is that while it may be important to value the views of all students regardless of levels of knowledge, there is no consideration of how that knowledge is actually formed. It is developed, as we know, by much of the material actually designed to help students 'access' works of art along with all the ideological baggage the material is expressing.

According to Bancroft, level two involves the information which cannot be constructed by the students themselves, such as facts about provenance. The contextualization is limited to that of the 'world of art'. The English National Curriculum for Art works at this level. Bancroft suggests that Rod Taylor's approach exemplified in *Educating for Art*[19] works within this level:

Rod Taylor's model of form, content, process, mood, would seem to provide an example of what might be achieved at this level, and also of the dangers. Despite his insistence on the importance of contextual knowledge, the examples he provides of students writing conform to a particular model. They provide imaginative and intuitive responses informed by second level knowledge, but show little evidence of critical distance or awareness of the paradigm that they are working within. It is too easy for this paradigm to turn into the right approach, and limit rather than empower looking, by failing to provide an awareness of alternatives.[20]

The third level she proposes deals with methods of analysis in a cultural, social and philosophical context. This can involve a re-examination of level two approaches and, quoting Hughes again, it seeks to empower them to make meaning for themselves. She argues that this level differentiates education from training, asserting that if we want to empower our students, it is essential that we do not predetermine the destination.

Given the low level of inquiry into this development of critical studies following Alison Bancroft's work in 1995 one would think that her article had never seen the light of day. The worrying signs she identified did much later, prompt UK government agencies to commission two pieces of research.[21] Most of this research led towards an identification of 'favourite' artists used in the classroom of which there was already plenty of anecdotal evidence of a 'hit parade'.

In the first piece of research, it was interesting that of all non-western cultures studied in art and design in the UK throughout 1995 and 1996, Africa was the most common, at 85 per cent across all age ranges. The fact that this was 'The Year of Africa', with the Royal Academy of Arts hosting a blockbuster show and a range of smaller events around the country seems to have escaped the notice of the researchers, but it does serve to remind us of the impact of major high-profile exhibitions on the art curriculum. Art examiners and moderators frequently testify to this and can almost predict the artists to be referenced by students prior to visiting schools each summer. When we add this to the barrage of associated ephemera, media attention, monographs and teachers' packs, we can see how and why schools are in the grip of the art publishers. The corporate publishing canon and the art-historical canon meets the pedagogical canon in the form of the National Curriculum; to ensure compliance this is policed in the name of 'good practice' by the Office for Standards in Education.

One revealing statistic showed that 80 per cent of published material being used in the sample schools made no significant reference to theory or research in either art or art education. We can relate this statistic to the observation in the findings that there was a general absence of discussion about the nature of art and education.

The second piece of research determines the extent to which certain artists were being used in schools, predictably, as noted by Grigg in the previous chapter, we have a top five of Van Gogh, Picasso, Monet, Matisse and Lowry. The researchers for the Qualifications and Curriculum Authority account for this list in a formalist tone reminiscent of the National Curriculum itself:

> Picasso's dominance is understandable in view of his enormous contribution to the development of painting and sculpture in the 20th century.

> The popularity of Matisse may be accounted for by the way that his work can be interpreted and responded to at different levels at different key stages.

> Van Gogh and Monet, for all their dynamic virtues, seem to be used as reference in primary schools because their use and application of colour is so evident and accessible even in reproduction.[22]

It is clear from the statements above that any 'official' analysis of what is happening under the guise of critical studies simply reflects the orthodoxy which critical studies itself should be critiquing. The research is predicated on the need simply to broaden the range of artists to reflect a multicultural world rather than examine what is being taught and learnt through the work of these artists.

THIS IS NOT THE NATIONAL CURRICULUM FOR ART

There have of course been some alternative resources for teachers generated by artists, teachers and children. *This is Not* is one such case that consciously and openly works against the canon with the involvement of younger students. The questioning of the question features strongly throughout; something ignored by most publications:

> When a teacher asks a pupil a question, the pupil seeks the answer most likely to please, least likely to exasperate. What then are teachers seeking? Conforming children. If it's true that teachers ask children about a thousand questions a week, children will ask more, especially if you encourage them, especially if you risk it. Questioning comes **from** those in power and not enough **to** them.[23]

This is Not draws upon the tradition of *Ways of Seeing* and integrates theory and practice in what could be termed critical making. It encourages teachers and youngsters to play with ideas and not just materials. The project is based upon process in a climate which measures product. It states that *This is Not a Teaching Pack*; certainly, in the sense that many other publications adopt the role of authority in relation to the artists being introduced, then it is not a teaching pack. However, it does highlight the strengths of teachers and students at a time when their confidence about art and art history has been undermined. It moves easily from the ideas of Foucault and Magritte to those expressed by the youngsters. The personal and ideological journey to and from the gallery is as important as the things to be experienced once there. How do these experiences relate? Why do we just assume that gallery education must automatically be a 'good thing'?

RECYCLING THE NATIONAL CURRICULUM[24]

In a follow up to *This is Not*, the artists, teachers and school students, with local authority help, engaged in a mass recycling of the National Curriculum documentation. The British Paper Company in north London pulped van loads of National Curriculum Orders and used the pulp to create blank drawing-paper embossed with the logo 'Recycled National Curriculum', and returned it free to schools. While this was happening at the macro level, youngsters in schools were shredding and pulping their own National Curriculum documents to make paper as well as paper costumes, wallpaper and all manner of artefacts from the recycled material. In addition, this hugely ironical project turned out to be therapeutic for all those teachers intimidated by the mountains of paperwork piling up in staffrooms. More importantly, it draws attention to the fact that art education is delivered via mountains of documents and exemplification material. The real world of art and visual culture is often about challenge and question; play and transgression; it will often run against the grain.

The National Curriculum was a defining period; it was also a lost opportunity. Yet because it enabled art education to sink into a deeper sleep while the world of visual culture was all around transforming itself,[25] the inevitable awakening has been sharper and more militant. However, the cultural exclusivity of the western European axis seems set to remain.

SCHOOL IS A FACTORY

Alan Sekula would go further in condemning the entire institutional framework in which art education takes place in a polemic from *School is a Factory*:

> School and the media are inherently discursive institutions, sites within which discourse becomes a locus of symbolic force, symbolic violence. A communicative relation is established between teacher and student, performer and audience, in which the first part, as the purveyor of official 'truths', exerts an institutional authority over the second. Students and audience are reduced to the status of passive listeners, rather than active subjects of knowledge ... Like home, factory, prison and city streets, school and the media are sites of an intense, if often covert, daily struggle in which language and power are inextricably connected.[26]

By way of contrast, Peter Jones, Her Majesty's Inspectorate, in *The Arts Inspected*,[27] as well as in much of the exemplification material emanating from government agencies) promotes examples of what is called 'good practice' from schools, yet fails entirely to mention the current debates in response to so-called 'good practice'. There is no mention of those schools attempting to provide an experience of art education based on challenge, risk or the unorthodox. Sometimes art can be bad for us, but children are often not allowed to address the difficult issues raised by and about art. They are, as a result, disempowered when they need to make judgements about much of what counts as art in the first place; as Adrian Searle expressed in the opening quotation. What values are expressed through art and the teaching of art and how do these relate to the values held by youngsters? As we have seen, the canon does not allow this debate and the censorship is enforced through the bulk of the published material, whether aimed at teachers, youngsters or parents.

Books, CDs, websites and TV programmes all form a part of the cultural climate for students and school. Many printed publications exploit the varied structural opportunities of the book format, for example the pop-up, in order to make them more interactive, yet still the content and the questions have not developed. This parallels one of the problems to have surfaced in the development the art CD-ROM, also aimed at youngsters – the lack of real interaction and the reliance on text/image relationships which adopt a didactic framework and content. Interestingly, Berger's *Ways of Seeing*, with its televisual concept, would seem to have offered a ready-made design for the CD-ROM before the CD had even been developed.

THE IMPOSSIBILITY OF ART EDUCATION[28]

Another school-based project aimed at undermining the divisions between art and education claims that key questions about art as education, and education as art, are not being addressed and that these must be central to any engagement with critical studies. The project quite deliberately sets out not to be an exemplification or model of good practice. It takes as its touchstone *Erased de Kooning* of 1953, by Robert Rauschenberg. In this work Rauschenberg literally rubbed out a drawing by the abstract expressionist Willem de Kooning. A group of upper-secondary-school students were duly instructed to erase drawings which they had earlier been instructed to make of their art room. This drew attention to a process of teaching art in the classroom in relation to an art event from the history of art. It raised key questions about the impossibility of assessment in relation to intention and whose art education is being addressed. Whose art work is being assessed? This became part of making the invisible visible in every sense.

Art education has a unique role to play in the cultural development of young people, but this can only have value if there is a willingness to allow the roles to be questioned as central to that cultural understanding. In fact the roles themselves can provide a rich source of ideas with which to play and create. This means that art education has to look afresh at its own structures and institutional frameworks to see what aspects can be shed and what new forms can be found. This was the Berger approach to visual culture. The forces of production and consumption pervade the art room as much as the factory floor, but reading the vast majority of art education publications one would think this was not the case. They remain rooted in a formalist tradition. A more recent survey for The National Association of Gallery Education

(ENGAGE) titled *Unpacking Teachers' Packs* analyses ten teachers' packs from ten London museums and galleries. It was found that the same assumptions about the elevated status of the unique work of art, and the aura surrounding this, still pervades.[29]

ART, ART BOOKS AND YOUNG PEOPLE

> Seeing comes before words. The child looks and recognises before it can speak.[30]

Berger in one of the *Ways of Seeing* programmes involved a group of very young children in a discussion about Michelangelo Caravaggio's painting *Supper at Emmaus* which revealed much about the reading of pictures by the young. Indeed, this fascinating sequence, which surprisingly was not referred to in the accompanying book, was another aspect of his project ahead of its time. Without any knowledge of the painting the children read the depiction of Christ as female. They were not approaching this image with an awareness of Caravaggio or his sexuality, the Bible or art history, but simply of their own experiences of their visual world. Added significance is given to the children's reading with the moment shown in the painting when Christ reveals his/her true identity to those breaking bread around the table. The picture is about identity as much as anything else. The biblical narrative of revelation and identity is mediated though the hands of Caravaggio.

Published materials about art aimed at young people seem to both draw upon and exploit the reader of visual and verbal text in the interest of certain ideological and canonical constructs of visual culture and remain a dominant force throughout these publications. Until the 1990s, books about art aimed directly at young people had been few and far between. The expansion of the popular art publishing industry, the introduction of a National Curriculum for art and the need for the museum and gallery to provide materials to support visits and promote their collections with the young, has resulted in an expansion of the market. This market appears to be directed mostly at a middle-income family audience and at schools. It is rare to find a current publication in this category which is affordable to those on lower incomes.

The target age range for many of the books has perhaps been affected by the improved quality of printing and colour reproduction developed over the past five years. Publishers now give designers the brief to create books able to meet the needs of the entire family age group, regardless of the text. They play upon the cultural appeal of the book as desirable object, the result of high-quality production.

There appear to be two main identifiable categories of publication: first, the art book, the youngster's 'coffee table' equivalent of an adult model, designed to introduce children to their cultural heritage. Well-designed and well-produced, these are often large and in some cases with a novel interactive element. There has been a revival and expansion of the 'pop-up' book and books which create optional ways of reading. Dorling Kindersley were quick to

Table 4.1: An Analysis of 43 Publications

Nationality	Number of images	Percentage of total
British	279	15.77
French	340	19.22
Italian	236	13.34
German	74	4.18
Spanish	118	6.67
Dutch	223	12.61
Other European	177	10.00
Total European	1447	81.79
N. American	122	6.9
S. American	22	1.24
Japanese	54	3.05
Indian	23	1.3
Other Asian	72	4.07
Australian	11	0.62
African	15	0.85
Other	3	0.18
Historical period		
Pre-14th C.	146	8.25
15th C.	176	9.95
16th C.	205	11.59
17th C.	191	10.8
18th C.	160	9.04
19th C.	482	27.25
20th C.	409	23.12
Women artists	61	3.45
Media		
Painting	1487	84.05
Sculpture	108	6.1
Textiles	22	1.24
Graphics	68	3.84
Ceramics	30	1.7
Other crafts	30	1.7
Other design	0	—
Architecture	18	1.01
Mixed media	2	0.12
Photography	2	0.12
Environmental	0	—
Computer	1	0.06
Performance	1	0.06
Other	0	—
Total number of books:	**43**	
Total number of images:	**1769**	

spot and exploit this market. Some of these publications are attempting to mimic the expensive adult art monographs, serving the dual role of ornament and magazine. Second, there is the art education book aimed specifically at teachers and their students, sometimes prepared within the parameters of the National Curriculum or some other framework for art as a teaching resource. The quality of design and printing for art education has in the past been poor in comparison to publications in the first category, reflecting a more limited market. This is now changing, and since the introduction in England of the National Curriculum, there appears to be an expanded market.

A content analysis of 43 publications aimed at youngsters, to be found in bookshops, school libraries and classrooms, from the last 20 years reveals a worrying yet not wholly unexpected result, as shown in Table 4.1. The data here are crude but they do reveal a great deal. Of course it would be more helpful to analyse how the images are used both by teacher and student, but the resources themselves represent an extremely narrow representation of the world of art through their pages. These books often claim to provide enlightenment and knowledge in relation to art and culture.

The evidence in this random selection indicates a clear bias that not only contradicts even the limited requirements of the National Curriculum for Art but also any equal opportunity policy in a school. There is a growing awareness of this situation. However, the simple provision of more non-European images, more work by women, more contemporary art and newer technologies avoids the issue of why we show what we do and why we use the work of artists in the way that we do. We have to reconsider whether it is art education that we need to see in schools or an education in visual culture of which art is a major part. Nick Mirzoeff argues that interactive visual media via the internet, virtual reality applications and the development with digital TV means that 'in this swirl of imagery, seeing is much more than believing ... it is not just a part of everyday life, it is everyday life'.[31] At the same time, whilst recognizing the interactive nature of a global visual culture, social political and cultural development is still experienced and mediated by local conditions and local struggles which artists reflect. Sarat Maharaj warns of the danger of hybridity, a type of visual Esperanto becoming the prime term, swapping places with a notion of stylistic purity. Difference can flip into sameness.[32] It seems to me that we are in danger of finding ways of *not* seeing.

POSTSCRIPT

I recently came across a little known 1977 publication by artist and teacher Jack Cross, titled *For Art's Sake* and part of a series called *Classroom Close-ups*.[33] The book is a classic 1970s humanist document questioning the amount of testing in art (even then!) and even includes at the end of the book a poem titled 'From Where Do We Begin' by a senior art inspector about his journey through life and art. It would be difficult now to imagine government inspectors writing poetry about art let alone going public with it: this is one of the sadnesses of our target-driven culture. Jack Cross, after exploring what art and an artistically educated person might be and what an art teacher might look like, at the end of his little book writes:

> When I started this book I planned to conclude it with some sort of statement of my own on the true aims of art teaching and offer some prescriptions by which these ends might be achieved. I was not absolutely sure what these would be, but after more than 30,000 words on a subject I have been teaching for nearly thirty years surely all would become clear – if only to myself? Yet I am not so very much wiser.

It does not matter whether or not we agree with Jack's ideas in his book, which is very much of its time. What is important is that he is surely 'very much wiser' in recognizing that there really are no conclusions where art teaching is concerned, just as in reality there is no beginning and no end to a lesson, except for the purposes of the timetable and school inspectors. This is one of the most difficult areas for the artist, craftworker and designer to face when embarking upon training for a career as an art teacher, and it is also an area that schools and art departments find most problematic because they are immersed in it and are under huge pressure to think only 'inside the box'.

Yet, what the artist/teacher and student have in common is the necessity to enter an empty space: not one filled with targets, visual aids and materials, but the void where ideas are not yet formed. This can be terrifying for both teacher and student and it shows that, before all else, the real challenge to orthodoxy in art education is not the risk involved in transgressive or controversial content (important though this might be), but the pedagogic power of not-knowing. This is the unthought space where 'art and teaching' should reside and it is here that the artist meets the teacher and roles become interchangeable. Freire says many teachers look for closure, for definite ways for themselves, students and knowledge to 'be', instead of 'becoming' as a method. For Freire[34] the ultimate form of pedagogy is 'dialogical cultural action': learning with, rather than teaching, transmitting or offering fixed models, or giving anything. He says that effective 'revolutionary leaders' (teachers) have to be both aware of the damaging effects of cultural invasion which brings about natural anxiety for things like closure, and try to think and work beyond that, beyond the 'deception of palliative solutions'.

Notes

1. Searle, A. (1999) 'Art'. *Guardian Weekend*, 16 January, p. 46.
2. Berger, J. (1974) *Ways of Seeing*. London: Pelican/BBC.
3. Benjamin, W. (1935/6) 'The work of art in the age of mechanical reproduction', in (1992) H. Arendt (ed.) (trans. H. Zohn) *Illuminations*. London: Fontana.
4. Clark, K. (1969) BBC. *Civilisation*. London.
5. Bourdieu, P. (1979) *Distinction: A Social Critique of the Judgement of Taste*. London: Routledge & Kegan Paul.
6. Cox, G. (1999) 'Be realistic, demand the impossible', in G. Cox, H. Hollands and V. de Rijke (eds) *The Impossibility of Art Education*. London: Camerawork.

7. NCET (1998). *Fusion*. Coventry: National Council for Education Technology.
8. See Meecham, P. (1999) 'Of webs, nets and lily ponds', in *Journal of Art and Design Education*, **18**(1), 77–82.
9. Hughes, A. (1998) 'A further reconceptualisation of the art curriculum'. *Broadside 1*, 1–14. Birmingham: ARTicle Press.
10. *Directions* is a special edition of the *Journal of Art and Design Education*, **18**(1).
11. Swift, J. and Steers, J. (1999) 'A manifesto for art education', in *ibid.*, 7–13.
12. Bancroft, A. (1995) 'What do dragons think about in their dark lonely caves? or critical studies: the importance of knowledge'. *Journal of Art and Design Education*, **14**(1), 21–34. The first part of the title is a question taken from C. Brigg and A. Penn (1993). *Art Pack: Animals*, Card 12. Philip Green Educational Ltd.
13. *Ibid.*, p. 22.
14. Hughes, A. (1993) 'Don't judge pianists by their hair'. *Journal of Art and Design Education*, **12**(3), 279–89.
15. *Ibid.*
16. Bancroft, *op. cit.*
17. Brigg, C. and Penn, A., *op. cit. Faces*. Card 1.
18. Dorling Kindersley Presentation at National Association of Gallery Education Conference (1995), *Out of the Frame*.
19. Taylor, R. (1986) *Educating for Art*. Harlow: Longman.
20. Bancroft, *op. cit.*, p. 30.
21. SCAA (1996–7) *A Survey and Analysis of Published Resources for Art 5 to 19* and QCA (1998) *Survey and Analysis of the Artists that Teachers Refer to and Use in Teaching Art 5–16*, p. 9. London: Qualifications and Curriculum Authority.
22. These quotes are taken from QCA, *ibid.*
23. De Rijke, V. and Cox, G., (1994) *This is Not the National Curriculum for Art: A Collaborative Project with Children on the Discourses of Art and Education*. London: Middlesex University.
24. Cox, G., de Rijke, V., Weeks, S. (1996) *Recycling the National Curriculum*. This project also resulted in an accompanying publication, *This Paper is Intentionally Blank*, by the same authors. London: Camerawork/Middlesex University.
25. See Hollands, H. (1996) 'Art: chance, opportunity and entitlement', in R. Andrews (ed.) *Interpreting the New National Curriculum*. London: Middlesex University Press.
26. Sekula, A. (1984) 'School is a factory', in *Photography against the Grain: Essays and Photoworks 1973–1983*. Halifax: Press of the Nova Scotia College of Art and Design, p. 228.
27. Jones, P. (1998) 'Art', in G. Clay, J. Hertrich, P. Jones, J. Mills and J. Rose. *The Arts Inspected*. Oxford: Ofsted/Heinemann.
28. Cox G., Hollands H., de Rijke, V. (eds) (1999) *The Impossibility of Art Education*. London: Camerawork/Middlesex University.
29. Clive, S. and Geggie, P. (1998) *Unpacking Teachers' Packs*. London: Engage.
30. Berger, *op. cit.*
31. Mirtzoeff, N. (1999) *An Introduction to Visual Culture*. London: Routledge.
32. Maharaj, S. (1995) 'Perfidious fidelity, the untranslatability of the Other', in *Global Visions: Towards a New Internationalism in the Visual Arts*. London: Kala Press, pp. 28–35.
33. Cross, J. (1977) *For Art's Sake*. London: George Allen and Unwin.
34. Freire, P. (1970) *Pedagogy of the Oppressed*. London: Penguin.

Chapter 5

Changing Practices: Art Education and Popular Visual Culture

DARREN NEWBURY

What is the relationship between art education and visual culture in the postmodern world? In the context of contemporary developments in the kinds of images available, and the ways in which they get made and seen, it is important that arts and media educators review the purpose and direction of current teaching. It is the aim of this chapter to consider the challenge to existing rationales presented by contemporary visual culture, in particular the implications of embracing a wider view of contemporary cultural practices. Examples of recent visual projects are considered in terms of their implications for the development of the visual curriculum. However, the question is not simply a technical, or technological, one. It is also my aim to draw attention to a debate around values that is at the heart of art education, though not always recognized as such: to reflect on the way in which visual education structures young people's engagement with their own and other cultures. Changes in the way art teachers view and categorize visual culture, including the work made by young people, are as important as changes in the way in which images are made and shown. It is argued here that the inclusion of examples from con-temporary popular and visual culture in the curriculum could be used to stimulate debate around the purpose of visual education in the twenty-first century, and to open up new directions for art education.

What is art education for? The answer to this question depends on the point at which one asks it, and to whom one is speaking. For my purposes here I would like to highlight two dominant versions. The first is identified by Romans in his research into the origins of the art and design schools in Britain in the nineteenth century.[1] Romans identifies two interlinked purposes which, arguably, have contemporary relevance: the idea that art and design education would add to the national competitiveness of manufacturing industry through an increase in the quality of output; and the education of the population in the appreciation of good design. The latter introduces a moral dimension, what Romans refers to as a 'democratization of taste'. The importance of this to an emerging consumer capitalism was, it seems, not lost on those who founded the art schools. This argument for art education implies a fixed body of knowledge about good art (and one should remember that, as conceived at the time, and still to some extent now, design was merely the application of the more abstract principles of art to specific material contexts) and hence suggests a straightforward pedagogy based upon instruction in the skills and techniques of artmaking and the inculcation of good taste through the introduction of students to the heights of artistic achievement. The universal principles of classical painting and sculpture informed both aspects. Alternatively, nearer to the present day it is possible to discern the emergence, of alongside, and sometimes in opposition, a different set of concerns. This second dominant version can be referred to as an 'expressive' tradition.[2] The components of the expressive tradition will be familiar to contemporary art teachers, placing its emphasis on the creativity of the individual; the notion of personal exploration is one that dominates much contemporary art educational practice. Pedagogically, the focus shifts to the development of the individual through practices of artmaking. Where works from an art-historical canon are referred to, the emphasis is on the making of a personal response. Though it is worth noting that this version does not initiate a challenge to the established canon of great works, instead it shifts the notion of appreciation to a more personal and subjective level. There are clear parallels here, it seems, with the subject of English and particularly the encouragement of creative writing, which Steedman refers to as 'a kind of ethical self-cultivation, to be achieved by children using the written word'.[3] The emergence in art education of work on the self as a recurrent theme, if not a genre, is arguably part of the same formation. Even photography, that most ubiquitous and modest of media, is co-opted in this way by the art curriculum:

> Photography provides a means by which students express and thereby develop themselves morally and aesthetically within the framework of the art curriculum. In this manner photography risks becoming restricted to one particular perspective – that of artistic phototherapy.[4]

There is both a moral and Romantic dimension to this practice, with such educational approaches considered as 'helping [students] to find the individual selves they have become ... protect[ing] them from that extreme awareness of individuality that we call alienation. Thus may education compensate for society.'[5]

Although aspects of both versions are often present simultaneously in contemporary classroom practice (along with more minor variations and some dissenting voices), there is clearly a tension between the extrinsic, worldly rationale of the former and the emphasis on the intrinsic value to the individual in the latter. Although the latter model offers greater autonomy of the subject from the social and economic pressures which attended its birth, and there are many reasons to welcome such autonomy, I want to argue here that there are attendant dangers which threaten to undermine the relevance of the subject in the early twenty-first century. Some of these have been only too evident in recent years, for example in Britain, where art has struggled to retain its importance as a core subject in the formation of a national curriculum. Stanley is also right to point out that the openness in this version is perhaps only apparent. In practice there are often quite fixed notions of where the subject is leading:

> Even art educational and museum models that promote the value of self-discovery and serendipity share the presumption that learning follows an evolutionary pattern where students acquire incremental knowledge so the world is gradually illuminated and properly understood.[6]

Ironically, perhaps, given the motivations that occupied the minds of those who contributed to the formulation of modern art and design education, the movement in art education, in schools at least, has been away from an engagement with the 'real' world, cultural and economic, in which the skills and knowledge that art education teaches will be tested, and towards an increasingly self-contained and other-worldly set of ideas and practices, viewed by some perhaps as a bastion against dominant values, but nevertheless remote from most young people's experience. My argument here is for art educators to look beyond the boundaries of the subject and to ask what is its place in the world. This will, I think, necessitate making new arguments for the relevance of the subject, but not in the sense of the narrow vocationalism that has dominated educational debate in many areas. For example, the issue of educating consumers of visual culture and design, that was present in the late nineteenth century, is arguably both more pressing and more complex in the current context. What contribution has art education to make here? I agree with Hall when she makes the following point:

> In Karen Raney's book[7] she said something like, 'Does understanding a Silk Cut advert help us to understand an abstract painting?' I think this sentence is the wrong way round, because actually, day-to-day, it's more important for young people to understand a Silk Cut advert, where it's coming from and what it's trying to communicate.[8]

Similarly, it may be antithetical to the way the subject is currently constituted at secondary level, but I think it is worth considering the relevance of the art curriculum to the world of employment. From my own research on the use of photography in secondary art it is clear that many students perceive the subject generally as unrelated to areas of future work. In a culture which, it is commonly accepted, is increasingly dependent on visual forms of communication this is a disturbing perception. It is the responsibility of art educators, I suggest, to envisage the value of the subject in these terms. As Bennett has argued for cultural studies there is a strong case for shedding the romanticism of the subject in favour of a more pragmatic approach, whilst holding on to the critical dimension.[9] The gallery and the studio are far from being the only contemporary cultural spaces where it is possible and necessary to foster creative and critical thinking about visual communication.

The problem with art education is not that it depends on a developmental instructional pedagogy,[10] indeed art education can be one of the areas of the curriculum where pedagogy follows Dewey's dictum that education be more than 'an affair of "telling", and being told, but an active and constructive process', using teaching methods that allow 'direct and continuous occupations with things'.[11] Instead, I would argue, the problem is the narrowness of the practice upon which the teaching of art is modelled. Hughes comes close to defining the problem in this way when he asks,

> Why have we apparently excluded for the present the possibility of an art curriculum based upon the critical, contextual, historical or cultural domains, and not predicated upon studio practice and the model of the artist?[12]

Should not the art classroom be a place where students experience something of the diversity of image-making practices that constitute contemporary culture? Although clearly within any one school there will be practical limits to the range of experiences that students can be offered, this is no reason to limit from the outset one's horizons to a highly specialized form of image-making which seems both anachronistic and remote from the everyday experience of the young people upon whom it is practised. The notion of the individual artist as creator which informs art education is a highly specific western construction, one which poses many problems for art education in dealing with the visual culture of other societies and, indeed, popular cultural forms in general. As one art teacher argues, 'the distinction between art and other kinds of representations is unhelpful to both formal education and the development of visual literacy'.[13] To accept such a claim is, of course, to do more than simply append design to art education; it is to undermine the status of the subject as currently constituted. This argument, with its focus on the contemporary cultural context and its ambition to embrace a broader range of visual practices, suggests the need for a radical rethinking of the purpose and direction of art education. Those who have fought long and hard for the autonomy of the subject may balk at such a suggestion. What is clear, however, is that without a clear understanding of its contemporary relevance art education is in danger of losing the argument.

My intention in this chapter is to reverse my initial question; instead of trying to understand the purpose of art education from within the subject itself and its history, I suggest that it may be useful to step outside the subject. Instead of asking, What is art education for? I will examine, momentarily, examples of visual cultural practice, and then consider how formal education can or should respond, and in order to explore these arguments further I will examine the relationship between education and popular culture; this is an area in which art educators are beginning to make a contribution to the debate.

ART EDUCATION AND POPULAR CULTURE

Calls for an art curriculum that is more responsive to the social and cultural experiences of young people are not new. Lister made this point over 20 years ago:

Firstly, traditional art practices and their values (ideas about art) now constitute a minor and peripheral area of contemporary cultural production especially in the field of visual culture (if there is such an isolated category). Secondly, the social worlds of a great many secondary school students are necessarily different from those of the individuals and communities in which these practices and ideas have their roots and development. They do not help them to see their world or to organise their experience of it.[14]

Writing more recently, Hughes echoes Lister's argument:

The time has come to consider opening up the definition and therefore the parameters of our subject, which may mean dropping the evaluative term 'art' in favour of a more neutral description of visual education or visual culture which exhibits greater inclusivity and a clear recognition that '21st century youth ... needs a visual vocabulary that enables them to decode visual images, not just the (technical) means of reproducing what they see'.[15, 16]

These are radical suggestions and imply more than a simple revision or extension of the syllabus for art.

The sense of an emerging commonality of interest between art and media educators suggests a recognition on the part of art educators of the need to engage with visual culture beyond the boundaries of the subject itself, and can be argued to indicate one direction for curriculum development and change. In a recent article, Freedman discusses the way in which an engagement with the popular is becoming inevitable, and is to some extent beyond the control of teachers.[17] Popular visual culture is shaping the way in which young people engage with the subject of art, although in Freedman's teacherly discourse it not clear whether this can be construed positively. Freedman insists on the need to teach students formally to be critical and suggests a role for media studies approaches and semiotic theory in the art classroom. However, beyond the acknowledgement of the presence of popular imagery in young people's art, and the need to somehow deal with it, which usually implies the addition of a theoretical or contextual component, one might argue for a recognition of the legitimacy and purpose of popular forms. This in turn could be used to encourage the critical development of such forms as purposeful means of expression by young people themselves. It would, arguably, also offer one way to obviate the pedagogic differences between media studies and art education, in particular the tendency within media studies to view practical work as a vehicle for theoretical knowledge and understanding rather than intrinsically purposeful.

One area in which the need to reconfigure the curriculum and to recognize common ground with other subjects is most pressing is in relation to digital technologies. Digital media are having a significant impact on contemporary culture and society; considerable investments are being made in the development of new technology-based teaching and learning at all levels of education.

And yet, arguments concerning the specific use or value of the technology are often vague and circular. The ability to use computers is often presented as a good thing independently of any purpose it may serve. Why is it important that young people learn with and about digital technologies? For art education, I suggest, two issues are of particular importance: the skills associated with contemporary forms of image-making and the relationship between education, access and cultural participation. As Sefton-Green argues:

> The increasing accessibility of these technologies has created significant new opportunities for young people to become cultural producers, rather than mere consumers. Using equipment that is now much more easily available, not just in their own homes or peer groups but also in formal and informal education, young people can participate much more readily in activities such as music production, image manipulation, design, desktop publishing and video making ... The educational implications of these developments are potentially vast, and extend well beyond the delimited area of 'information technology'. They indicate the need for an expanded notion of literacy, encompassing the social processes involved in understanding texts ('reading' in its broadest sense) and the range of competencies brought to any form of expression, be it painting in oils or conventional domestic photography.[18]

Although subjects such as art and English are often perceived to be providing young people's main opportunity for cultural participation, except as consumers, they do not always contribute positively to the shaping of young people's patterns of cultural activity beyond school.[19] One reason for this may be the gap between the formal curriculum in these subjects and young people's experience of contemporary media culture. If art education is to have a role in the twenty-first century then it has to engage with popular culture, with the everyday world of visual and technologically mediated culture that constitutes the experience of the majority of young people. As Stanley argues, 'Put bluntly, the working of visualisation is too important to relegate to commercial operators without intense and continual scrutiny from us all.'[20]. This is not to argue that the introduction of computers in the art classroom will resolve the current crisis in the art curriculum; instead the challenge faced by art educators is wide-ranging and includes theoretical, pedagogical and technological issues as well as familiar practical problems.

In order to explore further what this argument means for practice I will consider two examples: the first concerns an internet-based project using domestic photographic imagery; the second draws on a recent project with young people around the use of digital imaging outside of formal education. Both can be used to suggest how popular visual practices can be utilized as the basis for curriculum projects.

DOMESTIC PHOTOGRAPHY AND DIGITAL TECHNOLOGY

One area of popular image-making that has been largely ignored by media educators, although it is present to some extent in art education, is that of domestic photography. Students are frequently asked to bring photographs of themselves into the classroom to be reworked. Such images are often used in the context of projects on the theme of 'The Self'. The emphasis in such projects is on the formal manipulation of the image, the photographic image reworked as a painting, for example, or on the use of artistic means to represent the notion of an inner self. The popular photographic image is conceived as a kind of raw material that can be reworked through art. Less often is attention given to the complexity of family photographs themselves and the narratives that surround them. As Pinney has demonstrated in his fascinating recent study of popular and commercial photographic portraiture in central India, the idea that domestic photographs are expressive only of a kind of trivial realism is mistaken. Not only are practices of making and displaying images the outcomes of complex social and cultural processes but the medium can provide for subtle and critical forms of expression. Pinney characterizes the Nagda photographic studios as 'chambers of dreams':

> The inventive posing that characterises much of the imagery produced within studios is concerned with the transcendence and parody of social roles. The photographic studio becomes a place not for solemnisation of the social but for the individual exploration of that which does not yet exist in the social world.[21]

A recent (and ongoing) internet photography project, 'Collected Visions', provides an interesting reworking of the practice of family photography that may serve as a model for cross-curricular educational practice. The project consists of an internet website or archive of domestic photographic images.[22] The site has a gallery and a museum section which consists of individual or groups of images combined with short passages of text, usually descriptions of or reflections on the particular images shown. Beyond browsing, visitors are encouraged to interact with the site in a number of ways. One's own family images can be submitted for inclusion in the archive. If one chooses one can submit the image or images with a written text or caption for inclusion in the gallery or museum sections. However, the testimony form of image-text display to which this gives rise is counterposed with the invitation to visitors to search the archive and select others' images to combine with their own text for exhibition in the gallery and museum spaces. This possibility works to destabilize the authenticity of the narratives presented and provides insights into this most ubiquitous of visual forms. The viewer is unsure whether what he or she is reading is a true or fictional account (some of the images are used more than once with different written narratives).

The siting of this material on the internet also opens up a number of cross-cultural possibilities. Although, in fact, most of the images and written contributions appear to come from North America, reflecting, no doubt, global patterns of access to this means of distribution, this is unlikely to remain static. Even within the selection one can discover variations in photographic practices. As well as the expected images of weddings, children and so on, the archive contains a small number of funeral images, prompting reflection on what may be considered acceptable subject-matter and what inappropriate.

The gallery and museum sections contain some fascinating combinations of images and text. One combination is entitled 'Chinese American Family'. It contains 24 images, all conventional family portraits, some in black and white and some in colour. The text is simple and straightforward:

> These are pictures of my family. There's Moon Fong Chau (my dad), Mee Siu (my mom) and my brothers and sister: Terry, Linda and Glen. These photos are all taken when we were living in Houston, TX. The older photos are from as early as 1954 and go through the mid-70s (notice my brother Glen, the long-haired surfer). Those were the days.

The construction is deceptively simple, but the sheer weight of images and the conjunction of people, time and place referred to in the text attest to lived histories and identities. Other combinations point up the disjunction between different actors' experiences of situations and the 'official' narratives often recorded by the family album:

> Everyone always wanted me to be a cowboy. To stand tall in the saddle. To look squinting at the sun to tell what time it is. To do what had to be done, even if means shooting your dog, or your best friend dying on the dusty streets of Dodge. To do what had to be done. To be a man, for Chrissakes. To die with my boots on.

Although educational work with the domestic snapshot imagery is not new, there is indeed a history of such work, much of it within art education, I think this example points up two relatively unexplored issues: first, the relation between visual and written narratives, and second, the consideration of audience. Popular culture tends to have less respect for boundaries and, as a result, the visual as a domain of practice is less distinct. This may be instructive for art educators. The opportunities for image/text production and dissemination made available by digital technologies offer new possibilities for educational practice. Historically, it is clear that the introduction of cheap and easily reproduced images changed the nature of photography as a social practice. Similarly, the impact of digital technologies on the dissemination of images, although apparently a quantitative change, has qualitative implications. The scanning and digitizing of family images allows for the easy reproduction and manipulation of what are often precious objects. Their placing on a website opens the work to potentially large and diverse audiences. The availability of this potential in schools will impact significantly on the way in which teachers and students think about what they are doing. A recent secondary-school project in conjunction with the English National Portrait Gallery, explored precisely this potential to construct visual narratives from young people's own domestic images.[23]

What does this offers to the secondary art curriculum? First, one way of reconceptualizing art education is to see it as a site within the curriculum where students gain a *practical* insight into the importance of the visual image and visual narratives to contemporary culture: where better to start than with a cultural form with which all students will have some experience? Further, it is not simply a case of incorporating popular cultural material into the practice of art; what one might call, bearing in mind the way fine art practice has incorporated material from other cultures, the primitivization of popular culture; but of exploring the critical and aesthetic potential of popular forms themselves. Art education work on The Self is often at pains to distinguish itself from more popular forms of self-representation, rather than engaging directly with the popular as a valuable and potentially critical form. Second, the response of art educators to contemporary culture should not be one of simply looking to include a greater element of theoretical studies (on the model of media studies) but rather should be offering students insight into the processes of construction – technical and cultural – of visual and cultural texts. It is significant that a project such as this may be equally, if not more, at home within English or perhaps personal and social education classes, and indicative of the problems of isolating the visual domain in relation to contemporary and popular cultural forms.

PROJECT WORK WITH YOUNG PEOPLE

A second way of exploring the development of an art curriculum that is more responsive to contemporary cultural concerns is to ask what young people want to do, and are already doing independently of school in some cases, with visual media. This was the approach taken by a research project with which I have been involved over the last two years,[24] the aim of which is to work with young people outside of formal education to explore aspects of their own visual culture on their own terms. This seemingly obvious strategy of seeking the voices of young people as a contribution to curriculum development is rarely taken up,[25] most probably, one surmises, because of the problems that are perceived to stem from ceding even the smallest control of the curriculum. Nevertheless, there is something to be learned from such an approach and the challenges it lays at the door of formal education.

The practical work with young people gives an indication of the scope of this project. 'Young, Queer and Safe?' was a project with a Birmingham (England)-based lesbian, gay and bisexual youth group. The development of the project had been influenced by research suggesting a relatively high level of use of the internet by the lesbian, gay and bisexual communities, and the desire to explore further the visual communication of identity in a context where the young people had control over the image-making process, but little control over the diverse and geographically distant audiences that may encounter the work. The theme of anonymity and visual reference to self-identity had emerged from an earlier pilot project; this was seen as an opportunity to pursue this exploration in more depth. Although the context of the project may seem to overdetermine the theme of identity to the point where alternative uses of the project are excluded, the resulting images suggest this was not in fact the case. The non-prescriptive methodology employed by the project workers, placing emphasis on the decisions of the young people involved as to how work developed, helped to ensure that the project reflected the participants' own concerns. Although, unsurprisingly, some of the work made reference to sexual identity, the resulting website touches on a host of areas in a playful exploration of youth, pleasure, popular culture, technology, relationships and the body. There is an issue here as to whether work defined in this way would be subject to censorship or self-censorship within the context of secondary education. However, I would also draw attention to a wider issue about the ability of this type of project to motivate young people and the kind of learning experience it offers. The pivotal point of the project was the publication and dissemination of the images, primarily in the form of a website, but also to more local audiences through exhibition at events. The young people's engagement with the project was as a form of visual cultural communication. The collaborative process of image-making and the time given over to editing and the consideration of meaning in relation to audience offers a marked contrast to art in schools where success or failure is considered to be a feature of (usually the formal properties of) a final image or portfolio of images. Interestingly, although the participants may not necessarily recognize it as such, the project has continued to offer a form of educational practice, through its support for the young people, in the writing of an article and in further collaborations with other similar youth groups. Educationally the project could be conceptualized as providing scaffolding to support the development of active and meaningful cultural participation. This project is a challenge to art education both in terms of the kinds of cultural practices it makes available and in terms of the extent to which art education recognizes students as purposeful communicators and image-makers. The project was a novel experience for the young people, as is evident from the difficulty they found in finding a frame of reference suitable for what they were doing. The following exchange comes from a feedback session on the project:

Project worker: So do you think this project was more interesting than it would have been had it happened in a school environment?
Participant: Well, it wouldn't have happened in a school environment – fullstop, really.
Project worker: Why?
Participant: Basically because of the nature of the website that we created and it was basically specifically for us. If we'd done it in a school environment there would have been a lot more restraint and, you know, you've got the teacher watching over you, so you're not going to start messing about and everything and also you treat it more like work and not actually a project, you know, a sort of hobby, although I hate the word hobby, but I can't think of a better one.[26]

Like this young person I find the word 'hobby' deeply inadequate as a description of the work accomplished, and yet the relative lack of resources and formal structures that support this kind of practice might explain why it comes to mind.

A second project further supports the need for opportunities for young people to develop purposeful approaches to the use of visual media. This project focused on the Bull Ring, a shopping and market area of central Birmingham that is currently being redeveloped. The aim of the project was to work with a range of young people that had different relationships to the same urban space and to use the production of visual work as an opportunity for them to communicate their views on the area and the changes that were taking place. Again, this example emphasizes the purposive nature of young people's image-making, not simply as work to be assessed but as a means of commenting on changes in their environment. The young people's relative unfamiliarity with this way of working suggests that formal education often does little to encourage young people to recognize the legitimacy of their own voices and the power of visual media as a means of their expression. Discussing gallery and museum education in particular, Stanley makes a similar point:

> I would argue that, with some notable and highly significant exceptions, art education, gallery education and museum education seldom welcome the students' real experience into the culture of the school and certainly not into the curriculum.[27]

It could also be argued that the project shifts the focus from the personalized notion of expression often present in art education, with its emphasis on states of feeling, towards representation, thereby adding a greater social dimension to the curriculum.

CONCLUSION

The argument put forward in this chapter has a number of implications for the way in which art education is both thought about and practised. First, the range of contemporary visual culture could be reflected in the visual curriculum to a greater extent than currently. This is not a call for art teachers to become specialists in all areas, but rather to recognize the diversity of visual and cultural practices within, as well as between, societies. A recognition also that practices of visual representation are pervasive and not the preserve of fine art alone. This is an argument against culturally exclusive forms of education which Bourdieu characterizes as teaching the majority to recognize the superiority of high culture and their exclusion from it.[28] In practical terms this means a change in the way in which art teachers resource their teaching. Rather than a reliance on the work of established artists as a point of reference, students could be encouraged to make use of other forms of contemporary visual culture, for example magazines, advertising, film and family photography to name just a few possibilities. Students might also be expected to do some of this resourcing and research work themselves, bringing into the classroom visual images and objects that they find interesting or meaningful. Importantly, this greater range of material should not simply be funnelled into producing the same type of art works but can itself be considered as forms within which the students should have the opportunity to work. For example, how might they retell family stories through images and text?

Second, that young people be conceived of as purposeful communicators. Whilst it is clear that art educators do not simply think of students as vessels to be filled with knowledge, it is also clear that the model of self-development through aesthetic expression begs its own questions. The focus on audience and communication that can be initiated through the introduction of digital technologies such as the internet into the classroom raises some interesting issues. Instead of alternating between observational drawing and the notion of personal expression, one potential strategy here might be to set students particular problems to be resolved visually. These could be devised in relation to other subject areas such as history (the representation of other times) or geography (other places). For example, the production of images or objects to commemorate a particular event or to represent a particular aspect of cultural identity could provide a useful vehicle to explore visual symbolism as well as practical art-making skills.

Third, the relationship between cultural theory and image-making practice in visual education pedagogy is an area in need of further reflection. For my part, I have tried to argue that it is not simply a case of introducing more or better theory into the classroom, especially if this is presented to students as academic approaches to images separated from their own making activities. Discussion around meanings and visual language needs to be an integral rather than a supplementary feature of the curriculum. In classroom terms students could be encouraged to discuss and explain how they think their work communicates and to whom. This would initiate a move away from the dichotomy between the notion of the purely subjective response and the ultimate authority of the teacher to award marks. Obviously this would require some careful structuring on the part of the teacher, but the reward would be to shift the focus away from the artwork as the end point and towards an understanding of visual things as only part of a process of communication, representation and expression.

Finally, all of these have implications for the way in which the visual work by young people is viewed and assessed. Instead of a notion of the aesthetic being the key criterion, it becomes modified by the inclusion of additional criteria such as communication, representation, and the making of a visual argument. This is perhaps the most difficult of all. Although the assessment of abilities in observational drawing, for example, does have the virtue of relative transparency, it is the responsibility of educators to negotiate the difficulties of assessing learning when and where it occurs, and not simply relying on that which is most easily assessable. However, if the art classroom is considered as a space for reflective and collaborative learning then perhaps the forms of material that this gives rise to – discussion, written commentaries, visual research sketchbooks – must also, increasingly, be the focus of assessment and evaluation, alongside finished work, as they already are in many successful art classrooms. My claim here is not to have available an alternative model, fully worked out, but to have shared some provocative questions and intriguing possibilities.

Acknowledgements

I am grateful to Nick Stanley and Roz Hall whose work and ideas have informed the writing of this chapter. They do not, of course, bear responsibility for the conclusions I have come to, nor for any of the imprecisions in my thinking.

POSTSCRIPT

Art education seems at the centre of a dichotomy. On the one hand visual practices and visual modes of knowledge and expression are clearly an important feature of our contemporary world; indeed, some would argue that from the latter half of the twentieth century 'images take precedence over words as the most significant realm of meaning'.[29] On the other hand, contemporary art practice is often presented as increasingly self-referential, and art education simply a welcome addition to the curriculum, but not at its core. I had this dilemma in mind when I originally wrote this chapter. At the centre was a simple question: what is the role for art education in the contemporary world, and how might art educators reconceptualize the practice of teaching art? My argument was that art education should acknowledge the many and varied image-making *practices* that are important in the world today, rather than base itself on the highly specialized model of practice of the studio-based artist. This is not an argument against the value of the studio, and certainly not the classroom, as a space of experimentation and critical reflection, but rather an argument for developing critical and innovative approaches to the making and using of images across many sites. The economic importance of the cultural and creative industries implies that an increasing number of people will find themselves working in the creation, support, distribution, marketing and interpretation of visual cultural products. Whilst clearly only a minority of young people will become 'artists', that is to miss the point. Only a minority of school students become scientists, but the practice of science is so fundamental to contemporary society that an understanding of this is a democratic right and responsibility.

I have not substantially changed my position on these issues since the chapter was written. With or without the interventions of art educators, popular cultural practices will continue to absorb the interest and investment of young people. And whilst the incorporation of popular forms into the curriculum risks subverting their value for young people, there is much educators can learn from them. The increasing combination of the means of production (digital cameras) with the means of distribution (the internet, mobile phones) in photography, for example, seems to shift the attention from the formal qualities of the image to a more sophisticated appreciation of timing, audience and communication style – all subjects worthy of academic exploration. If anything, the transformations in popular image making practices have been accentuated over the last two or three years. The original failure of digital photography to engage with the ways in which people use images – as material objects – is rapidly being overtaken by new uses of the digital photograph. Photography placed in the context of the new mobile technologies has become intertwined with the everyday lives of many young people. The association of the digital photograph with pleasure and playfulness, an aspect of the medium's transience perhaps, should not be a barrier to its exploration through visual practice in schools.

For art educators the visual diary might be of particular interest, as it cuts across popular culture and existing educational practice, having origins in both spheres. As Nick Stanley has noted, the self-reflective diary has huge potential within art and design education.[30] At the same time, the web-based photographic/text journal, or photoblog[31] is one of the new forms emerging from digital photographic culture. There is a paradox perhaps in that these new creative cultural opportunities go hand in hand with the increasing penetration of consumer products and technologies into our everyday lives and relationships. Nevertheless, if art educators are able to capture just a small portion of the energy and investment involved in these kinds of practices, and harness it to the development of a critical visual literacy, then that would be a valuable achievement.

Notes

1. Romans, M. (1998) *Social, Political, Economic and Cultural Determinants in the History of Nineteenth Century Art and Design Education in Britain*, PhD submission, University of Central England.
2. I have borrowed the formulation from Christopher Frayling's keynote presentation, 'Head, Hand and Heart', to the 1997 International Design and Technology Education Research conference at the University of Loughborough, 1–3 September. Frayling outlined three traditions: the normative, the critical and the expressive.
3. Steedman, C. (1997) 'Writing the self: the end of the scholarship girl', in J. McGuigan (ed.) *Cultural Methodologies*, London: Sage, pp. 106–25.
4. Stanley, N. (1996) 'Photography and the politics of representation'. *Journal of Art and Design Education*, **15**(1), 95–100.
5. Thomas, G. quoted in Steedman, *op. cit.*, p. 111.
6. Stanley, N. (1999) 'The war between the Tates or reflecting elements of popular entertainment in art educational and museum practices'. *Journal of Art and Design Education*, **18**(1), 83–8.
7. Raney, K. (1997) *Visual Literacy: Issues and Debates. A report on the Research Project 'Framing Visual and Verbal Experience'*. London: Middlesex University.
8. Quotation taken from transcript of discussion between Roz Hall, Alistair Raphael, Steve Herne and Rebecca Sinker published as 'Whose art is it anyway? Art education outside the classroom', in J. Sefton-Green and R. Sinker (eds) (2000) *Evaluating Creativity: Making and Learning by Young People*. London: Routledge.

9. See Bennett, T. (1997) 'Towards a pragmatics for cultural studies', in J. McGuigan (ed.), *Cultural Methodologies*, London: Sage, pp. 42–61.

10. I think the argument put forward in Stanley, *op. cit.* overstates the pedagogic uniformity of art educational practice.

11. Dewey, J. (1966) *Democracy and Education*. New York: The Free Press.

12. Hughes, A. (1998) 'Reconceptualising the art curriculum'. *Journal of Art and Design Education*, **17**(1), 41–9.

13. Kennedy, M. quoted in Raney, *op. cit.*

14. Lister, M. (1978) 'Art, schooling and contemporary culture'. *Schooling and Culture*, **1**, 24–65.

15. Hughes, *op. cit.*

16. Meeham, quoted in Hughes, *op. cit.*

17. Freedman, K. (1997) 'Curriculum inside and outside school: representations of fine art in popular culture'. *Journal of Art and Design Education*, **16**(2), 137–46.

18. Buckingham, D. and Sefton-Green, J. (n.d.) 'Digital visions: new opportunities for multimedia literacy'. Institute of Education, University of London (unpublished project report). See also Buckingham, D. and Sefton-Green, J. (1996) 'Digital visions: children's "creative" use of multimedia technologies'. *Convergence* **2**(2), 47–79.

19. Harland, J., Kinder, K. and Hartley, K. (1995) *Arts in their View: A Study of Youth Participation in the Arts*. Slough: National Foundation for Educational Research.

20. Stanley (1999), *op. cit.*

21. Pinney, C. (1997) *Camera Indica: The Social Life of Indian Photographs*. London: Reaktion Books.

22. The website has been created by Lorie Novak and can be found at http://cvisions.cat.nyu.edu/

23. This website is hosted by the London-based arts organization Artec, and can be found at http://www.artec.org.uk/npg/

24. This is a three-year collaborative project between the University of Central England in Birmingham and Jubilee Arts in Sandwell, funded by the Arts Council of England and West Midlands Arts. Information and links to project web pages can be found on the Birmingham Institute of Art and Design research website at http://biad.uce.ac.uk/research/ I draw in this section on written accounts of project work by the project researcher Roz Hall. Reports on various aspects of the project have been published, see for example Hall, R. and Newbury, D. (1999) 'What makes you switch on? young people, the internet and cultural participation', in J. Sefton-Green (ed.) *Young People, Creativity and the New Technologies: The Challenge of the Digital Arts*. London: Routledge.

25. There are some significant exceptions. Martin Kennedy's work with secondary students in South East London would be one example: see Kennedy, M. (1995) 'Issues-based work at Key Stage 4: Crofton School: a case study'. *Journal of Art and Design Education*, **14**(1), 7–20.

26. Transcript taken from research diary, Roz Hall, October 1998.

27. Stanley (1999), *op. cit.*

28. Bourdieu, P. (1986) *Distinction: A Social Critique of the Judgement of Taste*. London: Routledge.

29. Chaney, David C., (2000) 'Contemporary socioscapes: books on visual culture'. *Theory, Culture and Society*, **17**(6), 111–24.

30. Stanley, N. (2003) 'Young people, photography and engagement'. *International Journal of Art and Design Education*, **22**(2), 134–44.

31. Cohen, K. and Wakeford, N. (2003) 'Photoblogging: digital photography and sociology as strange chronicles'. *Images of Social Life: The New Foundations of Visual Studies,* 8–10 July, University of Southampton; Ward, M. (2003) 'A blog for everyone'. *BBC News* [online]. Available at http://news.bbc.co.uk/1/hi/technology/3078541.stm [accessed 21st June 2003].

Chapter 6

Bite the ICT Bullet: Using the World Wide Web in Art Education

ANDY ASH

INTRODUCTION

Information and communications technology (ICT) can take many different forms: computers, video and audio recorders and players, telephones, facsimiles, photocopiers and so on, combining electronic texts, words, sounds and images; and all being combined in ever more complex and interesting ways. This chapter is concerned primarily with the use of the internet, particularly the World Wide Web, in teaching and learning about art. The Web gives art teachers and students access to a world of electronic texts and images; it is a vast stockroom of free material to manipulate – malleable and waiting to be used. Students can pick it up, play with it, explore and investigate it, push it about, modify its meaning, and create new meanings through links with other texts and images.

I intend to offer an insight to those who wish to find out more about the Web, or those who may need more information to convince them of its potential for development. I would argue that the Web is an important tool for learning in art; a contemporary resource which is linked to resource-based learning. It is also a revolution happening at breakneck speed; if art departments in schools and colleges do not engage with it, art departments compete with other departments in schools for control of it, innovate and 'think big' about it, art departments will be left behind and their resources will be further controlled by others. Where possible, throughout the text I will give a website, so that the chapter can act as a resource; however, it should be kept in mind that such addresses do go out of date very quickly. I will endeavour to show how to access and integrate Web information. The discussion will act as a springboard to sites for art teachers to investigate and develop for their particular circumstances and environments.

THE INTERNET AND THE WORLD WIDE WEB

The internet started as a military initiative by the USA during the Cold War; it was a way to connect their computers, and therefore personnel, in the event of a nuclear war. The system they developed was called ARPANET, a communications network where the messages would always get through – if one place was removed from the maze, then the message would find another way to get to its destination. This continued to be developed in the 1960s by the military, business and university academics. They built their networks for their own purposes and wanted to link them to others, a network of networks, or the internet. The internet supports several different services, e-mail: the World Wide Web, newsgroups (or Usenet Newsgroups) and file transfer protocol (FTP) are probably the four most common. People visualize the internet in many different ways:

> some compare it to a transport system or a map; some see it as a gigantic library or an infinitely big encyclopaedia. It has been described as a jungle or ocean of information and as a spider's web.[1]

The World Wide Web was born at CERN Switzerland, invented by a group of physicists looking for a way to share scientific data around their laboratories over their computer network.[2] The Web is offered over the internet which allows computers to access each other and to view and copy information presented mainly through text and graphics on computer screens. It uses a language, or protocol, called hyper text transfer protocol (http). This is an agreed standard which allows the transfer of hypertext documents across as many computers as possible. Files that support this language are called Hyper Text Markup Language (HTML) files. Hypertext is text that can be navigated in a non-linear way. A word in a page of hypertext can be linked (e.g. clickable) to another place on the same page, or another page on the Web.[3] In the next section I would like to explore the relationship between resource-based learning and the WWW.

ART EDUCATION, RESOURCE-BASED LEARNING AND THE WORLD WIDE WEB

As an art educationalist I frequently find myself having to go back to a basic issue and justify the importance and role art education plays in educating the next generation of young people. The debate is not just a concern of academics, however; many, if not most art teachers have at some time been asked to justify their position in an ever-expanding school curriculum and densely packed timetable. Education, including art education, has often been caught up in a game of political football, trying to respond to different needs and being kicked about. We need to ask some simple questions about our plan for the future. What is our vision? How are we to make it happen? The Web is at present offering a partial glimpse of that vision and where we could be heading. It is up to us to be proactive, to initiate and shape the future.

As Isaac Asimov once said, 'the important thing to forecast is not the motorcar but the parking problems; not the television but the soap opera. The two most common errors in technology assessment are overestimating the speed of diffusion of an innovation and underestimating its eventual consequences.'[4]

What are art education's parking problems? What are we saying the future of art education should be? John Swift and John Steers, in their Manifesto for Art in Schools[5] make a brave and bold attempt at defining the future direction for art education. I am not able to be so precise or comprehensive, but I will be unequivocal about one aspect: if we are in the business of planning for equipping students for the twenty first-century, we should be using the tools and machinery which will drive it.

When we consider the nature of our aesthetic experiences and our relationship to art, we find that they are essentially personal and should be given room to be driven by the personal. Students' learning should therefore identify with students' concerns in a contemporary context – the 'now' is very important to young people. They are motivated by the issues and values which directly relate to and affect them, and being able to express personal and shared insights about these issues is valuable. Learning about art and using art language offers them the opportunity to articulate values of the 'now' and to discuss subjects which are real to them.[6] It also gives students control over the learning process; it is not someone else's knowledge passively received; it is *their* knowledge, gained from active engagement.

This kind of 'now' relevance is exciting, and when art is committed to the exhilaration of discovery it gains pace and momentum. Problem-solving is an important part of discovery; it involves taking risks, making mistakes, questioning and trying out new and different solutions. If you constantly know what you are going to find there will be no surprise or, to paraphrase Picasso, if you know what you're going to do, what's the point in doing it . . . it's better to do something else.[7] Discovery, solving a problem and being committed to the creative process of questioning gives the student a sense of achievement and consequently gives the result currency, importance and value. If students search, rather than being led, if they are offered challenging ways of engaging with art rather than predictable ones, a deeper learning will occur.

The Web gives access to the new; it allows students to keep pace with current practice. By using it as a part of his/her research strategy the student gains reasonable freedom and control to develop his/her own ideas and interests. This can still be done within a broad and flexible scheme of work, so teachers need not be unduly concerned when replanning for the whole-class use of the Web. This kind of divergent approach gives teachers with mixed-ability groups opportunities for differentiation, extension work and work for students with learning difficulties; divergent approaches also allow for exploration of a range of media, not reliant on one fixed response but control over what students want.

When we investigate the definition and usage of resource-based learning we can see why it is important and connected with this argument about Web usage. Lesley Burgess describes the difficulties resource-based learning had in establishing itself within and impacting upon the general curriculum in the 1970s.[8] It has, however, found a home in many art departments and still exists to an extent, as Binch and Robinson define:

> The concept of 'Resource based Learning' ... developed from successful teaching and learning methods which were based on extensive provision of an appropriate range of learning resources. In the main, these consisted of collections of objects, reference materials used both as stimulus for practical work and 'research' as work progressed ... An essential characteristic of this movement was to insist upon work which arose from 'direct experience'.[9]

By working from 'direct experience', students can be empowered and given opportunities to make choices. Giving learners choices makes them responsible for their learning, at least in part, and an opportunity to be active in the creative process of art-making. Museums and galleries are increasingly seen as integral to resource-based learning as are other outside agencies such as artists, craftspeople and designers. The introduction in England of the National Curriculum for art continued the trend by emphasizing the importance of students' engagement with art objects, and according to Binch and Robinson

> created a surge of activity in the use of external resources and increasing use of the references to 'works of art'. There has been an increased emphasis on education in the priorities of museums and galleries. This is exemplified in many of the case studies and there are numerous examples throughout the country of exhibitions which are influenced more by education than by curatorial needs.[10]

Art departments in schools often make excellent use of a wide range of resources. These may include artists-in-residence and regular use of museums and galleries in addition to books, slides, videos, artefacts, postcards and posters. The use of ICT as a resource is relatively new. Several commentators, in addition to Binch and Robinson, have highlighted concerns that orthodoxies continue to be generated, notably Arthur Hughes[11] and that 'school art' continues to be divorced from contemporary art practice.[12] Growth in the use of CD-ROM, the intranet and the internet has made some changes to art education pedagogy, and in teachers' strategies for delivering their schemes of work, but a more fundamental change is needed. In the UK, the expansion of ICT use in schools has been pushed by the government's claims of 'connecting the learning society', in its highly publicised 'National Grid for Learning' and an ambitious timetable for implementation:

> By 2002, all schools will be connected to the superhighway, free of charge; half a million teachers will be trained; and our children will be leaving school IT-literate, having been able to exploit the best that technology can offer.[13]

The Web is seen as the vehicle for accessing a rich and diverse range of material and at the core of the agenda of raising standards including new targets for literacy and numeracy. So how will it improve learning?

LEARNING AND THE WORLD WIDE WEB

The British government has set up pilot projects looking at how the Web can support learning. Some 1000 schools and 30 colleges of further education across the UK have been involved in the Education Department's Super-highways Initiative (EDSI). Its conclusions, in terms of learning, show six main effects:

- improved subject learning;
- improved vocational training;
- improved motivation and attitudes to learning;
- the development of independent learning and research skills;
- social development; and
- the development of network literacy.[14]

From the art teacher's perspective it has been widely accepted that, as a resource, this kind of usage can 'improve subject learning'. The importance to learning has already be touched upon earlier, and this kind of access should build upon existing good content and practice. Using the Web, students can gather, select and collect resources and record findings in diaries and sketch-books. These could be thoughts as well as information from the Web. Students should be encouraged to organize their materials, analysing critically sources and their quality. This is a common method of research in art education and an important aspect of examinations and helps students to be active learners and to develop creative-thinking skills. Using the Web in this way will also enable teachers to emphasize the importance of studying images in a variety of contexts and to adopt a culturally diverse perspective. Viewing information from contemporary art, craft and design in museums and galleries from around the world is a crucial aspect of this. Having such breadth of vision, and being able to interact with it, and even respond to it, is noted by Pachler:

> Computer-mediated communications (CMC) allows students to engage in exchanges with peers or experts from outside the classroom, school and even the country. The two main modalities of CMC are synchronous and asynchronous. Interchanges, be they real-time or delayed-time, tend to be authentic and, consequently, motivating for students.[15]

Museums and galleries are keen to develop extensive use of the Web and linking themselves with schools. As noted by the UK's department of National Heritage, it needs to be viewed as a positive challenge which is in their interests to take up:

> It is probable that technology will not undermine but stimulate the public's desire to have a gallery experience; the 'virtuality' offered by

new media may balance and complement, rather than erode, the 'actuality' that is to be found in real human relationships and contact with authentic objects in museums.[16]

In the next section I would like to offer some of the current sites I have found which may give art teachers opportunities to explore the Web further.

USING WEBSITES: SOME CONSIDERATIONS

The Web is of obvious interest to art educators, with its vast arrange of free resources across the world, and the opportunities it offers to communicate with others. However, it is not without its problems and issues, as Selinger describes:

> The Internet is the world's largest library, but it is also a huge junkyard, and has been described as a library where all the books have been thrown on the floor.[17]

In order to find and gain access to useful and relevant material you need to

a)   know where it is – you have a Universal Resource Locator (URL) – an individual address, that only one document can have; or

b)   search for it.

Using your browser, probably Netscape Navigator or Microsoft's Internet Explorer[18] you can access web sites, which are typically addressed: http://websitename.com/

If you know the name of a site you simply type in the address and hit return (or enter). If the address is correct, your server will receive the request, look for the site and, if it is there (and functioning), serve the page to you. You may also want to make use of general educational sites like the Virtual Teachers Centre[19] and RM Eduwebsite[20] looking at possible links for your purpose. The Arts Ed Net Getty Foundation[21] is a source that is more particularly suited to art teachers and students and provides an extensive list of museums around the world. This will save you and your students valuable time and avoid the trawl through cyberspace and all the distractions en route. Using these kinds of sites which have links to other relevant and useful sites improves your 'surfing' efficiency, and it is a good idea to store them under 'bookmarks' for easy access in the future.

There are several other sites specifically designed and targeted at art teachers, Schoolart[22] being one such example. It claims to be '[a site where] innovative and originality in art education thinking can be set alongside down to earth advice'. These kind of sites are only accessible on payment of a subscription, usually annual. Before spending capitation budgets on pay sites, it is important to examine the demonstration pages carefully, discuss the alternative pay sites with other art colleagues and, finally, evaluate whether a pay site provides and delivers what you need for your teaching (see 'evaluating website materials' below). You may want to encourage art staff and students to record any relevant websites they come across and set up an art directory for the department. Acting upon recommendation is a valuable technique when using the internet and saves time and money.

If you are looking for a site but do not know its address, you should use a search engine. The main ones are: Altavista, Excite, Northern Light, Yell!, Yahoo, Lycos and, a search engine of search engines, Ask Jeeves.[23] Type what you are looking for in the text entry box, (for example an artist's name) and click on 'search'. The search engine will check its records, and send out small applications called 'spiders' or 'robots' which search the Web for pages containing your words, and will return a page with the results. A results page will typically say 'displaying a number of records (per page) out of a number of records found'. These will be listed by their relevance and by percentage. How you plan your search and choose the search words will be crucial to how successful, or useful, the results will be. Keep the search focused, hone your terms rather than be too broad, and keep a record of the different combinations tried with the different search engines, as they do not all search in the same way. Typing in slightly different key words, or words in a different order will generate different responses. For example, using Ask Jeeves, typing in the question 'Where can I find sites about artists using computers?' yielded 42 different sites from the above search engines, while typing in 'Where can I find out about computer art?' yielded 47.

You can download the text or images from the Web to your hard disk. Text can be saved in several ways. You can simply highlight, copy and paste it to a text editor, you can save the whole page as text or you can view the whole Source of the page. The latter is useful if you want to know how a page has been made. You can either save the Source code, or choose View > Document Source from the browser's menu, and the browser will open the Source code in its own Source window or in a text editor (SimpleText on a Mac). You can copy and paste any code, and this is how many people learn how pages are made.

Any image can be saved by simply clicking and choosing 'Save Image As' from the pop-up menu. RealPlayer[24] and Flash[25] are examples of 'plugins' which give authors more control over copyright. A plugin may be needed to stream video and/or audio, which can be copy-protected. You can listen to it while you are connected but you cannot save it to disk.

EVALUATING WEBSITE MATERIALS

The quality of websites varies greatly. Once your search has identified apparently suitable websites it is important for you to evaluate them carefully and systematically. You should devise for yourself a series of questions which may cover the following areas:

> **Content:** What information is available and which themes or topics does it cover? Does it include diverse cultural perspectives? Is it balanced, inclusive and does it avoid stereotypes (gender, race, social class, religion)?

Subject skills/knowledge/understanding: What aspects of these are being developed? What learning objectives does it support? What questions might it provoke? Is it flexible and does it allow for individual investigation and development?

Examination syllabus/National Curriculum: What elements does this resource cover?

Timing: When in the Scheme of Work do I use it? Is there sufficient time available for the activity?

Management: How do I use this resource? Is it to be used for individual student work, pair work or group work?

Teacher's role: What strategy will I need to employ?

Language: What specialized art terminology will the learners be engaging with in the resource?

ICT skills: What level of competence will the student need to use this resource? What ICT-specific skills, knowledge and understanding are being learnt?

Extension and differentiation: How does this need to be considered?

Assessment: What assessment criteria will be used for the work?

An art teacher can save a lot of lesson time and optimize the students' learning by preparing thoroughly. By browsing a range of sites in advance, discovering and questioning what works well and incorporating these ideas into programmes and schemes of work, websites will be more efficient in delivering the desired outcomes. The next section looks at a range of resource sites as a starting point for exploration.

METAPHORS AND DIFFERENT RESOURCE TYPES

The development of websites as a publishing medium in their own right has meant that Web designers have tried to form them into a shape that users can understand. This has often meant a dominant metaphor is used alongside the design features. The metaphor may be faithfully carried through or just employed as an overall structuring device. Web designers are experimenting with graphical language and structures and pushing the concepts of how content and information can be provided. Some of the more commonly found metaphors are listed below,

Websites as books

It is not surprising that this format exists as it was the Web's original purpose to share academic information in a digital form. 'What is?'[26] provides a comprehensive guide to terms you will encounter on the Web. Its structure is that of an electronic encyclopaedia or dictionary: close-packed information leading to an explanation, with a menu bar at the top of the page.

Website as magazines

These are similar to books but more like journals or periodicals in format, with short pithy texts and punchy headlines; some have paper equivalents, others are purely digitally-based. They are produced at frequent and regular intervals and fit in well with the websites' ever-changing pace. 'Suck'[27] is a good example of a chatty, cutting, satirical online journal. It has daily editions with two or three articles picking up on current events, with a slant on American and digital communities. 'Rhizome'[28] is a critical art magazine with interviews, coverage of art events and links to art sites in the same theme.

Websites as art, craft and design galleries/museums

There are many variations of use in this category. Some established institutions either provide information about physical operations, providing tasters of images from their collection which can be accessed. 'The Louvre'[29] is an example of a practical guide to the real archive. Using the Web allows greater numbers of students to view artefacts and visit collections such as 'Design Museum',[30] or the 'Cooper Hewitt National Design Museum' (Smithsonian).[31] Students and teachers can compare collections, for instance, of contemporary exhibitions in London, 'ICA'[32] and 'Lisson Gallery'[33], to New York, 'MOMA'.[34]

Some sites develop the notion of the metaphor further and use the Web itself as a virtual gallery. They may cross boundaries between media, real space and virtual space and produce artworks to be experienced in both, investigate 'Digital Graffiti'[35] and 'ARIADNE'[36] as examples.

Other sites are offered as space for artists to show their work and give contact details. 'ArtNet'[37] has developed as an online art resource and encompasses links to other sites, contact details to art galleries and their shows. Other sites are bringing particular collections, individuals, artefacts and works together to act as a collaborative source or to highlight and promote their particular cause; see 'Institute of International Visual Arts'[38] or 'Finnish Design'.[39] As the Web expands so does its range of users and purposes, with increasingly complex links. A multi-layered example is the 'Dia Center for the Arts'[40] as described by Burgess,[41] which contains arts projects for the Web, long-term installations and information about art education in the USA.

Websites as websites

There are many designers who are now transforming the Web and using it as a medium for art, giving it a new identity rather than emulating an existing medium. One place which promotes this use is 'Arts Electronica',[42] which holds a festival every year to promote electronic art. 'Irrational'[43] is a London-based website which plays with the structure of the Web, and 'Recycler'[44] takes images from web cameras from around the world and recycles them into combined images.

Websites as radio

The potential to offer sound on websites has grown quickly and provides an interesting base for student investigation into multimedia content. Sound archives like 'Vincent Voice Library'[45] and music magazines like the US-based 'Reverb'[46] all provide interviews, speeches and sound samples to use in multimedia production. Record companies have sites, some large, for example the global 'BBC World Service'[47] and some small radio stations, even 'Pirate Radio'.[48] Almost everything imaginable is available; you can even download bird sounds from Australia at the 'Australian National Botanic Gardens'.[49]

Websites as TV channels

As with the radio stations, the ability to move around video assets has meant the development of webcasting. With a large enough memory capacity and the appropriate software, students can experience clips and broadcasts on the Web. It is a still a growing media and clips tend to be short. However, one of the first stations to broadcast over the web was 'CNN'.[50] Students may be interested in the 'Learning Technologies Channel'[51] which hosts NASA's educational web channel.

Websites as webcams

These are similar to TV channels but are online and live. Webcam sites offer fleeting views of people, places and objects around the world. Whilst taking care to avoid the unsuitable material, it is possible to view the silly to the sublime. For a sample of the sheer number of webcam sites available try using the search engines. You can even tour the world via webcam using the worldcam compendium at 'AT&T Labs'.[52]

Teachers may be interested in using a webcam in school and in creating their own clips and publishing artworks, people, places etc. on the Web. You can either purchase a commercial webcam set-up or assemble the hardware and download the software needed to get a basic site functional without cost. There are sites where other webcam enthusiasts are happy to explain, step by step, how to set up: try 'Sam's Web Cam Cookbook'.[53] You can get the software at 'Cam Central'.[54]

SUMMARY

In this chapter I have explored how the Web offers exceptional opportunities for individual and social learning. This is, however, only one aspect of the bigger picture of learning in art education; the Web as a resource is not necessarily better or worse than other resources, it's just different. Art teachers should consider carefully all options when selecting materials for teaching and not limit themselves in their choices. If the Web supports good practice in the teaching of art then teachers should use it. If it does not, then avoid it. I have tried to show how teaching and learning can be enhanced through the use of the Web, but there are problems; I agree with Li-fen Lu:

> The impact of technologies, however, might not always be positive. Although new technology has become a fashion, it is risky to assume students will always benefit from its use in art instruction. It is imperative that art educators and teachers face the problems that arise from using technologies in teaching art and explore ways to deal with these problems.[55]

Ultimately it is the teacher's responsibility to ensure that students receive a positive experience when using the Web. If students are left to their own devices, time may be wasted in browsing endlessly on the Web. They may become frustrated and switch off from the Web's potential or they may become hooked and insist on engaging only with the Web. It is the teacher's role to prepare, plan and monitor carefully its usage and to design teaching strategies that are appropriate. Teachers will need to make the purpose of the learning clear to students and shift the students' focus from the technical effects of the Web, which are enticing, to the underlying concepts and ideas of the information retrieved.

Art teachers will need to consider their role-shift, as the Web encourages questioning and the empowerment of students. The approach used by art teachers in the past, with more traditional media, may not be suitable any more. Furthermore, students' responses to the new media may be different and teachers need to be prepared to react:

> they [teachers] assume students will have the same responses they would have to traditional art forms. When teachers are not sure what students' reactions to computer art may be, they are not well prepared to teach students to critically appreciate or judge computer art.[56]

A new critical art education pedagogy for the Web will need to be developed and piloted in the art departments. Students will need to be trained in the analytical skills of researchers, questioning what they see on the screen and referencing their sources. Even though the use of computers in art education is not new (Guy Hubbard describes his struggle to use them since the 1960s!),[57] the Web is a new resource, and so is a lot of its content. It has brought changes, and art teachers cannot ignore it. They need to prepare to embrace those changes for the students' sake: 'Will students have to wait before these changes begin to take their rightful place in the classroom throughout the world?'[58]

The Web acts as a gateway for students to investigate resources from diverse cultures, and teachers as the gatekeepers have an important role to play. Denying access to students will restrict learning opportunities and the possibilities of contemporary art, craft, design and popular culture. There could arise in art departments 'haves' and 'have nots'.

If teachers continue to rely exclusively on monographs of well-documented painters, they will be discounting not only many black and female artists but equally also important histories of craft, design and popular culture.[59]

Students need access to cultural resources, and art departments in schools need policies to enable their students to flourish with the Web, and to capitalize on the opportunities it presents. An information and communications system which is shared around the world demands a new approach. The ground rules have altered so sharply that even an erstwhile 'star' can be left behind by the pace of change; radical change can only be pursued successfully on a radical timescale. Pam Meacham, writing in *Directions*,[60] notes that the 'search for a digital aesthetic has proved elusive and/or illusory'. This may be so, but it need not prevent us from making full use of the available technology, both as a medium for creating and as a research tool. To paraphrase Heller, writing in *The Observer*, art teachers need to bite the bullet of ICT or prepare for their subject to die.[61]

Acknowledgement

I would like to thank M. Gaved and J. King-Farlow for their support and guidance with technical information and Web sources.

POSTSCRIPT

> As the new media are inventing culture, they also reinvent the disciplines we are teaching, the institutions in which we are teaching, the way in which we are learning.[62]

Looking back on this chapter and reflecting with the benefit of hindsight, I note how the final sentence makes a dramatic concluding prediction – a warning to art teachers to 'bite the bullet of ICT or prepare for their subject to die'. Whilst I muse over the excitable language, I still believe that the message is valid. In the UK considerable sums of money have been given to schools:

> Since 1998 there has been a very significant investment in ICT in schools through the National Grid for Learning Programme [...] nearly all schools are now connected to the Internet and the average number of computers in school for teaching and learning has virtually doubled.[63]

ICT's integration into the curriculum is calling for adjustments of approach and thinking about teaching and learning. With teachers adopting these principles, a realization is taking place that puts 'digital literacy'[64] central to the key skills – key skills that young people require when entering an information age society. Art teachers need to be at the forefront of this debate, for they have much to offer in the understanding of digital literacy. If they do not contribute to the process then there are other subjects that will shape and colonize their territory. ICT and 'e-learning' can have a major part to play in the development of art departments in schools; this will, however, require every art teacher to be 'e-confident'.[65]

Charles Clarke, Education Minister for the UK, believes that in the UK 'the potential for real transformation still remains largely untapped'.[66] I feel that this is an accurate assessment of UK schools – but what of their art departments, and what will this mean in practice? At this point it might be helpful for us to consider a number of common characteristics which the use of ICT either enables or enhances, particularly for the learners and their teachers. For the learners, lessons can be made more individualized, differentiated and customized to individual needs. The use of ICT should also facilitate the delivery of a more engaging, exciting and enjoyable learning process that encourages better learning outcomes, as well as broader horizons with more opportunities for creative expression. It should also provide flexibility to study where, when and in what ways are best suited to individuals' needs and preferences, with smoother transitions between different phases of education. This increases student motivation through learning that stimulates, stretches and takes into account prior and concurrent experiences in and out of school.

Through the appropriate use of new technologies, the teacher can provide more personalized feedback on progress and achievements can be more effectively recorded and shared with others. Learners will have wider access to learning and participation; better informed choices through greater access to information, guidance and support services; and the ability to make sensible choices about when, when not, and how to use new technologies to enhance, extend and enrich their learning, reflecting the increasingly ICT-rich environment in which they live and learn. For teachers, all of this increases opportunities to develop innovative and creative ways of supporting students' learning, enabling seamless links with experiences beyond the conventional classroom and timetable.

Notes

1. Moore, P. (1997) *Teaching Learning with the Internet*. British Telecommunications plc, p. 8.
2. 'History of the WWW' is available at: http://www.w3.org/WWW/
3. If further definition or explanation of terms is needed please see 'What is ...?' – an encyclopaedia of computing terms and definitions, available at: http://www.whatis.com/
4. Strack, G. (1995) 'The future: the computer as ubiquitous as the pen', in B. Tagg (ed.) *Developing a Whole School IT Policy*. London: Pitman Publishing, p. 195.
5. Swift, J. and Steers, J. (1999) 'A manifesto for art in schools', in J. Swift and N. Stanley (1999) *Directions: Journal of Art and Design Education*, **18**(1), 7–13.
6. See for example Hickman, R. (1994) 'A student centered approach for understanding art'. *Art Education*, **47**(5), September, 47–51.
7. Picasso, P. (1974) 'La tete d'obsidienne', quoted by A. Malraux in E. Cowling and J. Golding (1994) *Picasso: Sculpture/Painter*. London: Tate Gallery.
8. Burgess, L. (forthcoming) 'Resource based learning', in N. Addison and L. Burgess

(eds) *Learning to Teach Art and Design in the Secondary School: A Companion to School Experience*. London: Routledge.

9.   Binch, N. and Robinson, L. (1994) *Resourcing and Assessing Art, Craft and Design: Critical Studies in Art at Key Stage 4*. Corsham: NSEAD.

10. Binch, N. and Robinson, L., *ibid.*, p. 113.

11. See, for example, Hughes, A. (1998) 'Reconceptualising the art curriculum', in *Journal of Art and Design Education*, **17**(1), 41–9.

12. See Ash, A. (1999) 'Sculpture in secondary schools: a neglected discipline', in N. Addison and L. Burgess (eds), *op. cit.* for a further exploration of this issue.

13. DfEE (1997) *Connecting the Learning Society: National Grid for Learning*. London: DfEE publications, p. 2. This can also be accessed through the DfEE home pages at: http://www.open.gov.uk/dfee/dfeehome.htm

14. DfEE (1997) *ibid.*, p. 16.

15. Pachler, N. (1999) 'Using the Internet as a teaching and learning tool', in M. Leask and N. Pachler (eds) *Learning to Teach Using ICT in the Secondary School*. London: Routledge, p. 61.

16. Anderson, D. (1997) *A Common Wealth: Museums and Learning in the United Kingdom*. A report to the Department of National Heritage, p. 16.

17. Selinger, M. (1999) 'ICT and classroom management', in M. Leask and N. Pachler (eds), *op. cit.*, p. 48.

18. Netscape Communications 4.5 is available on: http://home.netscape.com/download/index.html Microsoft Internet Explorer 4 is available on: http://www.microsoft.com/ie/

19. Virtual Teachers Centre available at: http://vtc.ngfl.gov.uk/

20. Eduweb available at: http://www.eduweb.co.uk/

21. The Arts Ed Net Getty Foundation is available at: http://www.artsednet.getty.edu/

22. Schoolart is a UK-based art education site and can be found at: http://www.arteducation.co.uk

23. These search engines can usually be found by adding .com/ to the name, e.g.:
     http://www.altavista.digital.com/
     http://www.excite.com/
     http://www.nlsearch.com/
     http://www.yell.co.uk/
     http://www.yahoo.co.uk/
     http://www.webcrawler.com/
     http://www.aj.com/

24. RealPlayer is available at: http://www.real.com/products/player/index.html

25. Shockwave Flash is available at: http://www.macromedia.com/shockwave/

26. What is? *op. cit.* at: http://www.whatis.com/

27. Suck is an online journal available at: http://www.suck.com

28. Rhizome is an art magazine available at: http://www.rhizome.com/

29. The Louvre Gallery, France, is available at: http://mistral.culture.fr/louvre/

30. The Design Museum is available at: http://www.design-council.org.uk

31. The Cooper Hewitt National Design Museum (Smithsonian) is available at: http://www.si.edu/ndm

32. Institute of Contemporary Art (ICA) is available at: http://ica.org.uk

33. Lisson Gallery is available at: http://www.lisson.co.uk

34. Museum of Modern Art, New York (MOMA) is available at: http://www.moma.org

35. Digital Graffiti is concerned with graffiti art in London and is available at: http://www.graffiti.org/dj

36. ARIADNE is a women's photography project at Staffordshire University available at: http:web.staffs.ac.uk/ariadne

37. ArtNet is available at: http://www.artnet.com

38. Institute of International Visual Arts (online) is available at: http://www.iniva.org

39. Finnish Design contains examples of Finnish Design and is available at: http://www.finnishdesign.fi/

40. Dia centre for the arts is available at: http://www.diacenter.org/

41. Burgess, L. Resource based learning in Addison, N. and Burgess, L. (eds) (2000) *Learning to Teach Art and Design in the Secondary School: A companion to school experience.* London: Routledge.

42. Arts Electronica is available at: http://www.prixars.orf.at/

43. Irrational is available at: http://www.irational.org

44. Recycler is available at: http://shoko.calarts.edu/~alex/recycler.html

45. The Vincent Voice Library at Michigan State University is a spoken archive available at: http://web.msu.edu/vincent/index.html

46. Reverb is a US-based ezine available at: http://www.reverb.com/

47. The BBC World Service is online and available at: http://www.bbc.co.uk/world-service/

48. Pirate Radio is available at: http://www.pirate-radio.co.uk

49. Australian National Botanic Gardens is available at: http://155.187.10.12/sounds/

50. CNN is available at: http://www.cnn.com

51. The Learning Technologies Channel is a NASA site available at: http://quest.arc.nasa.gov/ltc/mars/workshop1/index.html

52. AT&T Labs is based in Cambridge, England and is available at: http://www.cam-orl.co.uk/world.html

53. Sam's Web Cam Cookbook is available at: http://www.teleport.com/~samc/bike

54. Cam Central is available at: http://www.camcentral.com/links/software.html

55. Li-fen Lu (1999). 'Using technologies in art education: a review of critical issues'. *InSEA News*, **6**(1), 5.

56. Li-fen Lu, *ibid.*, 5.

57. Hubbard, G. (1999) 'Recollections and visions for electronic computing in art education'. *InSEA News*, **6**(1), 4.

58. Hubbard, G. (1999), *ibid.*, p. 4.

59. Burgess, L. and Holman, V. (1993) 'Live art'. *Times Educational Supplement*, 2 June, p. 9.

60. Meacham, P. (1999) 'Of webs and nets and lily ponds'. *Directions: Journal of Art and Design Education*, **18**(1), 80.

61. Heller, R. (1999) 'Bite the bullet or prepare to die'. *The Observer*, 23 May, p. 16.

62. Soetaert, R. and Bonamie, B. (1999) 'Reconstructing the teaching of language: a view informed by the problems of traditional literacy in a digital age'. *Journal of Information Technology for Teacher Education* **8**(2), 123–146.

63. DfES (2003) *Fulfilling the Potential: Transforming Teaching and Learning through ICT in Schools.* Nottingham: DfES Publications.

64. Buckingham, D. (2002) 'New media literacies – informal learning, digital technologies and education'. in Buckingham, D. and McFarlane, A. *A Digitally Driven Curriculum?* London: Institute of Education, p. 11.

65. DfES (2003). The National College for School Leadership has developed ten key features which define e-confident. These are:

- high levels of staff confidence, competence and leadership;
- re-engineered teaching learning and assessment, integrating effective use;
- leading and managing distributed and concurrent learning;
- effective application within organizational and management processes;
- coherent personal learning development, support and access – for all leaders, teaching and non-teaching staff;
- secure, informed professional judgement;
- appropriate resource allocation to ensure sustainable development;
- availability, access and technical support;
- pupils/students with high ICT capability;
- school as the lead community learning and information hub.

Further details of this framework, including examples of the characteristics that underpin these features, can be found on NCSL's website: http://www.ncsl.org.uk/slict.

66. Charles Clarke, in DfES (2003) *Fulfilling the Potential: Transforming Teaching and Learning through ICT in Schools*. Nottingham: DfES Publications.

Chapter 7

Critical Studies: Values at the Heart of Art Education?

MICHELE TALLACK

INTRODUCTION

Critical studies – the study of works of art, craft and design – is now embedded in art education in many countries. For many years, art education publications and periodicals have been packed with passionate proselytizing by committed art educators intent on putting the case for particular methodologies through which students can engage with and acquire knowledge and understanding of the works of artists. At the heart of the debates over critical studies methodology lies the crucially important question of what constitutes the essential character of critical studies as a discipline and the contribution it makes to art education. It is apparent in the debates that there is no real consensus about its character and, therefore, little agreement regarding its contribution. This should not surprise us since there is also little consensus about the types of knowledge and content that constitute and define art education itself as a discrete domain.

Despite the lack of agreement about the essential character of critical studies, most secondary-school art teachers would support the view that critical studies should be delivered within the context of art education. Despite the disagreements about methodology there is one model for delivering it within art education which has, to date, dominated, at least in England. This model, which might be called the 'exemplars of good practice' model, primarily values critical studies for its ability to act as a means of improving students' artwork. In this model, works of art and artists are used to introduce students to exemplars of good practices in art-making. Content, style, techniques and media are examined in order to enable them to enhance their art-making skills. Whilst the primary purpose is to improve students' art-making, this model of critical studies also enables teachers to introduce students to their artistic heritage. Although the 'exemplars of good practice' model dominates, there is no consensus about how it should be delivered or about its content. There are arguments over the question of how and when to introduce students to past and present exemplars of good practice without impeding their ability to express personal feelings and ideas. Another battle focuses on the establishment of criteria for selecting exemplars to introduce to students. The latter is a particularly lively battle where defenders of established canons of taste – the hierarchies of named 'greats', perceived by some to be fundamental to any understanding of western culture – are in conflict with others who see such canons either as elitist, Eurocentric or sexist; and sometimes as all three.

A different perspective on critical studies which has emerged is the 'critical studies as an independent discipline' position. A few voices are now articulating what is perceived to be a radical and highly contentious question: whether critical studies, because of its essential character, should be tied to art-making activities in the classroom or whether it should exist as a discipline worthy of study in its own right. This is not as radical as it may seem. It is an old question about which art historians in particular have felt very strongly. Those who take this position argue that its essential character is such that teaching it within school art departments, whose primary purpose is often seen to be concerned with enabling students to engage with making processes, distorts its very nature and makes it a servant to art production. This is the perspective that I shall adopt in this chapter.

I shall begin by outlining some reasons why critical studies has become so closely allied with art-making, show why I believe the 'exemplars of good practice' view, though extremely valuable, is insufficient as a model and put forward for consideration a model in which the essential character of critical studies is defined in a way which demands that it be taught as an independent discipline. I shall argue that its role as an adjunct to art-making should be seen as one element within this independent discipline and that even this role requires revision. I shall also argue that, because of the systems of knowledge that characterize it, there is a strong case for putting critical studies into a wider educational context rather than expecting art departments to be entirely responsible for its delivery. Last, and most important, I shall argue that this model needs to be seriously considered for adoption if, in art education, we wish to educate students, in a cosmopolitan sense, to prepare them to take their place as consumers, critics and appreciators who value the visual arts, whether they become art practitioners or not, in a world where cultures are not static but are shifting rapidly, changing and merging.

THE ART DEPARTMENT: A HAVEN OF CREATIVITY

Before beginning to address the question of what constitutes critical studies as a discipline, it is useful to start by identifying some fundamental ideas about art education that are prevalent in the art departments of secondary schools in England. These, I would suggest, are not peculiar to England. Patricia Sikes, using data collected during her research into the careers of secondary-school art and science teachers, outlines ways in which art teachers perceive themselves, their educational roles and their departments. Describing the secondary art department as 'a kind of oasis', she notes that art rooms are frequently to be found away from main school buildings and that they have a different atmosphere to the rest of the school. She maintains that art teachers she worked with placed a higher value on creating a certain atmosphere than teachers of other subjects; that 'they talk about cultivating and fostering a climate which is conducive to creativity and self-expression, both in terms of producing work and of enabling students to relax and be themselves'.[1] She notes that the art teachers she worked with 'shared the aim of offering and making art available as a means of self-expression and communication, as a source of personal satisfaction and achievement, and as a way, or a valuable part of life', but did not 'realistically expect any of their students to become artists'. Instead the teachers saw themselves as facilitators, perceiving their job to be 'to draw out, or to facilitate the expression of, potentialities and possibilities already within and possessed by the child', which, she argues, contrasts with the aim shared by the teachers of other subjects she worked with whose aim was to transmit knowledge.[2] Sikes draws many positive conclusions in her study showing that, among other outcomes, 'art teachers set out to encourage self-respect and a positive self-concept' and that 'they encourage individuality'.[3] These are admirable, if not essential, educational objectives if one believes that a liberal education system enables students to take control of their own learning under the guidance of teachers who have the vision and qualities to create an atmosphere where independence of thought can be fostered. However, leaving aside the disputable question as to whether it is only art teachers and art departments that can provide such an atmosphere, if one believes that self-expression and self-determination are only part of what art education should be about, one might be somewhat worried by this 'oasis' view of the art department being physically as well as philosophically set apart from the rest of the school.

Physical separation can be a factor that contributes to a particular view of art education. An 'oasis' can become metamorphosed into a fortress where the art department is seen as a last beleaguered bastion in the war against the Philistines. Art education can become perceived to be a discrete domain within education, one that has no connection with other subject areas. Teachers can become unaware of, even uninterested in, the types of knowledge and understandings that are transmitted in other subject areas; knowledge which may be crucial to understanding the visual arts. It is, of course, not only art departments that have this tendency. In England, erecting barriers between disciplines is a tradition that Herbert Read noted sadly decades ago when he argued that a major flaw in the system was 'precisely our habit of establishing separate territories and inviolable frontiers'.[4]

If physical distancing of the art department is combined with a philosophy that argues that art education differs from other subject areas in that it does not involve the passing on of knowledge and facts but has, as its primary aim, the development of self-expression and self-realization, then some serious consequences result. Barriers are erected between art and other subjects that prevent students from having access to knowledge, facts and ideas that are fundamental to understanding the visual arts.

The nature of critical studies as a discipline is such that it cannot be properly delivered under conditions where the above philosophy is adopted. If we wish to enable students to understand the roles that artists and art have played, and continue to play, across the world; if we wish to prepare them to be consumers and/or artists in their adult lives who will be working and living within the framework of a global community which is drawing closer and closer together; we shall have to redefine our aims in relation to critical studies and our view of where and how it will be delivered, and stop being isolationist and territorial. Whilst art education in secondary schools is partially about realizing innate creative abilities (and there is considerable doubt as to whether all students have innate creative energies and ideas waiting to be released), it ought also to be about enabling students to understand the visual arts in the widest possible sense, to understand why the visual arts have been, and continue to be, a fundamental part not only of their own culture, but of cultures across the world. We need to help them to understand how the visual arts impact on them individually and how they, individually and collectively, will have an impact on art production at a national and a global level. We need to enable them to see this impact will take place whether or not they become professional artists. To do this we have to shift from an 'oasis' model where critical studies is seen primarily as an adjunct to self-realization through art-making, to a very different model with much of its delivery taking place outside the art department; a model which has as its central role the bringing about of an understanding of the visual arts.

THE USE OF CRITICAL STUDIES IN ENGLISH SECONDARY SCHOOLS

So far, it has been argued that there has been a tendency to deliver critical studies within a conceptual framework where not only is art perceived to be the only means whereby students can express themselves and realize their individuality, but where creating is the major focus, with process and product driving the art curriculum. There is substantial evidence that in the English system this perspective dominates. Critical studies, once admitted on sufferance into art departments, is now well-established as a major contributor to raising standards in practical art-making. It is not, however, used to its full potential, as it has no role as an independent discipline and has been given a subservient role within art education. As David Thistlewood points out, 'it is a discipline within a discipline (it has no role outside the context of art and design), and it is a servant discipline'.[5] In England this view of the role of critical studies is compounded by a National Art Curriculum which, while wishing to introduce students to the history of art, primarily ties critical studies to art-making.

This relegation of critical studies to servant status is reflected in recent official publications on English art education. The 1998 publication by the English Office for Standards in Education (OFSTED) picked out instances of good practice in arts education in 98 English schools.[6] In reporting on good practice in secondary-school art departments, the focus is primarily on good practice in relation to students' making activities. Most references to critical studies are related to its function as a support for making activities, through the use of visual materials, gallery visits, or artists-in-residence.

There are some instances where good practice in enabling students to understand the visual arts is praised. Praise is given to secondary-school art teachers who help students, through gallery visits and other strategies, to understand the works of past and present artists. There is also some praise for vocational courses for post-16 students that enable them to learn about the roles of artists within business and industry.[7] In the section on good practice in primary schools, it is stated that 'much can be learned from the masterpieces of famous artists, but only when students are taught to look carefully at the subject matter and techniques involved, and can use this knowledge to support their work'.[8] While this publication is very encouraging in pointing out that making practices are obviously being improved through critical studies and that critical studies is being used to foster an atmosphere where understanding of works of art, past and present, is being encouraged, it is very worrying in some respects. It does not set out to articulate the range of aspects of critical studies and the types of knowledge and understanding that ought to be introduced as part of good practice. The references to ways in which critical studies is used are often vague. For example, a project in a secondary school, cited as a model of good practice, shows how native Australian art was used as stimulation for high-quality, practical work, and the project was praised for the ways in which students' imaginations were stimulated in relation to practical work. Excellent practice one would agree. However, no mention was made of how native Australian art was discussed, what concepts, information and issues were raised in relation to it, or whether such issues were raised at all, since 'books and illustrations of native Australian art have provided the source of inspiration'.[9] This is a prime example of critical studies being praised for being there, but without articulating what good practice in relation to it means as a discipline.

Part of the problem is that the OFSTED publication is addressed to a very broad constituency of teachers, school governors, parents, inspectors and professional artists. Inevitably this leads to the adoption of a general, rather bland tone, but it does purport to articulate what constitutes good practice. Therefore, the rather generalized comments in it do nothing to help improve the 'poor relation' status of critical studies, but instead go some way towards confirming it. Because its function is to report on the way in which the English National Curriculum for art is delivered, it also reflects the ambiguities present in that curriculum. Consequently, it does not begin to suggest that a model of good practice in art education might be one which gives equal weight to art-making and to developing critical understanding of the works of artists. There is also no suggestion that a structured, developmental approach should be adopted in relation to critical studies.

Not only is it the problem that critical studies is almost exclusively tied to practical work, but also that it is seen in very limited cultural terms. In the 'exemplars of good practice' model, teachers draw, naturally enough, on the cultural heritage to which they have had access through their education. For example, when choosing examples from art of the past, white, western teachers tend to draw on white, western artists.

Both Grigg and Hollands, in earlier chapters, refer to the 1998 Qualifications and Curriculum Authority survey on teachers' use of artists in their teaching. The subsequent report was based on data collected by questionnaires from teachers in 248 secondary schools and 373 primary schools. It showed that critical studies was primarily used as an adjunct to art-making activities. The report maintains that

> Discussion, and teaching students about how artists make work so that they can apply this knowledge to their own work, are considered to be the most effective ways to extend students' knowledge and understanding of art.

It provides data showing that only 23 per cent of secondary-school teachers teaching students aged 12 to 14, and 35 per cent of teachers teaching students aged 15 to 16 made some use of the strategy of 'giving pupils an understanding of the social and cultural context within which an artist works', and draws the conclusion that 'Learning about an artist's life, about the purpose and meaning of the work, and about how ideas develop and change in art, are viewed as being of comparatively little importance.'[10] The report also noted that teachers used a Eurocentric range of fine art exemplars for critical studies work. When asked to list artists, craftspeople and designers, or schools of art or cultures used in each year of their teaching, and to list these in order of their importance, it was found that 'four-fifths of all references favour the European tradition, and a tiny minority refer to craftspeople and designers'.[11] Data showed that 74 per cent of works shown were European, 8.5 per cent came from the USA and 11.5 per cent from other civilizations.[12] The report's data suggest that the critical studies curriculum, therefore, is strongly directed towards art-making, is Eurocentric and is fine-art-focused.

The English experience suggests that any art education system that combines the 'oasis' model with the 'exemplars of good practice' approach to critical studies, and lets these drive the curriculum, will not address the issue of preparing students to take their place as cultural consumers or as artists working within the global community.

THE ESSENTIAL CHARACTER OF CRITICAL STUDIES AS A DISCIPLINE: SOME METHODOLOGIES

Whilst the 'exemplars of good practice' model dominates, models have been provided that have sought to provide a balance between linking critical studies to art-making activities and introducing students to the contextual, historical contexts within which artworks exist. These models have defined critical studies in ways that make clear that the transmission of facts to students is also required.

The 'discipline-based' model, referred to in previous chapters, has been promoted in America by several well-known authorities, such as Elliot Eisner, for many years; it is a model which is now firmly established in many American schools. Eisner argues that there are four crucial ways in which we come to understand art: making, looking, understanding its place in culture over time and making judgements about quality. These are presented as four routes into understanding and are translated into art production, art criticism and art history, using aesthetics to deal with qualitative judgements.[13] These four aspects provide a model for art education that is integrated with each of the four elements contributing to its basic structure.

Michael Buchanan has offered a model that offers routes to understanding by providing a structured approach to discussions of artworks in which students may use different approaches to acquire and develop progressively their understanding. His model provides stages through which students pass – the 'knowing, decoding and exploring' model. It starts with 'knowing' – the giving of information derived from known facts, followed by 'decoding' – description elicited from students based on close observation, description and analysis. This, he argues, will lead on to 'exploring' – interpretation, involving the 'use of deduction and the formulation and testing of hypotheses'.[14] Buchanan also argues that critical studies can be used for different ends, as

> historical sources in the pursuit of knowledge and as extensions of cultural horizons ... Analytically to learn about form and process ... evaluatively, to elicit from them interpretations of meanings, ideas, beliefs and personal, social and cultural values.[15]

He argues for a need to recognize different, discrete domains in art education that can be used at different times for different educational outcomes to provide a holistic model in which all the domains, including art-making, play contributory roles.[16]

The strength of Buchanan's model lies in his identification of the need to provide critical studies with a progressive developmental structure within which facts, interpretation, criticism and evaluation can take place. However, one might have some real concerns about starting with facts, and there are real problems in trying to separate out the three areas of 'knowing, decoding and exploring', because they are inextricably entwined. The most significant phrase he uses is when he argues that students should evaluate works of art to 'elicit interpretations of meanings, ideas, beliefs and personal, social and cultural values'. If we are to enable students to become educated artists, critics or consumers, as adults, I would argue that this last point provides a route to critical studies that should be given priority, using facts, decoding and exploring to discover meanings, ideas and beliefs. The three approaches need not necessarily be used sequentially, because different works of art may need different combinations of these approaches according to the questions to be addressed in each case. What is significant is the types of questions we encourage students to ask about works of art, as they research facts, decode and explore. Furthermore, if we take 'personal, social and cultural values' as our starting point when thinking about critical studies, these would not only enable students to uncover the meanings, ideas and beliefs that inform art-works, but may provide us with a series of questions that could act as components to help us build a structure for critical studies. We need to make it very obvious to students that in order to understand the visual arts, funda-mental questions have to be raised about the value that they have had and continue to have today. Such an approach would still enable teachers to focus partially on methods and media to inform students' artwork, and it would also enable students to understand the ways in which their own values feed into their personal art-making activities. In Buchanan's approach, questions about the range of values that inform the visual arts may arise as students analyse facts, decode and explore, but I would suggest that these are more important than that: they need to be brought to the fore; indeed they should provide the structure for critical studies as a discipline.

VALUES AND THEIR RELATIONSHIP TO ART PRODUCTION

There is a wide range of fundamental questions that need to be asked. For instance: What values affect the ways in which artists think and feel and thus inform their art-making? Why have societies and cultures considered the visual arts to be of value? Are the personal values that underpin the works of artists the same as the values of the society or culture within which those artists live and work? Do artists, and those who see, commission, buy or use their works, value the works for the same reasons? Do personal, social and cultural values shift and change over time? Does one value a work for the same reasons that another values it? Values is the key word; if we start thinking about values then we start to ask a range of interesting questions about the reasons which lie behind art production. A model with values as its basis can be used to address a wide range of factors that affect art production and the reception of art. The number of questions that can be asked, taking values as a starting point, are infinite, and the problem is to bring them together into an order which might provide a proper structure for critical studies. If we are aiming at a model that ultimately provides us with visually literate, globally knowledgeable art critics and consumers, we need to think about organizing our questions into groups that provide paths for students to follow; to move their thinking outwards from the personal level to the global.

The values model: (i) personal values

We begin by focusing on artists' personal values and the values to which they subscribe which inform their art-making activities. It could be argued that art-making is derived from what makers personally value and that these personal values are derived from a range of personal, social, political and cultural life-experiences. In England, Louis Arnaud Reid has explored the embodiment of values in works of art. Pointing out that works of art are rooted in life-experiences he argues that 'the life-resources of art are events or facts or concepts or images as experienced, and as experienced with feeling'[17] arguing that what is expressed through art are values which are felt. That is to say that works of art embody the values of artists; what they have chosen to explore, to present or to interpret. He has argued that these values become metamorphosed during the processes of making art, maintaining that 'The processes of art-making in a medium transform and transubstantiate the infinitely ranging values of human experience, and what comes out is new meaning', which he calls 'new concretely embodied meaning'.[18] Reid has pointed to the personal choices that artists make, derived from what they see, know and feel. If one accepts the view that artists' values inform their artworks in this sense, one can then begin to see that the range of such values is indeed infinite, as he maintains, and that there is no aspect of human experience that does not inform art. The whole history of the visual arts supports this view and shows us that artists have been interested in all aspects of human experience and areas of knowledge. They have been interested in mathematical, philosophical, moral, religious, historical, metaphysical, scientific, political, sociological and psychological as well as aesthetic questions. Reid has pointed out that poetry and drama 'are, in an important sense, about life – love, hate, tragedy, mortality, nature-mysticism'.[19] By extension, the visual arts have also dealt with and embody all the great timeless universal themes that underpin human life.

Much of Reid's work has concentrated on the ways in which these values get transformed into his 'new concretely embodied meaning'. He presents complex arguments to show that what counts is the new meanings that emerge in the works themselves – meanings which are different to the values which informed them – and argues that it is to these meanings that we need to attend. While one would agree that in art appreciation the outcome of the transubstantiation processes, the new meanings that the work itself conveys, should be of first concern, I would argue that we also need to identify the values which underpin it in order to explain the genesis of the work. Process, manipulation of form and media, is driven by the artist's need to realize and transform, as it were, these values as felt. Students need to see that this is also true of their own making activities and that learning to use media and techniques is a means to realize and transform feelings, concepts, ideas and *values* into expressive form, and to become aware of how values inform their own work.

The values model: (ii) artists' values and their relationship to cultural values

The next step would be to look at the extent to which an artist's values are rooted in life-experiences that are socially and culturally determined. As Anthony Dyson has argued, 'an art object is the work of a human hand and mind, the evidence of a particular moment of history, the product of a certain geographical region and the expression of a culture'.[20] This could be expressed another way: a work of art is an embodiment of what an artist values, thinks and feels, and such valuing, thinking and feeling is not just personal but is in some way related to, or is a response to the values that underpin the artist's particular culture at a specific moment in history in a particular location. Values are not just personal but are culturally determined in a variety of complex ways. It is the interaction between personal values and culturally determined values that is significant.

Within art education, there has been a tendency to place too much emphasis on the idea of artist as genius who works away in hermetic isolation, driven only by personal values and feelings. Historically, there are many reasons that explain how this idea has come about. As an idea, it crops up in many periods and takes many forms, such as the notion of the artist as set apart from society in a shamanic role, acting as a mouthpiece of the Divine, or as an imaginative genius forging *avant-garde* artistic creations in the crucible of a lonely studio. But these ideas are themselves culturally determined and students need to recognize them as such. These culturally derived ideas are important in that they can identify some of the values that underpin the production and reception of art in a range of cultures. The idea of genius itself, taken out of cultural context, does not go very far towards enabling students to understand works of art. Neither does it help them, if they wish to become artists, to understand and to make decisions as to what their roles and activities as artists should be. We need to replace the 'artist-as-genius' notion with a model of critical studies that evaluates artists as art producers who work within the framework of given cultural values; whose works are the result of the interaction between *their* values and those of the culture they belong to. By evaluating these interactions, students will be enabled to see that artists' values can either reflect established cultural values, ideas and beliefs at particular moments in time in particular locations, or challenge them. While artists can act as a mirror to reflect cultural values – like all of us they carry cultural baggage that affects their personal value systems – they can also have a vital role within cultures in that they contribute to cultural, social and political change by challenging established cultural values and ideas.

The history of art shows that throughout history artists have acted like grit in an oyster, irritating the society in which they live yet producing pearls through their challenging or subverting of beliefs, ideas and conventions and by articulating new ideas and beliefs through their work. In doing so they have changed ways in which individuals or groups have been perceived, valued or treated within a society through focusing on issues such as poverty, the treatment of minority groups, the mentally ill or gender, either by observing these groups objectively or becoming a member of them. They have challenged ideas and beliefs about universal and timeless themes like birth, death, war and the nature of good or evil, and they have reflected and articulated, or presented for re-evaluation, the range of passions, feelings and relationships which are part of human experience.

Students need to confront questions that raise issues about the interaction of artists' personal and cultural values, and to learn that if they choose to become artists they have important roles to play within the society they inhabit, for which they have to take responsibility. If we use critical studies only as a means of self-realization in the classroom, there is a danger that self-expression may come to be seen as the only rationale for art production. Such a model does not prepare students who want to become artists for their roles as citizens within the world community. It does not help them to identify the values which inform their works, nor to be aware of how these may interact with, or impact on, the bodies of cultural norms that inform their own multicultural society.

The values model: (iii) values that inform ways in which cultures use the visual arts

Having looked at artists' values and some of the ways in which these interact with social and cultural values, the next step might be to raise questions which shift the focus away from the artist. Although the last set of questions would appear to shift the focus towards an examination of cultural values, we need to ask specific questions about the extent to which values inform the ways in which cultures use the visual arts, and to consider the value the visual arts have for the societies and cultures within which they are created. This provides a range of questions relating to function, purpose and the transmission of values and ideas.

First, there is the question of the value the visual arts have as means of giving pleasure. Those who take this view often subscribe to the utilitarian notion that good art is that which provides the greatest pleasure for the greatest number. Undoubtedly, the visual arts do provide a great deal of pleasure for individuals, and for many that is sufficient reason for their existence, but this is a dangerous rationale. They can come to be seen as peripheral, there to be consumed when the economic climate ensures that there is surplus wealth, but redundant in times of economic hardship. The questions about the extent to which art gives pleasure and the relationship between pleasure and quality are interesting ones, but provide only one route towards understanding the range of values that affect art production and consumption. Notions of pleasure alone will not enable students to come into contact with the range of factors that lie behind art production, nor enable them to understand why the visual arts have been valued and supported, and why artists have been enabled to produce art, throughout history. We cannot begin to explain why the visual arts are such a fundamental part of cultures unless we look at the multiple roles they play *within* cultures.

Questions about patronage characterize many of these roles. While these do not sit comfortably within a conceptual framework that sees art as the product of self-expression and self-realization, they are crucial to understanding cultural value systems that affect art production. Historically, artists have been employed by individual patrons, groups or institutions to provide images and objects designed to educate populations, to convey religious ideas, to reinforce ideologies, values, beliefs and customs which act either to weld individuals together or to promote divisions and conflict. Furthermore, art production has always been in some way connected to power, status or wealth, and the value systems that underpin these. Architecture provides obvious examples of this. A tour around any city, town or village in any country will provide numerous examples of public or private buildings that embody ideas about status, wealth and value. The way in which form and function are linked in buildings –

churches, mosques, temples, banks, hospitals, town halls and schools – reflects ideas about what is central to the wellbeing of a culture. Architecture, whether public or domestic, combines form and function to express ideas about what institutions, groups, societies or cultures value, and ideas about how members of a community ought to live and relate to each other. Buildings do not just provide shelter, they also embody cultural values. This is true whether we are talking about Ledoux's working community at Arc-et-Senans in late eighteenth-century France, nineteenth-century English garden cities, the temples to Mammon that dominate New York and Tokyo or the Haida villages on the north-west coast of North America.

Similarly, portraits, whether painted, sculpted or recorded on film, remind viewers of the value and status that societies accord to certain individuals or groups, and enable individuals or groups to indicate their power, wealth, status or the contributions they have made to the value systems of a society. Unknown artisans carved their self-portraits into the fabric of European cathedrals to show their contribution to these great stone monuments. Icons of all kinds have abounded in, and continue to form a substantial part of artistic production across the world. Sub-groups within societies have their own icons that they value for a range of reasons, as heroes, role models, for religious or other reasons. Some sub-groups use icons on banners or posters deliberately to cause controversy and to challenge dominant values. The visual arts have always provided what Margaret Thatcher, during her time as Prime Minister, memorably called (in quite another context) 'the oxygen of publicity' for groups and individuals who have used them to challenge ideologies and values and to promote their own.

Because the visual arts act as a means of establishing, reinforcing, challenging and changing cultural value systems, students need to understand not only the roles that artists play, but also that they as viewers are affected by the ways in which the visual arts are used and presented. They need to understand the relationship between patronage and the uses to which the visual arts have been put in the past, and the ways that they are used today. The range of images and objects that they encounter in their daily lives, through film, television and other visual arts forms is enormous, and the values that inform these shape their view of themselves, of others and of their cultural environment. The power that the visual arts have, in the age of film, video and television, to shape our sense of self should not be underestimated: we are what we see.

Values model: (iv) The relationship of artists and art consumers with other cultures

Many of the questions raised in the previous three sections can be addressed from a multicultural standpoint. There are, however, further questions to be addressed. These are questions about the values that underpin the use by artists in one culture of art objects and formal devices belonging to other cultures. There are also issues about the values that underpin consumption, by members of dominant cultures, of the arts of cultures not their own.

Artists have engaged in cross-cultural borrowing of subjects and forms for thousands of years. Artists' works have often been related to what they see as being of value in other cultures, either within a continent or globally. Cultural interaction did not start with Picasso and other icons of modernism. An examination of the factors which have fed the relationship between content and style throughout history shows that art production exists within a continuum in which there has been constant cultural interchange, of ideas, methods and techniques. For example, the 'squash blossom' necklaces of the Navajo of North America have, built into them, silver crescents derived from silver decorations on the horses of Spanish conquistadors. These horse decorations were themselves derived from the crescents of the Moors of Spain.

An awareness of cultural interaction would raise further questions related to values. Some would focus on cultural appropriation and recontextualization: Why have individual artists valued and used the artworks of other cultures in their own work? Why do we as consumers value the works of other cultures? What happens when we take them out of context and place them in our galleries and museums; does this affect how we see and value them? What effect is the international art market and tourism, with its limitless appetite for artworks, having upon art production across the world?

Some questions may focus on the criteria we apply for judging the arts of others. What values underpin our notions of 'authenticity' in relation to works of other cultures? What values and stereotypical ideas inform our thinking about national or regional art, or colour our judgements when we see works that mix cultural styles and ideas? How do we value the works of artists who, by circumstance of their birth, relate to more than one culture and encapsulate in their works values drawn from each? Are our values different to those of the makers; do they use a different set of criteria and value their works for different reasons?

Another important question for teachers and students is the extent to which limits should be set for questioning the processes that are used in forging an understanding of the works of other cultures. In our search for knowledge which will inform our understanding of other cultures, do we place a higher value on acquiring that knowledge than on respecting the values of art makers in other cultures and the rules they abide by to regulate who has access to their artefacts? As I have argued elsewhere, the Aboriginal clans of Australia have complex rules about who sees, or has access to, their imagery and symbolism, and these rules can conflict with our desire as teachers to impart knowledge to our students.[21] In other words, do the values which underpin multicultural art education in the west conflict with values held in other cultures and lead to a new, well-intentioned, but damaging form of cultural plundering?

CONCLUSION

The values model of critical studies outlined above suggests that there are many questions that students need to explore if they are to become makers and/or art consumers. Values-related questions inevitably connect with many other areas of the curriculum because personal and cultural values governing art production and consumption operate in innumerable different and complex ways. It could be argued that there is no area of life-experience that does not, through the medium of ideas, beliefs and values, inform the visual arts. Therefore, they are related to every subject area of the school curriculum. This makes it inevitable that, to put a model such as this into place, we have to cross subject boundaries.

Many values-related questions can be dealt with within the context of the art department and may be connected with the processes of making. Others may, perhaps, be best dealt with in other subject areas. The relationship between art and other subject areas has been explored many times by other writers, and we are all aware of the range of problems encountered when we try to work across the curriculum in secondary schools. If we place a high value on giving our students a cosmopolitan art education we have to find ways of overcoming these problems and delivering critical studies across the curriculum.

The values-related model can provide a framework that would gradually introduce students, over the period of their secondary-school career, to the variety of ways in which a work of art relates to contextual and cultural factors. A progressive model could be adopted which would enable students to engage with increasingly complex questions. Teachers could, depending on the abilities and the needs of their particular students, select questions from the four values-related areas of enquiry to use at any one time. Some examples of values-related questions that might be addressed are grouped below. These are, of course, only examples and do not in themselves constitute an all-inclusive list. Furthermore, whatever examples of questions are given, such questions only provide a basis for discussion; the direction such discussion takes will take will vary enormously, according to the types of factors that may have influenced the work under discussion; psychological, sociological, political, metaphysical, to name but a few. Values-related questions raised by a work being discussed may indicate to teachers that they should also be addressed or investigated within other areas of the curriculum.

Values model: (i) personal values

Focus

The artist/maker's personal values, ideas and beliefs that inform content and style.

Questions

1. What has the artist/maker chosen to represent; what values, ideas, beliefs and feelings are embodied in the work and how does the form relate to these?
2. Are any other works by this artist/maker related to these values/ideas/ beliefs/feelings?

3.   Do any of his/her other works express different values/ideas/beliefs/feelings?

Values model: (ii) Artists' values and their relationship to cultural values

Focus

The way that content and style relate to values and ideas current at the time of production.

Questions

1.   Is the subject/style related to works by other artists/makers of the time?
2.   If so, do they express similar, or different, ideas, values, beliefs and feelings?
3.   Does the work relate to any values/ideas/beliefs/feelings expressed in other art forms?
4.   Does it embody values, ideas or beliefs then current in that culture?
5.   Does it question or challenge values, ideas or beliefs then current?

Values model: (iii) Values that inform ways in which cultures use the visual arts

Focus

The original purpose/function of the work, its reception then and now.

Questions

1.   Was it commissioned? If so, by whom?
2.   Was it sold? If so, what kind of person bought it?
3.   Where was it intended to be placed; what was its purpose?
4.   What values, ideas, beliefs and feelings did it convey?
5.   How was it perceived at the time of its making?
6.   Is it likely that there would have been a range of reactions to it at the time?
7.   What is its function now?
8.   How do we see/understand/value it now?
9.   Does everybody see/understand/value it the same way?

Values model: (iv) The relationship of artists and art consumers with other cultures

Focus

The use by western artists of non-western artefacts.

Questions

1.   Why did the artist borrow these ideas/images/forms?

2. Did he/she understand the original values and purposes that informed this artefact?

3. How would the original makers of the object feel about their artefact being used in this way?

Focus

The values, ideas and beliefs that inform artefacts from non-western cultures. The values, ideas and beliefs we bring to our understanding of them.

Questions

1. What values, ideas, beliefs and feelings are conveyed by the maker(s) of this object?
2. Do we share these? If not, how do they differ from those of the makers?
3. What was the original purpose/function of this artefact?
4. Where is this artefact now? Does its placing within a gallery, museum, tourist-shop or in this classroom affect our ideas about it?

These questions provide paths for exploration. Discussion of these questions may be open, discursive and relatively uninformed at the outset, and move on to more focused, informed discussion based on research by students. For an interesting model of how research can assist informed discussion of artworks in the classroom, see Richard Hickman's 'four Rs' approach: React, Research, Respond, Reflect.[22]

The four sets of values-related questions may provide routes to the understanding we need to engender in our students, which is to understand the reasons why the visual arts have been, and continue to be, so important, and to place the visual arts within the context of the world they inhabit. The 'oasis' model of art education, with its exclusive emphasis on self-realization, has not served the visual arts very well. In the minds of the general population, self-realization has too often become equated with self-absorption, and the visual arts are often perceived as being self-indulgent, elitist and divorced from the concerns and needs of most of the population. If we wish to educate students to become *responsible* makers, critics and appreciators, we have to put the visual arts back where they belong – in the context of the societies and cultures which produce, shape and use them – and identify, for our students to evaluate, the matrix of values which inform them. The questions raise issues that affect them as consumers and as makers of artworks. The values model enables them to examine relevant questions about the visual arts that surround them and influence their lives and to identify the values and ideas they wish to inform their own artwork. It may help prepare them for their future roles as critics, consumers and tourists, and to be aware of the impact they have as individuals upon art production in their own culture and in other cultures. It may also prepare them to value and defend the visual arts from a position of understanding and knowledge when attempts are made to marginalize them.

The sets of values-related questions offer the visual arts curriculum a different kind of integrity. Self-expression and self-realization is part of this integrity, but in this model they become part of a sounder understanding of where personal ideas and feelings come from. It clarifies intentions and ideas for students who are seeking to understand exactly what they are trying to express through their works. For them, and for those students who, as adults, may choose not to become artists, the questions provide a means of understanding, enjoying and having a positive influence as consumers on what is made.

The questions identified in the model vary from simple to extremely complex. Teachers need to exercise their own judgement as to when they might introduce them to students. The values model above sets out the questions in groups in order to provide a general structure, or pathways for teachers to follow. It may well be that these groups provide a developmental pathway, or that questions might be selected from groups to be used together at different times. Questions could also be revisited in increasing depth throughout students' school careers.

I am not suggesting these values-related questions are the *only* ones that need be raised with students. There are important questions to be raised about media, form and techniques that are not values-related. However, it is surprising how often personal or cultural values inform the choice of media and techniques in the visual arts. What I have suggested is that, in art education, if we wish to prepare our students to be ready to take their place as informed art lovers and art makers in a world where cultural interaction is on the increase, we have to approach critical studies in a completely different way and focus on the important questions that will enable them to do so. I have also suggested that many of these questions will inform self-expression in new ways; that knowledge and understanding, as well as the facts given in this model can help to develop students' art-making activities.

Lastly, I have indicated that many of the questions, because of their nature, are strongly related to other subject areas. Therefore, this suggested values-related model for critical studies demands that as art educators come out of 'oases', our fortresses, and fight to put art back where it has always belonged historically – in the real world, and at the centre of so many human experiences.

POSTSCRIPT

This chapter argues that there is no area of life experience that does not inform the visual arts and has, therefore, put the case for the cross-curricular delivery of values-related critical studies. In Essex, we are currently engaged in an arts project that operates in a wide range of curriculum areas. Using fourteen artists, from a range of ethnic backgrounds and arts disciplines, we are promoting and supporting intercultural education in six primary schools.[23] Although the project is based in the primary sector, the concepts that underpin it and the way in which it draws on a range of subject areas – in particular the cultural aspect of the 'spiritual, moral, social and cultural' (SMSC) dimension – provide a way forward that could be adapted for the 11–18 sector.

The project uses the arts as a focus to promote a respect for, and understanding of, the wide range of cultures that make up the population of Britain. The brief for the fourteen artists is to work with the teachers and schools to show how the arts relate to personal and cultural ideas and values. They are delivering in-service training for the teachers and practical arts related residencies in the schools, focusing on the cultural and contextual aspects of art production. A description of the model being used follows.

During the in-service days and the residencies:

i)   teachers and students are asked to identify the cultural experiences that were most significant to them personally in forming their ideas and values about their own culture and that of others;

ii) the artists engage in discussions with teachers and students during which they make clear the ways which their own work has been informed by ideas, feelings and values related to cultural factors;

iii) the artists, in partnership with the teachers, help the students to draw upon their own cultural experiences, ideas and values, or upon the new culturally related ideas they are acquiring about other cultures, for imaginative work in art, music, dance and writing.

The project draws heavily on the critical studies values model outlined in this chapter, in that at the outset the artists were briefed to show how the art-forms they engaged in and their own work:

i)   draw upon *personal* ideas and values;

ii) relate to events, ideas and values *from their own culture*, or in some cases cultures;

iii) are *perceived, valued and used* in their culture.

Some artists are also showing how their art-form has changed as it has travelled across the world and has been taken up and used in new ways by other cultures, thus relating their work to values model (iv), the relationship of artists and arts consumers with other cultures.

Using the arts curriculum as a focus, the artists and teachers on the project collectively use all aspects of the school curriculum. All residencies are giving students experiences and understandings relating to the SMSC and intercultural aspects of education. The students engage in discussion, research and practical arts making activities, all of which are related to asking fundamental questions about personal, social and cultural values.

This project, which at the time of writing is nearing completion, has shown that a values-related model is a natural and creative way of enabling students to understand the factors that inform artists' works. It is enabling students, some as young as seven, to begin to understand the ways in which personal and cultural ideas, feelings and values feed into their own arts related work, as well as enabling them to begin to understand how people from different cultures think and feel. In this way, arts are being put back where they belong, at the forefront of education: not separated from other curriculum areas or servicing them, but working within a matrix in which curriculum areas mutually support each other to generate understanding.

Notes

1. Sikes, P.J., (1987) 'A kind of oasis: art rooms and art teachers in secondary schools', in L. Tickle (ed.) *The Arts in Education: Some Research Studies.* Beckenham: Croom Helm, p. 143.
2. *Ibid.,* pp. 145–6.
3. *Ibid.,* p. 162.
4. Read, H., (1943) *Education Through Art.* London: Faber & Faber, p. 11.
5. Thistlewood, D. (1993) 'Curricular development in critical studies'. *Journal of Art and Design Education,* **12**(3), 305.
6. OFSTED (1998) *The Arts Inspected.* Oxford: Heinemann.
7. *Ibid.,* p. 17.
8. *Ibid.,* p. 12.
9. *Ibid.,* p. 21.
10. QCA (1998) *Analysis of Educational Resources in 1997–8. Survey of the Artists, Craftspeople and Designers Used in Teaching Art 5–16.* London: QCA, p. 9.
11. *Ibid.,* p. 2.
12. *Ibid.,* p. 4.
13. Eisner, E. (1989) 'Structure and magic in discipline-based art education', in D. Thistlewood (ed.) (1989) *Critical Studies in Art and Design Education.* Harlow: Longman and National Society for Education in Art and Design, p. 17.
14. Buchanan, M. (1995) 'Making art and critical literacy: a reciprocal relationship', in R. Prentice (ed.) *Teaching Art and Design: Addressing Issues and Identifying Directions.* London: Cassell, p. 43.
15. *Ibid.,* p. 44.
16. *Ibid.,* p. 45.
17. Reid, L.A. (1961) *Ways of Knowledge and Experience.* London: Allen & Unwin, p. 65.
18. Reid, L.A. (1981) 'Art, feeling and knowing'. *Journal of Philosophy of Education,* **15**(1), 50.
19. Reid, L.A. (1973) 'Knowledge, aesthetic insight and education'. Proceedings of the Philosophy of Education Society of Great Britain, no.1.
20. Dyson, A. (1989) 'Art history in schools: a comprehensive strategy', in D. Thistlewood (ed.) *op. cit.,* p. 128.
21. Tallack, M.L. (1996) 'Aboriginal art', in L. Dawtrey, T. Jackson, M. Masterson, and P. Meecham *Critical Studies & Modern Art.* New Haven, CT and London: Yale University Press, p. 158.
22. Hickman, R. (1999) 'Language and learning in Art', in E. Bearne, *Use of Language at Key Stage 3.* London: Routledge.
23. Tallack, M. and Essex County Council Learning Services (in press) *My Culture, Your Culture, Our Culture – the Essex Intercultural Arts Project.* Chelmsford: Essex County Council.

Chapter 8

The Meaning and Value of Craft

RACHEL MASON

INTRODUCTION

This chapter seeks to clarify the meaning and purpose of craft in art education. It does so by drawing on recent research into craft education at lower-secondary-school level, sponsored by the Crafts Council and carried out at the University of Surrey Roehampton between 1994 and 1997. The chapter also draws on parallel research carried out in Japan.[1]

Both Britain and Japan have long-standing traditions of craft that are recognized internationally as living embodiments of their respective cultures, and as epitomizing the highest human achievements in the use of materials and craft skills,[2] but at the close of the twentieth century the meaning and value of craft is unclear. Whereas some people view it as essentially backward-looking and opposed to new technology, for others it represents a counter-culture. The tendency of more and more craftpersons to adopt the role-model of the designer or artist and prioritize originality and ideas over and above technical virtuosity reflects a western modernist aesthetic stance that devalues tradition and practical craft skills. It is noteworthy that, while 'making things by hand' is no longer necessary for human survival, the last decade has witnessed substantial growth in small crafts businesses and hand crafts as hobby activities.[3]

Although craft education is interpreted differently in Britain and Japan, it reflects the dilemmas above. A cross-national concern about craft education, at the time the research began, was the need for accurate demographic data on provision and practice for the 11–16 age range; in Britain, to determine the effects of the new National Curriculum which had dropped 'craft' from its nomenclature; and in Japan to ascertain its role and status at a time of impending educational cutbacks. There was public concern also about the growing attention both governments were giving technology, to the detriment of art, craft and design.

CRAFT EDUCATION IN BRITAIN

The research, as designed in Britain, had the following stated aims: (i) to determine the nature and extent of learning through craft activity; (ii) to determine the extent to which knowledge and understanding of craft inheritance is included; (iii) to establish the degree to which such learning is valued by teachers; and (iv) to identify the quality and quantity of provision for learning. The research was in two parts. Part one took the form of a nationwide questionnaire sent to the heads of art, design and technology in all secondary schools in England and Wales, and part two involved interviews with 126 teachers and 239 students. This chapter focuses mainly on the findings about craft education in art.

A major concern underpinning the British research was the Craft Council's need to obtain evidence about provision and practice in four material areas: metal, clay, textiles and wood. These materials were chosen because 'designing and making with them requires a sound understanding of their properties and potential as well as the specialist processes required to make with them'; 'they are materials in everyday use'; and '[because] they are also the materials used most frequently by professional craftspeople'.[4] That the concept of craft education is unstable was evident in the inclusion of the following definitions in the survey questionnaire:

> **Craft activity:** Students should be actively involved in the designing and making of one-off individual artefacts encouraging the development of imaginative and practical skills, visual sensitivity and a working knowledge of tools and materials.
>
> **Craft inheritance:** Learning targeted at developing knowledge and understanding of the historical, technological and cultural context in which artefacts have been and are being made.

Many respondents found these definitions either too narrow in terms of curriculum content and/or materials, or 'too traditional'. Typical comments were, 'It's backward rather than forward looking'; 'The segregation of craft into materials gives it an old-fashioned flavour'; '"Design and making activities" is a more appropriate term.' Where they judged the definition too narrow in terms of materials, art teachers wanted it to include printmaking, photography, sculpture and 3-D work of all kinds, and design and technology teachers wanted it to include food, electronics, control technology, plastics, print, photography and mixed media. The view that craft involves one-off activity was challenged, as was the emphasis in the questionnaire on opportunities for students to acquire craft skills. Some respondents indicated that 'craft' was no longer an appropriate concept for their subject, or that it should be given less emphasis. Only 7 per cent commented on the definition of craft inheritance, of whom several suggested it was irrelevant. There were similar objections to the categories of 'women's crafts' and 'rural crafts' used in the survey.

The survey questionnaire achieved a 21.2 per cent response rate overall. A key finding highlighted in the executive summary report[5] was that craft education is provided for differently in the two National Curriculum subjects, in that making in ceramics is almost entirely located and resourced in art, and wood and metal in design and technology. No predominant location was established for making in textiles which is the least well resourced of the four areas. Provision for computer-aided craft design and manufacture is slight. The most common justification for including craft activity in secondary education (agreed by 80 per cent of all respondents) is that 'it gives students a sense of pride and achievement'. Whereas art teachers are more positive about the effects of the National Curriculum on craft than design and technology teachers, there is general concern about the effects of decreasing consumable budgets and increasing class sizes on the quality of craft teaching and learning. Regarding craft inheritance, knowledge and understanding of the historical, technological and cultural contexts in which artefacts are made is given considerably less attention that craft activity, and students' ability to talk about artefacts is not afforded much importance in assessment. The Crafts Council was disappointed about the low priority that schools give to building relationships with the professional craft world.

At the end of part one, the steering committee agreed there was a need to ascertain how representative the survey findings were, and that they should be followed up in more depth with students and teachers using qualitative research methods in schools. In view of the objections to part one, they elected to use the term 'making' instead of 'craft'. The discussion of findings in the next section of this chapter is derived mainly from part two.

STUDENTS' AND TEACHERS' VIEWS OF CRAFT

Students

Part two of the research found that British students' views of craft-based learning are extremely positive. For example, many of those we interviewed named design and technology and art as their favourite school subjects, and we found that 'making' is far and away the most popular aspect of project work (designing, researching ideas and evaluating received short shrift by comparison). That students gain enormous personal pleasure and satisfaction from hands-on experience of, and engagement with, craft materials and processes is obvious from the following quotes:

> I like working with my hands, using my hands to actually construct something.

> You have something to show for your time. There is all that research and stuff and that takes time, but it's worthwhile. When I've made something, it feels really good. To other people it might not matter, but to me it does.

> I think people are missing out if they don't get a chance to do things like that.

When it is interpreted broadly to encompass model-making, do-it-yourself, sewing, cooking, fixing bikes, clothes, furniture and electrical goods etc., the majority participate in some kind of craft activity outside school:

> In our cellar there's a complete Victorian kitchen range which I have put back together again with my brother. We repaired all the panel doors and re-hung them, as well as dismantled and repaired a mangle.

Some students expressed thought-provoking views about why they preferred making at home to making at school. They explained that it gives them more ownership over projects; they can spend more time on them and are not distracted by other students:

> I don't have to make it at home and I don't have to do what I'm told, what and where and how. I like it better at home because I can ask for help when I want and need it and not when the teacher thinks I've done something wrong.

They clearly did not regard making as a 'soft' educational option. They recognized that it requires more than innate talent and ability and is demanding and challenging educationally. In discussion of artefacts made in school and brought with them to interview, they were able to offer reasoned judgements about the quality of processes and outcomes and were keenly aware of personal strengths and weaknesses:

> My clock [is the best thing I made]. It was very curvy and I carved it all out. There was a sun and it had flames around it and I had done it all on a coping saw – all on my own – and I filed it as well and the finishing paint was very ... was all different colours, blotched together and I really liked the effect it had and enjoyed making it.

Moreover, they recognized that making in art and in design and technology serves different educational purposes and knew which subject they preferred and why. They voiced strong opinions also about how practical subjects should be taught and what they did and did not like to make in school:

> [I like Art] because in Design and Technology you are always using different tools and the more tools you use, you never really learn how to use any of them properly.

> I like Design and Technology because you can make things; in Art you have to draw.

> Well we were told to make a money box and there was no research material there at all apart from shop catalogues which we were supposed to go though and find anything that we liked. I just couldn't. I refused to get into it because I just thought it [the project] was so badly thought out and I made a very naff money box.

Arguably, our most important finding about students' views was that their motivation for making is positively affected by the level of skills they are able to acquire in handling specific materials and vice versa.

It's easy if you know what you are doing, but it's difficult to learn to use new tools and things. But once you learn, its easy.

In other words, they want to develop skilled knowledge for working with craft materials, such as wood and clay and are dismissive of 'cardboard technology'.

To conclude this section, not only do students enjoy making, but they afford it high educational value in terms of its relevance to their future lives:

It might be the grades in the other subjects that gets you a job, but having good grades in practical subjects shows you are a more independent practical person.

Although robots and computers are taking over, skills are needed to make them and will always be needed.

Their viewpoints contradict common perceptions of employment patterns as moving away from jobs that are dependent on manual skills, because a clear majority of those we interviewed thought practical skills and knowledge would be more useful than academic knowledge. Moreover, when pressed to say whether manual skills are gaining or losing significance, most of them stated they are actually becoming more important, for vocational and utilitarian reasons.

Teachers

From part one of the research, it was difficult to determine what teachers value about 'craft' as distinct from design and technology and from art. When the word 'making' was substituted in part two, however, the majority of those interviewed provided good reasons for why it is a uniquely important general educational tool.

The most common intrinsic justification given was that it fulfils a basic human need for sensory experience that is otherwise unavailable to students in the secondary-school curriculum. This argument is well supported, by Ellen Dissanayake and Seonaid Robertson[6] among others, in the specialist literature on craft. The other common reason given for the intrinsic educational value of making was that it provides an alternative teaching–learning mode to so-called academic school subjects:

Making is different from other areas of the curriculum; the students behave in a different way because of the different relationship. You can address their learning differently, particularly those who find written work very daunting.

Turning the two-dimensional into the three-dimensional doesn't happen anywhere else and also, the application of a broad range of knowledge, through to the final effect of everything you know coming together to produce something which will last. I see them using mathematical solutions, their language skills, the way they appraise and evaluate their work ... making brings other areas of the curriculum together.

Again, this justification is supported by Howard Gardner's theory of multiple intelligences and his notion that bodily kinaesthetic intelligence is uniquely developed through craft.[7] The most commonly quoted extrinsic reasons given for the educational benefits of making were that it contributes to knowledge and skills developed in other school subjects, develops higher order thinking skills (such as problem-solving, imagination and ideas, managing time, co-ordinating resources etc.) that are useful both vocationally and in everyday life and enables knowledge and understanding of all kinds to be demonstrated in tangible form. Whereas the transfer of knowledge and skills has not yet been proven by research, evidence is beginning to emerge that making in school may contribute to employability in general. In 1998, for example, Cave, Neale and Tuffnel found that employees rated practical competence much higher than cognitive abilities or personal qualities, and the craft graduates studied by Press and Cusworth in 1995 found their specialist training useful in a wide range of jobs.[8]

At the same time, the teachers we interviewed were very conscious that both 'making' and 'craft' are low-status concepts in British society. Typical comments were, 'Society doesn't value it' and 'The way education is going there is less emphasis on it.' One person said, 'There has been a de-craft or non-craft focus in schools for so long that really positive work needs to be done to improve its status in relation to art and that of skills.' Another said, 'Before we can get anywhere, we need to raise the profile of the crafts.' As the above comments show, the low morale among teachers suggests that, if craft education is going to continue to flourish at this educational level, it has to be more actively promoted by external agencies, including National Curriculum policy-makers, regional arts boards and local education authorities.

CRAFT EDUCATION IN CRISIS

A conclusion from research as a whole was that recent educational policy has reduced provision and practice; pockets of excellence notwithstanding, in Britain there appears to be less sustained 'making' in art and in design and technology since the introduction of the National Curriculum and local management of schools: 'There is less making. I just don't think they get the satisfaction out of what they are doing now. It probably has a wider range, but in a way they are doing it superficially.'

Of particular concern for everyone who believes that craft-based learning in art is important is the dramatic decline in opportunities for students to work with clay and textiles. Of the 36 art departments visited in part two of the research, only ten offered specialist courses in ceramics. One had never had specialist provision. Since 1994 it had been terminated in eight of the schools and reduced in another fourteen. Opportunities to study textiles were unevenly distributed between the schools and across both art and design and technology; seven of the 36 schools had no textiles provision. There were only seven specialist, trained teachers in textiles employed full-time in art departments and 16 in design and technology, which suggests it is taught more often as a discrete subject area in the latter. We found concrete evidence of wide variations in budgeting between the departments and schools and of reduced opportunities for students to become skilled manipulators of materials, or to make completed artefacts.

Although the majority of the art and of the design and technology teachers we interviewed were convinced that making is central to learning in their respective subjects, large numbers were struggling to deliver quality teaching and learning in the face of increasing class sizes, shrinking resources (including technician support) and timetabling constraints that make extended project work almost impossible. Another problem we identified in both art and in design and technology departments was a significant lack of expertise, in teaching basic and specialist craft skills, and a low level of participation in professional development courses:

> We haven't got a lot of time in the lesson to do it, so you rush to try to get as much done as you can [student].

> There's a lot of things I've put off this term because I'm trying to help them finish their projects [teacher].

> I feel very sorry for the young teachers coming out who haven't got the skills. After 26 years of being in the job, and being traditionally trained, I feel confident that whatever pupils might throw up, I can find an answer ... I think the young teachers have got a mountain to climb and they are being asked to do the impossible.

Other problems detected in part two of the research were a lack of commitment from educational policy-makers towards transmission of historical, technological and cultural knowledge about craft, and low levels of collaboration between art and design and design and technology departments with regard to sharing of resources and expertise.

Why this situation, given Britain's international reputation for excellence in craft-based learning? The answer lies in a combination of factors, including the truism that good-quality craft education is expensive and complex to deliver. As the teachers we interviewed pointed out, it necessitates a balance between doing and knowing, and opportunities for students to experiment with and investigate materials, analyse contemporary and historical artefacts, make maquettes and solve problems; moreover, students need access to a variety of specialist resources including information and communications technology, books, videos, worksheets, gallery visits, visiting craftspeople and CD-ROM. But we know from our school visits that craft can and still is being successfully learned and taught.

More significant obstacles to the future development of craft-based learning stem from government policy, fuelled, no doubt, by a mistaken assumption that new technologies have obliterated the necessity for making by hand. The absence of the term 'craft' from the National Curriculum nomenclature and the inadequate criteria for assessment of skills-based learning in examinations are especially damaging. Craft, in design and technology, is not helped by the limited education-cum-vocational-training model the present government is promoting, which uses terminology that is relative only to making things for mass production. A negative factor impacting on craft education in art is the establishment's failure to grasp that the aesthetic, moral and cultural significance attached to artworks are as much a function of their technical excellence as are so-called 'creativity' and intellectual ideas.

The final report of the British research, published in 1998, included a list of recommendations centred on the need to ensure that all secondary-school students continue to have opportunities for craft education. It urged schools to capitalize on the extent to which students enjoy making and find it educationally beneficial, and identified an urgent need to halt the rapid decline of provision in ceramics and textiles in art. The report mentioned inadequacies in basic- and specialist-skills training of teachers, especially in design and technology, and called for a more consistent national approach to professional development. Most significantly, in view of its social status, it argued for improved advocacy for the distinctive educational benefits of craft that demonstrates that it is fundamental to human development.

Whereas some of the recommendations (such as making it a requirement of art examinations that all students show evidence of having engaged in and developed skills in at least one craft-based activity) would be quite simple to effect, others clearly require long-term reflection, commitment and thought. Crossley and Broadfoot[9] have argued that comparison can assist solutions to educational dilemmas. So is there anything to be learned from the parallel research in Japan? In the next section the findings of the British and Japanese research are compared with a view to clarifying the meaning of craft education in art, and the reasons why it should continue to be taught.

CRAFT IN ART EDUCATION IN JAPAN

Replication of the survey in Japan was facilitated by the fact that both countries have a national curriculum for art which organizes learning into productive and theoretical domains. A significant difference, however, is that the Japanese National Course of Study[10] specifies five study areas with distinctive learning objectives, one of which is *kogei* (the Japanese equivalent to 'craft'). Another significant difference is the extensive use of three sorts of Ministry-approved art textbook that includes technical instructions for, and exemplars of, *kogei*. Replicating the survey, therefore, necessitated extensive collaboration with Japanese colleagues on modifications to the design of the questionnaire and involved exchange visits of British and Japanese researchers. According to Stenhouse, educational development rests on reflection and critical analysis of relations between intention and practice, and is greatly aided by the phenomenon of surprise.[11] Consequently, this comparison begins by identifying surprising findings (from a British perspective) about Japanese craft education derived from my first-hand observations of *kogei* in action, and analysis of variations in the design, and results of, the two survey questionnaires.

Differences

That the Japanese questionnaire did not include definitions of craft is a measure of the stability of the concept by comparison. The National Curriculum learning objectives for *kogei* which are functional and utilitarian were surprising to a British-trained art teacher used to promoting non-functional artist-crafts. They require students, for example, to 'express individual ideas in the design of functional objects based on specific purposes for craft education', and propose that students 'appreciate a range of designs and processes' and 'value the role of craft in everyday life'. Unlike in Britain, the concept of *kogei* is exclusive to art and has not been associated with technology (the Japanese equivalent to design and technology) for some 40 years.

The lack of specialist resources in both art and in technology, by comparison, was surprising. At the equivalent of secondary level, *kogei* is taught in standard classrooms without any specialist equipment or workshops, by art teachers who are trained as generalists in both fine art and crafts. Since popular wisdom in Britain holds that good-quality work is directly related to good resources, and vice versa, I was surprised and impressed by the high quality of student outcomes.

The comparative-education literature confirms that western observers routinely extol the technical excellence of Japanese students' art and craft work.[12] I am aware that this viewpoint is suspect in Japan where art teachers have repeatedly told me they disagree with teaching techniques or skills, and identified 'creativity' as their most important educational aim. However, I believe cultural factors work within Japanese society and education to ensure that technical excellence *is* afforded a great deal of significance nonetheless. (As evidence, I cite observing students following how-to-do-it instructions from textbooks to make artefacts, and the time Japanese teachers allocate to teaching children the correct way to handle specialist tools. In my experience, art teachers in Britain do not give this the same attention.)

The Japanese survey listed no less than eleven craft areas, so Japanese students have opportunities to learn a wider range of craft traditions. Studying craft education in Japan introduced me to some uniquely Japanese crafts, such as *bankin udaishi*, *kami* and *tenkoku*, of which I was previously unaware. Seeing so much wood being used in art was a surprise (the British survey found that wood is only rarely used in art, although it is the most popular material in design and technology). I am reliably informed that Japanese people are party to 'a long-standing love affair' with wood which, together with the fact that it is one of the easiest materials to resource and use, probably explains its popularity. Another surprise was the absence of textiles in *kogei*. I hesitate to speculate, but since this craft medium has traditionally been gendered, and equal opportunities policies are non-existent in Japanese schools, I assume the system is more sexist.

It was a surprise to find that learning about local and national craft heritage is considered very important – for example the teaching of uniquely Japanese crafts, mentioned previously, and an emphasis on celebrating traditional, regional crafts. Another difference is the relative significance the two national curricula give to western and non-western arts and crafts. Whereas both national curricula for art (and, by implication, craft) specify that children *should* learn about a variety of arts and crafts in different places and times, there are very few non-western exemplars in the English and Welsh statutory orders. In Japan, on the other hand, the government-approved textbooks are virtually 'bicultural' in their inclusion of western and Japanese cultural content.

In comparison, there is very little use of external resources, such as museums and galleries, or artist residencies, to enrich the craft curriculum in Japan. Other surprising things about the theoretical curriculum domain in Japan include the emphasis given to understanding the contribution of craft in everyday life (in Britain, craft in everyday life features mainly in design and technology) and on the enjoyment and appreciation of art, craft and nature (rather than on analysing, evaluating and talking about art and craft). Finally, assessment of students' work focuses on motivation and effort, rather than product and process, and I was surprised that neither art nor craft is included (very often) in testing or in exams.

ALTERNATIVE MODELS OF CRAFT EDUCATION

Reflection on the above suggests that alternative models of craft education are in operation in Britain and Japan. Since this chapter does not allow for extended analysis of these models, the alternative cultural conceptions of aesthetic value, pedagogy and worthwhile knowledge that inform them are presented in Table 8.1.

CONCEPTS OF CRAFT

That the concepts of *kogei* and craft are not synonymous is no surprise given their different cultural histories. In Britain, there is a tradition dating back to the Renaissance of distinguishing between 'crafts' catering primarily for the satisfaction of functional and utilitarian needs (e.g. ceramics, textiles, leather work and jewellery) and 'fine arts' (painting, drawing and sculpture), which give scope for imaginative self-expression and intellectual speculation.[13] In this tradition, art has been afforded a higher social status. Until the modern period, there was traditionally no distinction between art and craft in Japan, and *bijutsu* (art) and *kogei* (craft) are translations of western concepts. The term *kogei* can refer to technical art, industrial art, fine and applied art or craft and design, which are understood to have both artistic and functional dimensions.

Table 8.1: Japanese and British Conceptions of Education, Aesthetics and Craft

Concept	Britain	Japan
Craft in society	Distinguished from art since Renaissance; afforded a much lower status.	Distinguished from art since modern period only (fine art is a translation of a western concept).
Craft education	Utilitarian and aesthetic strands of craft education in two separate school subjects (art and design and technology). Emphasis on the role-model of professional craftsperson.	The concept of *kogei* is exclusive to art. Emphasis on general educational benefits of craft.
Worthwhile knowledge	Individualist. Worthwhile knowledge arises from in-depth study of a small range of academic subjects (vocational subjects not valued).	Group-oriented: emphasizes filial piety and loyalty to state. Acquisition of knowledge, character-building and cultivation of personality go hand-in-hand.
Curriculum	Essentialist model in which specialization is encouraged early on.	Combination of European encylopedism, American pragmatism and Japanese morality. Students study a broad range of general education subjects.
Cultural policy	Neglects to address core social values. A functional national culture is compatible with a significant degree of pluralism.	Legislates for conscious transmission of core cultural values, beliefs and practices from one generation to the next. Understanding and engaging with other cultures necessitates knowledge of, and pride in, own culture.
Aesthetic value	Analytical and objectivist view. Necessitates training in critical reasoning and judgement, and learning the language of art.	Emotionalist and subjectivist view. Is about cultivating pleasure in and enjoyment of nature and art, and doing things well (aesthetically), which is a mark of good character.

Table 8.1: *Continued*

Concept	Britain	Japan
How children learn	Through exposure to cultural exemplars appropriate for their varying individual capabilities. Training in critical reasoning.	Through self-discipline and hard work. Full development of personality.

Moreover *dento kogei* covers living artisan traditions of crafts such as textiles, pottery, joinery etc. that were virtually wiped out by the industrial revolution in Britain. There has been significant cross-fertilization of Japanese and British crafts this century, however. The British Arts and Crafts movement was influential in effecting the development of the 'modern' or 'contemporary' craft tradition in Japan, and Japanese traditional ceramics were the impetus for a studio-pottery revival movement in Britain.

CRAFT EDUCATION

Craft education in both school systems originated in the late nineteenth century as manual training in vocational and domestic skills (woodwork for boys and sewing for girls). An aesthetic strand of craft education, influenced by the Arts and Crafts movement, was gradually established in first the primary and then the secondary art curriculum after the First World War. In Britain, aesthetic crafts spread rapidly in the 1940s and 1950s when traditional handcrafts experienced a revival. The expansion of craftwork (in the form of studio pottery, furniture-making, hand-woven and embroidered textiles and jewellery) at this time coincided with the spread of the expressive paradigm for art education and it was justified, together with painting and drawing, not as skill-based learning but to develop self-expression in the child.[14]

In British secondary education, at present, the concept of craft surfaces in a confused manner, in discussion and analysis of productive and artistic technologies in both design and technology and in art. *Kogei* on the other hand refers to functional items decorated and/or made with aesthetic intent during art lessons. Moreover, it is a reflection of the 'dualism' of modern Japanese life that while western aesthetic concepts like 'creativity' and 'free expression' are much sought after and admired, an alternative cultural aesthetic continues to be taught. One way of explaining the perceived technical excellence of students' craftwork in Japan, given the lower standards of specialist provision in schools, is that this is achieved because of the high value traditional Japanese culture places on 'spirit in technique'. Unlike their British colleagues, Japanese craft teachers understand lifelong training of the spirit, through concentration on learning craft techniques, as the key to establishing 'original' work. The nomination by government of 'National Living Treasures' from master craftspersons exemplifies this cultural belief. Moreover, the concept of *kogei* is closely associated with a pre-modern apprenticeship model of learning that emphasizes discipline, technical competence and the spiritual and moral value of learning craft skills.

WORTHWHILE KNOWLEDGE

According to Holmes and McLean, the secondary-school curriculum in Britain traditionally operates with an essentialist view of worthwhile knowledge derived from Plato and Aristotle.[15] Fundamental to this view is a belief in the value of in-depth study of a few academic subjects with clearly defined criteria. This academic curriculum was originally designed to develop future leaders, and it excluded practical, useful or vocational knowledge, which was reduced to the inferior category of training (this included, particularly, those manual activities associated with craft occupations having a distinctly lower status in the social structure). Its main tenets were adopted into comprehensive schooling after the Second World War and, despite strenuous government attempts at reform, vocational education has continued to be sharply differentiated from the mainstream system.

Holmes and McLean claim that the traditional Japanese model of curriculum, on the other hand, is a mixture of American pragmatism and European encyclopedism, with an inner spirit that remains essentially Japanese.[16] A European encyclopedic model of curriculum, that represents an attempt to include all human knowledge was adopted during westernization, 100 years ago in the Meiji period. The pragmatic model of curriculum introduced by the Americans during the occupation in 1945 has since been modified by strong indigenous Japanese moral values. Holmes and McLean describe the Japanese system today as more of a 'mass' one than in any other country in the world, save the USA. They say it is extremely competitive, and it is the knowledge needed to pass university-entrance examinations that is most highly prized. However, the system has been slow to respond to changes in the economic life of Japanese society since 1945.

CULTURAL POLICY

The British essentialist curriculum is notorious for its neglect of cultural values and the socializing functions of schooling.[17] Vigorous and bitter struggles to define and control the notion of national identity and culture have been a feature of recent National Curriculum planning, but, to date, no firm policy decision has been forthcoming as to how education contributes to national and cultural identities. In strong contrast, Japanese educational policy states clearly that in an increasingly global society, Japanese cultural traditions and values should be transmitted and preserved. It seems that only the Japanese Ministry of Education recognizes that conscious transmission, through education, of values, beliefs and practices, from one generation to the next, is essential in the face of the worldwide progress of market economies that are everywhere deeply subversive of tradition.

AESTHETIC RESPONSE

The Japanese and British national curricula promote different models of art criticism and response. Mention of 'deepening (students') concern over the relationship of life to beauty' and 'experiencing the pleasure of art, craft and design works' in the Japanese art curriculum implies a subjective emotional response arising from a person experiencing something in common with an artwork or a natural phenomenon. On the other hand, references to 'analysing images and artefacts' and 'using appropriate art and design vocabulary' in the English and Welsh Statutory Orders imply an objective response involving judgement and some form of empiricism. In this regard it is important to note that, whereas contemporary western aesthetic theory has tended to dispense with the notion of the beautiful as a symbol of the moral and good, the concepts of nature, beauty, morality and art have long been interrelated in Japanese aesthetics. Moreover, the separation of fine art from art of everyday life is a western, not a Japanese, aesthetic principle. According to Roger Scruton, an emphasis on developing critical reasoning in relation to high culture is central to the British liberal tradition of education, and it is this that is understood to distinguish education from training.[18] The fact that craft education relies heavily on transfer of skills and a body of knowledge from acknowledged experts, without undue questioning of received wisdom, undoubtedly contributes to its low status. Japanese education, on the other hand, does not teach children to express personal opinions and judgements about art and craft, and the system as a whole does not contain the principle of internal criticism to the same degree.

HOW CHILDREN LEARN

The British, essentialist view of curriculum incorporates a cultural belief that learning is the outcome of interaction between the innate qualities of individuals and their exposure to external cultural exemplars, and that a wide range of such exemplars is needed to cater for their differing academic abilities. In Japan on the other hand, the child's inner motivation to learn, character-training through self-discipline, hardship and education of the personality, are afforded the most significance. Likewise, it is understood that acquisition of knowledge and cultivation of personality go hand in hand and the amount of continuous effort in study, rather than levels of academic achievement, is measured in assessment (including high-school entrance exams). 'Shido', the Japanese word for teaching, embraces much more than British concepts like academic guidance and instruction; the responsibilities of Japanese teachers with regard to pastoral care involves associating with students, both mentally and physically, to encourage full development of character. It is said to be a characteristic of the traditional British model of curriculum, however, that students are taught to question and criticize, to seek fair play and be impartial.[19]

COMMONALITIES

Not everything about British and Japanese craft education was a surprise to me and the similarities are equally important in determining a way forward. The key finding was that craft education is declining in both systems as a component of the National Curriculum for art. Art teachers claim there is insufficient time to implement craft, as opposed to art, and are pessimistic about its future. The specialist materials and equipment it requires are expensive and many of them lack sufficient specialist training in craft knowledge and skills.

Whereas craft is understood as 'other than drawing and painting', the way it is taught and promoted is dominated by modernist beliefs about the educational value of fine art. Art teachers give the highest priority to so-called 'contemporary crafts', and regard developing individual students' imaginations and creativity as more significant than teaching techniques and skills. They regard making (and to a limited extent, designing) artefacts in a range of recognized 'craft materials' as more important than appreciation, knowing about or understanding craft. Craft education in art continues to signify making by hand, and experimentation with industrial processes or new technologies is rare.

Teachers in the two surveys justified craft and art education mainly on psychological and individualistic grounds. They viewed making as educationally significant because it gives individual students pride and confidence in their own achievements and develops imagination and expressive skills. The traditional artisan role of craft education as manual training and preparation for work and everyday life are played down in both countries and are largely ignored in Britain.

Overall it could be argued that this reflects a dominance of expression theories of art and humanistic or liberal education ideals which fail to take account of postmodern developments in art and education (for example, the de-centring of the subject and rejection of universal theories of art). Most importantly, the western modernist paradigm of art education, which is either practised or aspired to in Britain and Japan, is misguided in its unquestioning belief in human progress, and elitist in its restriction of curriculum content to contemporary studio and/or artist and designer traditions of craft.

LESSONS FROM JAPAN

The comparison has confirmed that there is a crisis of identity in craft. A very important strength of the Japanese system is the specification (in national curriculum documentation) of distinctive objectives for craft. On reflection, I think the insistence on function, materials and process to distinguish craft from art is crucial if it is to survive. Whereas I have difficulty understanding the theoretical domain of the art curriculum in Japan, the aim of developing an appreciation of the aesthetics of function seems important for craft education, and I want to argue that this should be emphasized much more in Britain. (I find it difficult to justify not including it in design and technology also.) I particularly like the emphasis, in the Japanese objectives for *kogei*, on appreciation of art and craft in everyday life, because this counteracts the elitist and idealist tendencies of modernist theories of art which postmodernism is currently challenging (e.g. divisions between high and low art and the separation of art from life). A problem with the Japanese objectives, however, is that they do not provide a logical rationale for teaching contemporary 'artists' crafts' which are non-functional.

Another strength of *kogei* is that it embraces a broad range of living craft traditions, about which many children are denied the opportunity to learn in British schools (e.g. folk arts, traditional artisan and rural crafts). Part two of the survey in Britain found that the majority of students who make and mend things out of school associate craft with do-it-yourself activities at home, tourist artefacts, cultural conservation and gift giving.

Recurring themes in the specialist literature about craft[20] are that it fulfils a basic human need for tactile sensory experience and necessitates 'making things skilfully or well'. The how-to-do-it instructions in the Japanese textbooks and the importance Japanese teachers attach to 'making things the right way' fit the second theme well. More importantly perhaps, these characteristics are compatible with the Japanese model of worthwhile curriculum knowledge in which character training and intelligence are inseparable.

Finally, the potential of craft to transmit cultural heritage and identity is well documented in the specialist literature, and whereas the Japanese system capitalizes on this, it is largely neglected in Britain. According to Gellner[21] a functional national identity *is* compatible with a significant degree of pluralism in society at the level both of beliefs and values, and of self-identification on the part of individuals and groups and the apparent failure of the educational system in Britain to address transmission of core social values is unfortunate.

THE WAY FORWARD

The British research confirmed that students' motivation for making is dependent on opportunities to develop in-depth craft knowledge and skills (craftpersonship). Learning a little about a lot of crafts and working with ready-made materials and prepared kits is demotivating. Students like making because they find hands-on experience with materials pleasurable and working skilfully with objects enables them to realize ideas and learning in concrete form. Incidentally, this also enhances their capability to recognize and appreciate craftspersonship and good-quality craft outcomes. Other arguments the specialist literature has put forward for the intrinsic educational benefits of craft are that is that it is spiritually enriching because of its close links with nature, and functions as an antidote to virtual reality. How else to explain the phenomenon of handcraft becoming increasingly important to the general public as a hobby or leisure-time pursuit?

By and large, it seems the British and Japanese governments prefer extrinsic to intrinsic educational rationales for craft. The Japanese emphasis on educating character and personality is well served by craft education so long as it emphasizes skills-based training and technical competence all of which necessitate patience, self-discipline and hard work on the part of students. Character formation does not feature in British educational discourse, however, and we have a long tradition of denigrating vocational educational aims. On the other hand, design and technology, and art, *are* currently being promoted for economic reasons. The former as a means of developing core life-skills and knowledge (e.g. informed decision-making, time-keeping, group work and habits of learning etc.), the latter as a means of supplying creative individuals to the 'culture industries'.

The potential of craft for transmitting cultural identity and heritage is a recurring theme in this chapter. A hundred years ago, craft education was being promoted strongly for community-building purposes in America[22] and as Britain becomes increasingly multicultural, the English and Welsh National Curricula are beginning to take citizenship education more seriously. People in Japan and in most other societies apparently agree that education can and should play a part in cultural transmission, and craft is admirably placed to fulfil this general educational aim. But, arguably, the most convincing rationale for continuing to teach craft into the twenty-first century is embedded in Howard Gardner's proposition, mentioned previously, that bodily and kinaesthetic intelligence are uniquely catered for and developed through craft.

In closing, I agree with Brian Allison that schools cannot be expected to function as training grounds or apprenticeship schemes for crafts. But at the very least, we should expect them to produce the kinds of experiences that develop a love for making artefacts and joy and satisfaction in things of endearing quality. In this sense, our children would be much poorer without the concepts of making, skilled knowledge (craftspersonship) and craft.

POSTSCRIPT

Making continues to be specified as a requirement within the English National Curriculum for both Art and Design and Design and Technology.[23] But is 'making' the same thing as 'craft'? The problem with making is that it omits reference to the quality of pupils' achievements, or efforts, in practical work. Historically, craft has been interpreted in the school curriculum in many ways: for example, as 'practical knowledge', 'technology', 'intelligent making' and the 'design-and-make process'. Central to all these is the notion of skilled knowledge acquired by engaging purposefully, at first hand, with materials and processes over time. I understand craft as skilled knowledge expressed through making and doing.

Skilled knowledge has always been undervalued in formal schooling because it differs from numerate and literate forms of knowledge. Yet it is essential for realizing and understanding the sorts of designs, materials and processes that are central to Art and Design and Design and Technology. Moreover, there are significant general educational benefits to be gained from acquiring skilled knowledge, which deserve to be better known (Houghton and Mason, 2002).[24]

The relative balance needed between making and other forms of knowledge in the school curriculum is difficult to determine at a time when new technologies are increasingly blurring these boundaries. However, the argument for students acquiring some form of skilled knowledge remains persuasive. The danger is that in trying to intellectualize this kind of intelligence we run the risk of destroying its essential character, which is tacit and intuitive and acquired through hands-on experience.

Notes

1. The Project Directors were Rachel Mason and Norihisa Nakase. Project Officers were Dorothy Bedford, Nicholas Houghton, Masako Iwano and Toshio Naoe. Information about the British project can be found in three research reports located in the Reference Library at the Crafts Council and at the University of Surrey Roehampton Learning Resources Centre, and in two executive summary reports published by the Crafts Council: Bedford, B. and Mason, R. (1997) *National Survey of Craft in Art and Design & Technology Curricula and Courses at Key Stages 3 & 4: Teachers' Views*, London: Crafts Council and University of Surrey Roehampton; Iwano, M. and Mason, R. (1995) *National Survey of Craft in Art and Design & Technology Curricula and Courses at Key Stages 3 & 4 in England and Wales*. London: Crafts Council and University of Surrey Roehampton; Mason, R. (1998) *Craft Education in Secondary Schools at Key Stages 3 and 4: Pupils as Makers*. London: Crafts Council; Mason, R., Nakase, N. and Naoe, T. (1999) 'Craft education in lower secondary schools in England and Japan: a comparative study' (submitted for publication to *Journal of Comparative Education*).
2. See Allison, B. (1998) 'Craft is more than helping in t'shed'. *Times Educational Supplement*, 3 April, p. 80.
3. See Knott, C. (1994) *Crafts in the 1990s*. London: Crafts Council.
4. Crafts Council (1995) *Aspects of Crafts in Secondary Schools in England and Wales: Pupils as Makers*. London: Crafts Council and University of Surrey Roehampton, p. 3. 5.
    Crafts Council, *op. cit.*
6. Dissanayake, E. (1992) 'The pleasure and meaning of craft'. *American Crafts*, **52**(2), 40–5; Robertson, S. (1989) 'The refinement of touch'. *Journal of Art and Design Education*. **8**(3), 241–5.
7. Gardner, H. (1985) *Frames of Mind: The Theory of Multiple Intelligence*. New York: Basic Books.
8. Cave, J., Neale, J. and Tuffnel, R. (1997) 'Learning through making: competencies and capabilities'. Unpublished research report, Middlesex University; Press, M. and Cusworth, A. (1995) 'New lives in the making: the value of craft in education in the information age'. Unpublished research report, Art and Design Research Centre, Sheffield Hallam University.
9. Crossley, M. and Broadfoot, P. (1992) 'Comparative and international research in education: scope, problems and potential'. *British Educational Research Journal*, **18**(2), 99–112.
10. Monbusho (1989) *Course of Study for Lower Secondary Schools*. Tokyo: Ministry of Education Press.
11. Stenhouse, L. (1978) *An Introduction to Curriculum Research and Development*. London: Heinemman.

12. Mason, R. (1994) 'Artistic achievement in Japanese junior high schools'. *Art Education*, **4**(1), 8–19.

13. Houghton, N. and Mason, R. (1997) *Students as Makers: Their Motivation For and Perceptions Of Craft Education at Key Stages 3 & 4.* London: Crafts Council and Roehampton Institute.

14. See Mason, R. and Houghton, N. (2002) 'The educational value of making', in B. Barnes, J. Morely and S. Sayers (eds) *Issues in Design and Technology.* London: Routledge.

15. Holmes, B. and McLean, M. (1988) *The Curriculum: A Comparative Perspective.* London: Unwin Hyman.

16. *Ibid.*

17. According to Beck, J. (1996) 'National curriculum and cultural identity in conservative cultural analysis: a critical commentary'. *Cambridge Journal of Education*, **26**(2), 171–18.
    Scruton, R. (1987) 'The myth of cultural relativism', in E. Palmer (ed.) *Anti-racism: The Assault on Education and Value.* London: Sherwood Press, cited in Beck, *op. cit.*, p. 193.

19. According to Gellner, E. (1983) *Nations and Nationalism.* Oxford: Blackwell (cited in Beck, *op. cit.*).

20. Dormer, P. (ed.) (1997) *The Culture of Craft.* Manchester: Manchester University Press; and Dissanayake (1992), *op. cit.*

21. Gellner, note 18.

22. Korsenik, D. (1992) 'Structure and transformation in art education', in D. Thistlewood (ed.) *History of Art and Design Education: Cole to Coldstream.* Harlow: Longman.

23. In the Art and Design programme of study for Key Stages one to three, the National Curriculum states: 'Teaching should ensure that investigating and making includes exploring and developing ideas and evaluating and developing work.' (DfEE/QCA (1999) *Art and Design – The National Curriculum for England*, London: HMSO, p. 20); in the Design and Technology programme of study, the National Curriculum for Key Stages one and two states: 'Teaching should ensure that knowledge and understanding are applied when developing ideas, planning, making products and evaluating them.' (DfEE/QCA (1999) *Design and Technology – The National Curriculum for England* London, HMSO, p. 16); for Key Stages three and four, the term 'making' is thus replaced by 'producing products'.

24. Mason, R. and Houghton, N. (2002) *op.cit.*

Chapter 9

Art Education and Spirituality

JAMES HALL

[W]hether art soothes or awakens, casts shadows or brings light, it is never merely a clinical description of reality. Its function is always to move the *whole* man, to enable the 'I' to identify itself with another's life, to make its own what it is not and yet is capable of being.[1]

[A]rtists are map-makers of consciousness and of the spiritual world as well as measurers and describers of the natural world, and their work demonstrates that consciousness is not divided one living thing from another, as the world is not so divided.[2]

INTRODUCTION

Recent educational policy, guidance and inspection in the UK and other western societies have given renewed prominence to students' spiritual development in all areas of the curriculum and school life. As part of a broader concern with young people's personal development and their preparation for life in society, these initiatives follow the UK's Education Reform Act of 1988, which gave birth to the National Curriculum, a principal aim of which is 'to promote the moral, spiritual and cultural development of students at school and in society'. A school's effectiveness in this area is also one of the four aspects of educational provision regularly inspected by the Office for Standards in Education (OFSTED).

The UK government therefore attaches considerable value to students' spiritual development and this might imply an important role for religious education. However, given the broad definition given to 'spirituality' by the UK government's curriculum agency, previously the National Curriculum Council (NCC) and then the Schools' Curriculum and Assessment Authority (SCAA), now the Qualifications and Curriculum Authority (QCA), I shall argue that art education also has a key role to play in students' spiritual development. These examples of policy and practice in the UK are used as characteristic of approaches to spirituality in a variety of contexts.

'Spirituality' is not used here in a purely religious or ecclesiastical sense but in the broader, secular terms determined by, among others, UK government agencies. In this definition, spirituality is seen as fundamental to the human condition, to do with the universal search for individual identity, the search for meaning and purpose in life, the values by which to live and the development of fundamental human characteristics. References to organized religion, or God, in the various guidance and discussion papers in relation to spirituality are minimal, and students' spiritual development is seen as the responsibility of all teachers and all areas of the curriculum.

Spirituality is inextricably linked to creativity and the creative act. The first artworks we create celebrate and validate our being and presence in the world. Art and religion have always had an intimate relationship and share a quest for meaning, purpose and direction in life. Both art and religion offer ways of exploring the fundamental nature of our being, comprehending the world and our experience within it, and have served as potential vehicles for spiritual knowledge. Art and religion share a common language, a 'spiritual language', as Halstead puts it, 'of symbols, myths, metaphors, parables and analogies rather than the more literal/rational language used in science and logic'.[3] In Western European cultures, as religion has had a diminishing influence on society, western art has become increasingly secularized and estranged from religion during the twentieth century, a process that, arguably, began with the Renaissance and accelerated with modernism.

This humanist and pluralist conception of spirituality is not far removed from, indeed shares common ground with, conceptions of art education. Many aspects of art education such as creativity, imagination, making and appreciation are spiritual in nature or contain elements of spirituality. I shall claim that art, with other arts-education disciplines such as music, dance and drama, is quintessentially the area of the secondary curriculum which supports students' spiritual growth and wellbeing. Fundamentally, the arts in education celebrate the uniqueness of each individual and the shared nature of experience. The arts, whether experienced through making or appreciating, like spirituality, are concerned with the inner life. In education systems that are increasingly driven by public accountability, assessment and that which is most easily measured, there is a vital place for the less predictable, less explicable and spiritual aspects of human nature.

There are contributions which art education can make to students' spiritual development which are unique to this area of the curriculum and others which overlap with, or are shared by, other subjects. I shall argue that the experiences of making and responding to art are essential to our spiritual wellbeing, and that learning, as a creative and personal process, is also spiritual in nature. Furthermore, artworks have the ability to reach across time and tell us what people from other times and places thought, felt and believed, and art plays an important role in students' multicultural and religious education.

This essential relationship between spirituality and art education will clearly have implications for the art curriculum, for its implementation in the secondary classroom and for assessment and this chapter concludes by addressing those areas.

WHAT IS MEANT BY THE TERM 'SPIRITUALITY'?

The National Curriculum in England and Wales defines ten foundation subjects, of which art is one. Religious education is also a compulsory part of the National Curriculum. The Curriculum has tended to reinforce subject definitions by encouraging teachers to focus on the distinctiveness of their particular subjects rather than on the common elements shared with other subjects. Spirituality is one of those common elements which is not the preserve or sole responsibility of religious education but is cross-curricular in nature, and is the concern of the whole curriculum. The term was defined in a discussion paper as

> applying to something fundamental in the human condition which is not necessarily experienced through the physical senses and/or expressed through everyday language. It has to do with the universal search for individual identity – with our responses to challenging experiences, such as death, suffering, beauty and encounters with good and evil. It has to do with the search for meaning and purpose in life and for values by which to live.[4]

Eight aspects of students' spiritual development were outlined in this paper and they are cited here in full to make explicit the common ground shared with the values and attitudes which art education helps students to explore and develop.

> *Beliefs* The development of personal beliefs, including religious beliefs; an appreciation that people have shared individual beliefs on which they base their lives; a developing understanding of how beliefs contribute to personal identity.
> *A sense of awe, wonder and mystery* Being inspired by the natural world, mystery or human achievement.
> *Experiencing feelings of transcendence* Feelings which may give rise to belief in the existence of a divine being, or the belief that one's inner resources provide the ability to rise above everyday experiences.
> *Search for meaning and purpose* Asking 'Why me?' at times of hardship or suffering; reflecting on the origins and purpose of life; responding to challenging experiences of life such as beauty, suffering and death.
> *Self-knowledge* An awareness of oneself in terms of thoughts, feelings, emotions, responsibilities and experiences; a growing understanding and acceptance of individual identity; the development of self-respect.
> *Relationships* Recognizing and valuing the worth of each individual; developing a sense of community; the ability to build up relationships with others.
> *Creativity* Expressing innermost thoughts and feelings through, for example, art, music, literature and crafts; exercizing the imagination, inspiration, intuition and insight.

Feelings and emotions   The sense of being moved by beauty or kindness; hurt by injustice or aggression; a growing awareness of when it is important to control emotions and feelings, and how to learn to use such feelings as a source of growth.[5]

In 1996, the then Schools' Curriculum and Assessment Authority created the National Forum for Values in Education and the Community, and charged it with making recommendations to the authority on 'ways in which schools might be supported in making their contribution to students' spiritual and moral development'. The forum was also asked to report on whether there is any agreement on the values, attitudes and behaviours that schools should promote on society's behalf. It responded by suggesting that students develop spiritually by 'learning to value themselves; learning to value relationships; learning to value society; and learning to value the environment ... '.[6] This broad, secular interpretation of spirituality reflects the increasing secularization of western society and the marginalization of organized religion. However, for Thatcher, the virtual omission of theological or overtly religious references, as well as the 'ahistorical' method of values-production employed by the forum, makes the claims for consensus highly suspect

> There is to be no discussion of the troublesome historical, social, ethnic, economic and religious differences and inequalities which constitute the actual society on whose behalf spiritual and moral development is being fostered.[7]

It is not the religious or secular interpretation of spirituality which is important in discussions of art education's possible contributions, for art can take either religious or secular forms, as Starkings reminds us:

> For some Christians the arts may reflect the divine creative power and be related perhaps to a divine incarnational theology ... where there may be no professed contact with the ideas or symbols of formal religion, the arts may be assumed to stand entirely free from religion as makers of meaning. But they are nevertheless makers of meaning.[8]

And, indeed, for some Christians, Muslims, Hindus, Sikhs, Buddhists and Jews, the arts may, or perhaps should, represent specific religious beliefs and doctrines. Historically, art has been inextricably bound up with religion and spirituality in virtually all cultures and religions. Late in the twentieth century, art might be thought to have grown away from organized religion, if not to have become completely divorced from it. Modernist and postmodernist art has developed new codes and new concerns; religion is seen by many people as having lost some of its significance and importance as church attendance falls in this country. For Ludovic Kennedy the arts have largely replaced religion:

> Winwood Reades' prophecy of 100 years ago that in the future art would take the place of religion is in the course of being fulfilled; and those whose spiritual needs were previously met by the church are now being met in various aspects of the arts.[9]

It is a view that Peter Hall shares: 'With the decline of religion, art becomes crucial to the health of a democracy. It helps society understand why and how it lives.'[10] Eagleton suggests this shift is nothing new, art as an alternative source of spirituality having been promoted by Ruskin and Arnold:

> Art would provide an experience of spirituality akin to religion; but it would be conveniently short of religion's embarrassing doctrinal baggage, preserving the aura and aroma of the sacred with nothing of its substantive content.[11]

However, Starkings suggests we need

> to recognise that where the arts (for example) appear to have achieved a status independent of religious inspiration they may not have ceased to carry the aspiration that is the hallmark of a spiritual quest.[12]

The aspects of spirituality as defined by UK government agencies relate to Fisher's domains of spiritual wellbeing, although he subsumes relationships and society into a single 'communal' domain and adds the 'global' domain:

> spiritual health is a dynamic state of being, shown by the extent to which people live in harmony within relationships in the following domains of spiritual well-being:
>
> **Personal domain** (wherein one inter-relates with oneself with regards to meaning, purpose and values in life. The human spirit creates self-awareness, relating to self-esteem and identity).
>
> **Communal domain** (as expressed in the quality and depth of inter-personal relationships, between self and others, relating to morality, culture and religion. This includes love, justice, hope and faith in humanity).
>
> **Environmental domain** (past care and nurture for the physical and biological, to a sense of awe and wonder, for some the notion of unity with the environment).
>
> **Global domain** (relationship of self with some-thing or some-One beyond the human level [i.e. ultimate concern; cosmic force; transcendent reality; or God]. This involves faith toward, adoration and worship of, the source of Mystery of the universe).[13]

I maintain that the descriptions of these domains hold few surprises for art educators, many of whom will draw close parallels with the aims, purposes and direction of art education in secondary schools. This is no less the case than in these concluding dimensions which Halstead deems to be necessary in the education of the human spirit:

1. Looking inwards: personal identity and individual development. This includes developing a sense of self and of identity within a group; personality and behaviour; educating the emotions; developing qualities of character; developing the conscience and the will.

2. Looking outwards: some spiritual responses to life. These include creativity; contemplation; personal commitments; the quest for meaning and for something beyond ourselves; living for others.[14]

ART EDUCATION AND STUDENTS' SPIRITUAL DEVELOPMENT

The arts need to have a central not peripheral role in this. Music, art, dance and drama, as well as being valuable in their own right, offer enormous possibility for developing sensitive listening, careful, selfless observation, awareness of others and respect for other cultures. They are literally vital: a life-giving vehicle for human creativity.[15]

The background

Learning in art can be seen as having three strands or elements:

*   learning about art through making;
*   learning about art through interpreting and responding to art; and
*   developing personal and social understanding, qualities and attitudes through art.

It is my contention that it is through each of these strands that art education contributes to students' spiritual growth. It can be argued that it is the third strand which is of the highest value as it subsumes the other two art strands and can be seen as the ultimate aim of education. As individuals we can acquire skills, knowledge and understanding, but these are not simply stored and accumulated as data or credit in a bank; human beings are not simply repositories of information. Learning is concerned with actively constructing your own world view and how you use this knowledge and understanding. Learning is necessarily a personal and therefore subjective process; it is about self-determination, change and personal growth; developing the flexibility to adapt and change with situations; and the critical awareness and empowerment to affect situations and to exercise your rights and responsibilities.

Developments in art education over the last 20 years or so in the UK, North America, Australia and elsewhere have seen a broadening of the art curriculum to educate students' critical responses to artworks in order to both inform, enrich and balance their practical responses in art. The former emphasis on the practical, formal and technical elements of art education has shifted to include a proper recognition and appreciation of the content and context of artworks. Both the discipline-based art education movement in the USA and the critical studies movement in the UK have been instrumental in helping to generate a more appropriate balance between content and meaning, as well as formal and technical processes, in art. The ideas and theories they generated are reflected in curriculum models developed in recent years. The first National Curriculum for art in England and Wales[16] defined a holistic model for learning in which students' investigating and making opportunities were integrated with their knowledge and understanding of art, each domain informing and enriching the other.

Additionally, we live in societies that are increasingly diverse culturally and ethnically and this fact should be reflected in the nature of the school art curriculum. Equal opportunities legislation has supported the development of a multicultural curriculum in which students learn about art from a diverse range of cultures. However, Rachel Mason[17] and others feel there remains a considerable gap between aspiration and practice. In Mason's view there remains a shortfall in art teachers' knowledge of art from non-western cultures. Furthermore, when these artefacts are sourced, Mason suggests art educators need to delve a lot further beneath the surface of the cultural artefacts from different times, places and countries if they are to do justice to their richness and to their educational potential. These shortfalls have important implications in terms of support for students' spiritual development, in which an important aspect is learning about the representation of spirituality and religious belief in art.

The three strands of art education identified above: making art, interpreting art, and personal and social development will be discussed in turn in relation to their respective contributions to children's spiritual development.

Making art

'In order to be an artist it is necessary to seize, hold, and transform experience into memory, memory into expression, material into form.'[18]

Art is a unique and non-verbal means of responding to experience and communicating that response through a visual statement. The art-making process is not replicated in any other area of the school curriculum and therefore has a rightful place in that curriculum. The making process is an *integrative* process, involving the human faculties of intelligence, skill, emotion and memory, and thus, in secondary art education, it educates the whole child.

Making is a *spiritual* process in that the transformative process described by Fischer above is mirrored by the transformation of oneself into a new and changed self. Students' artworks have the potential to give shape and form to their ideas, thoughts and feelings and through reflection, understanding and assimilation lead to a growth in their self-knowledge. As Lowenfeld and Brittain indicate, in the process of drawing and painting, the child gives us 'more than a picture'; he gives us 'a part of himself; how he thinks, how he feels and how he sees'.[19]

The making process involves a *dialogue* between maker and material, between painter and canvas, carver and stone, potter and clay, weaver and loom. 'It is a meditative process allowing undistracted concentration on the emergence of a form'.[20] For Prentice,[21] the creative process amounts to a 'conversational exchange', not only between maker and material but also between the artist as maker and the artist as critic, which continues as a discourse between the image and the viewer. It is these reflective processes which lie at the heart of the making process and of art education. However, this special dialogue between maker and object, which seeks to fathom the truth of experience is no self-indulgent or simple therapeutic exercise. The making process also involves deep practical knowledge: a coming to terms with the disciplines of the material and form which is being grappled with and an appreciation of the language of visual elements through which the maker speaks.

The making process can involve a deep engagement with materials and processes. The meditative experience of making, or indeed the engagement with another's artwork, can reach a transcendent level, an experience of being at one with nature or one's materials. Time is suspended. It is possible for students to experience a sense of wholeness and completeness which is perhaps rare in lives that are regimented and controlled by the school timetable. Any sense of separation or self-consciousness is lost. This experience relates to the 'conversive trauma' described by Hargreaves[22] and the related 'illuminating experience' described by Taylor.[23] This is no experience of idle day-dreaming or fantasy, but, according to Housden, one of transcendence.

> Such a moment is not one of unconscious idyll, or infant paradise; on the contrary, beauty requires an unusual degree of consciousness to enable its manifestation. It is not though the consciousness of the self-reflecting, separate ego; it is the presence of the person in us, which fosters a condition of intimacy with each other and with all things.[24]

Making in art can also be a social activity. Group creativity can involve unusual degrees of collaboration, co-operation, negotiation and compromise, mediated non-verbally through tacit understandings and intuition. Many craft activities, in a variety of times and cultures, have involved groups: quilt-makers, basket-makers, weavers, dyers. Design is inherently a social activity and process; printmaking and sculpture can often involve extraordinarily creative relationships between artist and printer, sculptor and foundry worker.

Recent research has shown that children 'enjoy craft-based activities, make and mend things at home, value and enjoy making more where there are opportunities to develop specific techniques and skills, want teachers to be makers who demonstrate craft processes and believe that practical knowledge will be useful to them in the future'.[25] Students also invest themselves – their time, care, attention and effort – in their art and craft work. These findings are backed by Ford[26] who suggests the crafts have been neglected in the curriculum yet have great potential for teaching 'caring' values. She refers to makers' intimate knowledge of their materials coupled with a deep emotional attachment to and care for their chosen materials, tools and processes.

Art education meets the deeply human and, I would maintain, spiritual need for an intimate engagement with materials and their manipulation. Complex skills are learned and assimilated so that they become 'second nature'; students need space in the curriculum to develop such craft skills and practical knowledge. Ford speaks of 'the fingers remembering', makers working in unison with their materials 'in rhythm with the land and close to nature'.

The notion of unity, and affinity with the natural environment is a further important contribution that art education can make to what Fisher has termed the 'environmental domain' of spirituality.[27] This can range from a more aesthetic 'sense of awe and wonder' about the world and its creation to a more immediate environmental awareness and a deep concern for its welfare by humanity. This developing ecological awareness and concern is reflected in students' interest in ecological forms of art.

The upsurge of interest in the art of Andy Goldsworthy, in my view reflects not simply its accessibility but students' profound interest in and concern for the natural environment and our relationship to it. Goldsworthy is capable of changing perceptions of how we view the natural environment and our impact on it; the concepts which Goldsworthy explores – the transience of the work, the materials, making processes, the site and the recording process – hold a deep interest for children, who can respond through their own making and evaluation. Peter Randall-Page is a sculptor whose work is also concerned with ecology and our relation to the natural world.

> [M]y work has always been more to do with my relationship with the world than a statement about art. For me, both [ecology and carving] share the idea of reconciliation between self and other, an ability to be the bit of creation that can stand back and look at itself, as well as being part of all the rest.[28]

Richard Long also explores our human nature and our relationship with the natural world. To me, Long is a 'map-maker of consciousness and of the spiritual world',[29] but for Peter Fuller, Long's work is 'simplistic and fetishistic [and] symptomatic of the loss of both the aesthetic and spiritual dimensions of art; he shows little trace of imagination, of skill, of the transformation of materials'.[30]

Such differences of view should demonstrate to students the complexities and difficulties of aesthetic judgement and interpretation in art. The absence of any consensual view, particularly where contemporary art is concerned, may bemuse or disturb some students. However, responding to and interpreting art is as important to students' developing spirituality as making art is.

Responding to art

In my own view and experience, one of the most significant shifts in developing students' knowledge and understanding of art, as far as its implications for spirituality are concerned, has been the shift from factual to interpretative approaches to art appreciation in education. As well as learning about the artworks being studied and locating them in a cultural and historical context, students are invited to invest the works with meaning themselves. Rather than passively receiving accepted, scholarly interpretations of art, students are encouraged to speculate, or engage in 'fruitful conjecture'[31] about artworks in order to arrive at their personal critical response to art. This more subjective approach is not mere fanciful, unthinking opinion, nor snap judgement, but is informed and disciplined by the student's own reflection, thinking and experience. Broudy[32] suggested we need to educate our students' aesthetic perception and analytical skills, in order to cultivate their vision and sensibility, and make aesthetic literacy as common as linguistic literacy. For Broudy, when imagination is disciplined by thought, and love is justified by knowledge, 'enlightened cherishing' can develop. Motivated by this more subjective but informed interpretative response, Taylor suggests students go on to research and learn more about the works, movement or artists in question, comparing their interpretations with those of others. This approach has important consequences, not only for students' aesthetic education but also for the education of their feelings and values, and, ultimately, for their spiritual development. For Fuller, aesthetic experience is greatly diminished if it becomes divorced from the idea of the spiritual.

Students can only be helped to form and develop their own values and attitudes through art education if their feelings are engaged. On the basis that our moral outlook and values are profoundly shaped by our attitudes and feelings and that our sense of meaning and purpose is derived as much from feeling as from understanding, it is argued that students' affective development is as important as their cognitive development.

> We would assert that the sense of awe and wonder, the sense of beauty and mystery which every subject can evoke and which leads to the deepest questions of human existence is at heart a question of feeling ... without [emotional education] students' search for meaning is barren and dry.[33]

The emotional learning which students derive from their art education is important for them to develop a strong sense of self and an empathetic respect for others and a tolerance of difference. Art education should thus enable students to become aware of, and to respect and celebrate, religious and cultural diversity. As I have suggested, art and religious belief have had an intimate relationship until recent centuries, when the divide has become ever wider. Students should have opportunities to learn about art from as many cultures and periods as possible and to appreciate and experience the spiritual in art, whether that art is religious or secular. Yeomans distinguishes between sacred art, religious art and spiritual art:

> Concepts of sacred art involve a special degree and status of sanctity which are usually intimately bound up with tradition, devotion and acts of worship. Religious art occupies a more generic category embodying elements of narrative and didacticism, as well as spiritual meanings and values; while spiritual art covers a much broader spectrum of human feeling and is not necessarily conditioned or bound by any religious creed. A spiritual art may be concerned with transcendental values on a grand scale, but it can also involve more personal and intimate feelings and beliefs which simply affirm and give meaning to our humanity.[34]

Despite western art's increasing secularization, as Yeomans reminds us, 'the Twentieth Century has been capable of expressing spiritual values equal to any other epoch'. Yeomans cites western artists in the twentieth century whose art has been spiritual on a 'grand, transcendental scale', such as Kandinsky, Matisse and Picasso and, after the war, the American Abstract Expressionists, in particular Mark Rothko and Barnett Newman. These are twentieth-century figures to whom many students will be exposed and with whose work they should become familiar.

There will be many art educators who suggest these artists perpetuate the outdated modernist emphasis of the art curriculum which should be reviewed and reformulated to take in the more diverse and challenging work by artists working in a postmodern context. As with any subject, curricula need to be continuously reviewed and revised to take in contemporary developments and knowledge; this is as true of science, history and geography as art. If a subject becomes immutably rooted in the past, as some claim,[35] then it will atrophy and become irrelevant to the needs of young people and society.

Art curricula in many countries require students to study art and artists in relation to their own practical work. In seeking to meet these requirements, it is likely that teachers will select art which is sacred, religious and spiritual, to use Yeomans' categories. Art from different times and traditions can be linked thematically. The symbolic significance of the 'circle' could be studied in relation to prehistoric stone circles, Native American art, and oriental and contemporary art. Art from the ancient civilizations of Egypt, Greece and Rome finds its way into secondary curricula as does, more frequently, art from Ancient Mexico and the African continent.

Through practical and critical work, students have the opportunity to study relationships between art and religious beliefs, magic and ritual. An interest in body decoration – face and body painting, tattooing and jewellery – has helped students to explore the cultural and religious significance of this form of art. Some departments explore the art of a range of cultures by basing their art curriculum on the study of art from the major religions of the world. Studying the visual representation of religious belief through artworks can support students' art education and their religious education. Art can help students understand different religions and cultures; for example, gaining insights into the Hindu religion through studying the various representations of the god Shiva. Students learn about the role art plays in religious festivals such as the *rangoli* patterns in the Hindu Diwali celebrations and the *mendhi* designs in the Diwali and Muslim Eid festivals. Students can also learn about the symbolic significance of geometric forms, of colours and of animals and plants through studying the art of different religions.

The studying of religious art is not without controversy and teachers must ensure they are well-informed and sensitive to religious issues and beliefs. Students will learn why the human form is not usually represented in Islamic art, but teachers may unwittingly ask their students to make a portrait without considering whether Muslim students' particular religious beliefs permit them to do this. Aboriginal art has been the subject of considerable interest and attention in secondary-art curricula in the UK in recent years. This interest has perhaps been given impetus both by a major exhibition held at the Hayward Gallery, London and by the increase in resources available to teachers. An Australian publication cautions teachers to become knowledgeable about sensitive issues to do with aboriginal art before attempting to teach students about it. For example, there are taboo topics and sacred and secret aspects of aboriginal art which should not be approached in the classroom.[36]

There is also the issue, not only with aboriginal art but with art of all kinds, that teachers can present the work from a formal and technical perspective, with a narrow focus on visual pattern and decoration, neglecting a fuller contextual understanding of the work and not encouraging students to look below the surface and engage with the meaning and purpose of art and its spirituality.

Self-knowledge

In addition to students learning about the significance of art in different cultures and religions, they should have opportunities, through their art education, to reflect on the meaning, purpose and direction of their own lives. Through making and responding to art we are helped to become most completely ourselves by making and remaking ourselves. Self-knowledge is surely the most valuable knowledge that the education system has to offer. Making art is an act of disclosure, of saying this is who I am, what I am, what or who I might be. Davey asks us to 'see artistic disclosure as being inseparably bound up with the question of what it means to be human, and insists that through making and contemplating art we dare look at what we have and are making of ourselves'.[37]

In art, students are not simply studying a subject; they are studying themselves. Art is a prime candidate for experiential learning and, as such, demands modes of teaching and learning which engage students meaningfully and purposefully in their own learning. Salmon suggests this is achieved through students reflecting on their experiences in their lives and in school. 'If it is to be personally meaningful, visual literacy has to be anchored in what is deeply felt and understood, at the level of lived rather than analysed experience'.[38] This is also true of other areas of art education: a child reads a Shakespeare sonnet or a Sylvia Plath poem and the emotion is their own. They do not experience an emotion which is then *related* to their own experience, they engage with the poem *through* their own experience. The meaning and value of the poem is in the context of the life of the student: thus the child is at the centre of the arts curriculum.

Sedgwick and Sedgwick also argue for a self-determining and constructivist standpoint for students' personal social and moral education, and regard art, along with every area of the curriculum, as having a major role to play.

> [Personal, social and moral education] insists that the learner is actively
> constructing his or her own world as s/he goes along, rather than merely

being filled with the inherited knowledge of previous ages. It acknowledges that right and wrong are difficult and shifting ideas not simple
matters. It is concerned with what we do in the classroom to help
children understand themselves and their responsibilities and duties to
each other. How they cope, in other words, with their intricate, loving,
sometimes hating, sometimes indifferent relationships.[39]

This is the most significant learning that takes place in students' lives – the
personally meaningful learning, which has the potential to transform their
lives. Art also helps students to develop self-esteem and identity through their
work, a sense of worth and value which can arise through a deep personal
engagement in the subject. Some students achieve very high levels of motivation and commitment, evidenced by students working outside the formal
timetable, both in school, at home and elsewhere. A glance at the sketchbooks
of some of these, often high-achieving and highly committed students shows an
extraordinary level and investment of care, effort, time and imagination. These
most personal examples of school coursework are cherished by students, who
take great pride in them and often decorate their books and personalize the
cover and endpapers.

A further example of this special worth and value which some students place
upon art is the depth and quality of the self-evaluations which students in some
departments routinely pen and discuss with their teachers and with one
another. This is further evidence of the depth of reflection in which students
can engage and the self-knowledge and self-esteem they derive from art. What
drives such students to invest so much of their own time, care and effort in their
artwork is surely the meaning and value the work has for them?

While working together in the classroom, there is also something distinctive
about some of the most creative and productive of art rooms; there is a buzz, a
creative atmosphere that is infectious, for students and adults. Indeed, there
seems to be a special kind of relationship also between teachers and students.
Ford recognizes that 'whilst making, children have an opportunity to talk to
each other about what is important to them in a way that is not possible in
other subjects'. She connects this observation to the fact that women in many
cultures have traditionally worked collaboratively, coming together to make
and to talk, quilt-making being an example. Students are allowed to play music
on cassette tapes or the radio in many art rooms, reinforcing the notion of the
art room as an oasis where students' own ideas, experiences and cultures are
recognized, welcomed and celebrated as material for their artwork. Students
relax in a purposeful and self-directed manner in some art rooms to an extent
that they are unable to in some other subjects.[40]

It is perhaps both unfashionable and cuts across subject-focused national
curricula to talk about 'child-centred education', but any education system
which ignores or underestimates the importance of the child and her or his
individuality, experience, ideas and emotions will be inadequate and, as far as
educating values and emotions is concerned, amounts to indoctrination. These
ideas are nothing new: the modern or progressive movement in education,

which placed the child at the centre of education, had its origins in art education. Frank Cizek (1865–1946) was a pioneer of the 'child art' movement which so influenced educational thinking at the beginning of this century. Herbert Read drew attention to the writings of Dewey, Pestalozzi, Froebel and Montessori. Following art, education was reconceptualized as developing to the full the innate and learned capabilities of the individual. Read advocated placing art at the centre of the curriculum as one of the chief means of knowing oneself. Read saw the child in a state of transformation, continuously adjusting himself to its social and cultural environment, and saw education as the means to uncover a student's identity. Read had a vision of art and the aesthetic at the heart of education, with knowledge of self as a primary goal and art as the key to unlock one's spirituality.[41]

IMPLICATIONS FOR THE ART CURRICULUM AND FOR CLASSROOM PRACTICE

Teachers committed to spiritual values in art education are those who challenge and support students to engage deeply with their artwork in ways which are personally meaningful to them in order to explore their own and others' ideas and values. It is not the teacher's place to impose upon or seek to control students' ideas or values. A department in which the students' ownership of their work in the context of a dynamic and negotiated curriculum is highly valued is a prerequisite for students to be able to engage in the spiritual in art. As national curricula increasingly focus on key, marketable skills in literacy, numeracy and information technology, the importance of visual literacy and its impact on students' language and communication skills is often overlooked. Fundamentally, however, art education is concerned with the development of the whole individual, looking inwards to the development of personal identity and the emotions, and looking outwards to the development of spiritual and creative responses to experience.

We need a curriculum which provides for all of our needs as human beings, both spiritual and material. A prominent art critic stated recently that we live in a world which is over-explained, so we go to art galleries to top up on the inexplicable. Those of us living both in developed and developing countries inhabit information-rich societies where unprecedented amounts of information are available to us continuously and globally, beamed through our radios, televisions, telephones and computers. We lack opportunities to absorb, assimilate and reflect upon this information in order for it to effect meaningful change and growth in our lives. We are swamped with information. Art offers a balance – for the subjective, the infinite, the inexplicable and the irrational to nourish us. Art education offers students a different way of knowing – aesthetically, through the senses, the intellect and emotions – through the whole being.

A characteristic of art in secondary schools is the opportunity students have to explore and make statements about their own ideas, interests and experiences. Of course, there are departments where students are not allowed sufficient freedom and ownership of their artwork but are over-directed by art teachers who are anxious to steer students towards prescribed outcomes and successful examination results. In these circumstances, there is unlikely to be the engagement with and investment in their work, which is essential for their spiritual and personal development.

There are professional development implications for an art curriculum with a strong spiritual dimension. In order to offer students an appropriately broad art curriculum, teachers need continually to update and renew their knowledge of art and art forms, particularly contemporary and non-western ones. There is a need to provide opportunities for teachers to engage with art at their own level, both through making and appreciating art. There are also resource implications to consider, such as meeting the need for students to experience original works of art and, if possible, to handle those works of art, an experience which museum loan-collection schemes offer students.

There are implications for teaching styles and methods – styles of pedagogy which emphasize personal and social values, and methods which emphasize the students' involvement and responsibilities in their own learning. There are also implications for planning, whereby the personal and social benefits of art education need to be made explicit in teacher's plans, 'mutually reinforcing'[42] objectives relating to art knowledge and skills.

As we have seen, there are implications for the ethos of the department. No two departments are alike but reflect the approaches and emphases of the teaching staff. Many good departments reflect the creative, informal, personal and relaxed purposefulness of the artist's studio. The ambience of colour, artefacts, posters, objects and plants help make the art department an environment in which students can flourish, which in turn implies a different order of relationships between teachers and students.

Just as creativity does not just happen, in a vacuum, but can be encouraged through preparation and setting up appropriate conditions, stimuli and materials, so, I would claim, can students be educated for the 'illuminating experience' to which Taylor refers. Art education would be failing its students were it not to do so; at the core of any programme of art education has to be the attempt to create the conditions and situation where art can be experienced at the most profound level, both through appreciation and making.

IMPLICATIONS FOR ASSESSMENT

If one accepts that art has an essential contribution to make towards young people's spiritual education, then how is this learning and development to be assessed? With the current emphasis on accountability and the measurement of students' achievements against common standards of attainment, we are in danger of moving too far away from the personal, idiosyncratic world of negotiated meaning, purpose and value. Perhaps we do go to art galleries to 'top up on the inexplicable', and Starkings argues that it is the ultimate indeterminacy and ambiguity of the art process which aligns it to the spiritual process.

[I]t is not the religious or the secular account of the arts that is most relevant to spirituality. It is rather the finally ambiguous (or multivalent) status of the art process. The human spiritual process (whether in its religious or its secular forms) itself aligns with the arts in having ultimate indeterminacy – so that there are no external criteria for determining its satisfactory completion.[43]

In this light, it is not only difficult to align students' achievements in art to common standards of attainment, it would be inappropriate to attempt the impossible task of assessing students' spiritual development through art in any simplistic, standardized or decontextualized way. Rather, teachers could look for signs of developing awareness and characteristics, and personal and social qualities and attitudes. Ross *et al.*'s work on assessing achievement in the arts is helpful here. Rather than seeing the artwork as straightforward evidence of the students' attainment of predetermined objectives,

It becomes the subject of an ongoing conversation between pupils and teachers, the purpose of which is to prompt an expansion and deepening of the pupil's self-understanding and to give the teacher a unique opportunity to explore the pupils' capacity for reflection as part of their experience in the arts.[44]

For Ross *et al.*, assessment in the arts had tended to neglect self-appraisal, and their project aimed to give students a voice and a role in the assessment process and sought to open up the students' subjective worlds, where their aesthetic responses are conceived. The importance of talk as an assessment medium is seen as especially valuable in eliciting the student's view and in developing the abilities of students to articulate their intentions and evaluate their own work. For Ross *et al.*, knowledge is seen as being concerned with interpreting individual experience.

This view is supported by Gardner's notion of 'process-folios' as vehicles for encouraging the formative and cyclical processes of artistic creation: exploring, making, reviewing, reflecting, revising, re-making. Gardner argues for assessment in the arts to occur in context, 'as part of the student's ongoing artistic activities'.[45] At particular points in a programme of study, teachers and students reflect on agreed goals, on what has been achieved, on the most or least effective outcomes and on the most promising directions for development. Through these methods, in which the role of teacher–student talk is fundamental, artistic and personal aims can be mutually reinforcing.

As art educators need to review, and update continuously their curricula, they also need to argue continuously for art's rightful place within the mainstream school curriculum. Art has the potential to contribute towards more balanced lives and a greater equilibrium in our social structures and attitudes, in which aesthetic values are not sidelined by functional, utilitarian values. Halstead argues that 'there is a danger that a despiritualised education could break down children's natural sensitivity to the inner world and imprison them in an impoverished non-human materialism'.[46] Art education has never been more important in providing opportunities for students to explore aesthetic and spiritual values so as to develop deeper knowledge of themselves and others and to realize more of their human potential.

Without curiosity, without the inclination to question and without the exercise of imagination, insight and intuition, young people lack the motivation to learn, and their intellectual development is impaired. Deprived of self-understanding and, potentially, the ability to understand others they may experience difficulty in co-existing with neighbours and colleagues, to the detriment of their social development. If they not able to be moved by feelings of awe and wonder at the beauty of the world we live in, or the power of artists, musicians and writers to manipulate space, colour and language, they will live in a spiritual and cultural desert.[47]

POSTSCRIPT

Reflecting upon recent developments in art education and education generally, it is difficult not to think beyond the professional confines of art education. No area of human activity has remained immune from the aftershock of the global events in the wake of 11 September 2001. Given art education's claim to be contributing to democratic values in society and to children's spirituality, we have to take account of events which cause us to stop, think and reflect upon our experiences in life and their representation through art. The human themes or abstractions of life, birth, death, love, fear, suffering, joy, despair and happiness are part of the grammar of the spiritual in art. Peter Hall is quoted above as saying that art remains crucial to the health of democracy: our faith in democratic principles and processes has been severely tested during this period. Ironically, this could have re-affirmed our faith in the importance of art in education.

Considering some implications of the UK government's recent education policies, it seems to me that the performative culture of accountability and audit in education has continued unabated and even gathered pace. The increasing emphasis upon results has contributed in inhibiting teachers and their students from taking risks, exploring their own ideas and making decisions for themselves. As teachers discover the kind of work, and therefore teaching, which achieves the highest examination grades, a reductionist and instrumentalist approach is evident, whereby art education can become little more than an unproblematic process through which students attain, at varying standards, the learning outcomes prescribed for them: an 'input-output' model. If there is no element of surprise, discovery and ownership on the part of the student, there is highly unlikely to be any spiritual dimension to their learning and development.

The paradox in this is that, were teachers to give more scope to their students to pursue and develop their own ideas and to use a greater variety of media and approaches, more closely reflecting the art of today rather than the art of earlier periods, grades and standards could not only be maintained but enhanced. As evidence in support of this statement, I would draw attention to work by some secondary students in which emotional and intellectual content is fused with understanding and appreciation of materials and processes in ways which are authentic, engaging, personal and often humbling in their humanity and honesty.

Increased accessibility to contemporary art, through the opening of Tate Modern and the Baltic in Britain, for example, has provided greater opportunities for students and teachers to engage with contemporary issues, including those of a spiritual nature. However, I would suggest that the pervasive culture of 'performativity' which dominates secondary education inhibits the potential of such increased resources. The introduction of a curriculum initiative such as 'citizenship', whilst having resonance with arguments for the spiritual in art education, only serves to re-affirm what was already evident in some schools, and may be marginalized as evidence of initiative overload in others.

Notes

1. Fischer, E. (1964) *The Necessity of Art: A Marxist Approach.* Harmondsworth: Penguin.
2. Anne Seymour's essay in Long, R. (1991) *Walking in Circles.* Catalogue to the 1991 exhibition at the Hayward Gallery. London: The South Bank Centre.
3. Halstead, M. (1997) 'Educating the human spirit: an approach to the spiritual dimension of primary arts education', in D. Holt, *Primary Arts Education: Contemporary Issues.* London: Falmer Press, quoting D. Carr (1995) 'Towards a distinctive conception of spiritual education'. *The Oxford Review of Education,* **21**(1), 83–98.
4. National Curriculum Council (1993) *Spiritual and Moral Development: A Discussion Paper.* London: NCC.
5. *Ibid.*
6. SCAA (1996) *The National Forum for Values in Education and the Community: Final Report and Recommendations.* London: SCAA.
7. Thatcher, A. (1998) *SCAA and the Eclipse of Theology.* Paper presented at the Fifth Annual Conference on Education, Spirituality and the Whole Child, 19–20 June, Roehampton Institute London.
8. Starkings, D. (1993) 'The landscape of spirituality', in D. Starkings (ed.) *Religion and the Arts in Education: Dimensions of Spirituality.* London: Hodder & Stoughton, pp. 9–18.
9. Kennedy, L. (1998) 'How I lost God and found faith', *The Sunday Times,* 27 December.
10. Hall, P. (1999) 'He was once our great young hope – today he leaves the country', in the *Guardian Saturday Review,* 27 March.
11. Terry Eagleton writing a response to 'Peter Fuller's Journey' *Modern Painters,* **3**(3), 45–9. (1990).
12. Starkings, p. 4.
13. Fisher, J.W. (1998) 'Helps and Hindrances to Fostering Students' Spiritual Health'. Paper presented at the Fifth Annual Conference on Education, Spirituality and the Whole Child, 19 and 20 June, Roehampton Institute London, p. 3.
14. Halstead, M.

15. Calouste Gulbenkian Foundation (1998) *Learning by Heart: The Role of Emotional Education in Raising School Achievement*. London: Calouste Gulbenkian Foundation, p. 9.
16. DFE (1995) *Art in the National Curriculum*. London: HMSO.
17. Mason, R. (1995) *Art Education and Multiculturalism*. Corsham: National Society for Education in Art and Design.
18. Fisher, *op cit.*, p. 9.
19. Lowenfeld, V. and Brittain, V. (1982) *Creative and Mental Growth* (17th edn). London: Collier Macmillan.
20. Miles, M. (1989) 'Celebration of nature'. *Resurgence*, 134, May–June, 32–3.
21. Prentice, R. (1995) 'Learning to teach: a conversational exchange', in R. Prentice (ed.) *Teaching Art and Design*. London: Cassell, pp. 10–21.
22. Hargreaves, D. (1983) 'The teaching of art and the art of teaching: towards an alternative view of aesthetic learning', in M. Hammersley and A. Hargreaves (eds) *Curriculum Practice: Some Sociological Case Studies*. Lewes: Falmer Press.
23. Taylor, R. (1986) *Educating for Art: Critical Response and Development*. London: Longman.
24. Housden, R. (1990) *Fire in the Heart: Everyday Life as Spiritual Practice*. Shaftesbury: Element.
25. Crafts Council (1998) *Students As Makers: Craft Education in Secondary Schools at Key Stages 3 and 4*. London: Crafts Council, p. 1.
26. Ford, R. (1998) 'Developing an understanding of worth'. Paper presented at the Fifth Annual Conference on Education, Spirituality and the Whole Child, 19–20 June, Roehampton Institute, London.
27. Fisher, *op. cit.*
28. Miles, *op. cit.*
29. Seymour, *op. cit.*
30. Fuller, P. (1990) 'Peter Fuller's journey'. *Modern Painters*, 3(3), 45–9.
31. Taylor, *op. cit.*
32. Broudy, H.S. (1972) *Enlightened Cherishing: An Essay on Aesthetic Education*. Chicago: University of Illinois Press.
33. Calouste Gulbenkian Foundation, *op. cit.*
34. Yeomans, R. (1993) 'Religious Art and Spiritual Art: Spiritual Values and Early Modernist Painting', in D. Starkings (ed.) *Religion and the Arts in Education: Dimensions of Spirituality*. London: Hodder and Stoughton, pp. 70–82.
35. See 'Directions' (1999), *The Journal of Art and Design Education*, **18**(1).
36. Department for Education and Children's Services South Australia (1994) *Aboriginal Art and Dreaming: Teaching about Aboriginal Art, Craft and Design in Secondary Schools*. Department for Education and Children's Services South Australia.
37. Davey, N. (1994) 'Aesthetics as the foundation of human experience'. *Journal of Art and Design Education*, 13(1), 73–81.
38. Salmon, P. (1995) 'Experiential learning', in R. Prentice (ed.) *Teaching Art and Design: Addressing issues and Identifying Directions*. London: Cassell, pp. 22–8.
39. Sedgwick, D. and Sedgwick, F. (1995) *Art Across the Curriculum*. London: Hodder & Stoughton.
40. Ford, *op. cit.*
41. Ross, M. (1993) 'Read's *Education through Art* 50 years on'. *Journal of Art and Design Education*, **12**(2), 135–41.
42. Halstead, *op. cit.*

43. Starkings, D. (ed.) *Religion and the Arts in Education: Dimensions of Spirituality.* London: Hodder and Stoughton, pp. 138–47.

44. Ross, M., Radnor, H., Mitchell, S. and Brierton, C. (1993) *Assessing Achievement in the Arts.* Buckingham: Open University Press.

45. Gardner, H. (1990) *Art Education and Human Development.* Santa Monica, CA: The Getty Center for Education in the Arts.

46. Halstead, *op. cit.*

47. NCC, *op. cit.*

Chapter 10

Diverse Directions? Visual Culture and Studio Practice

RICHARD HICKMAN

Since writing the introductory chapter to the first edition of this book, debate has intensified with regard to the nature and purpose of art education. The polarized positions of this debate can be characterized by the view that art education should be primarily concerned with studio practice, informed by reference to accepted canons of art, and the view that art education should be concerned primarily with 'visual culture' (this side of the debate has now acquired its own acronym, VCAE: Visual Culture Art Education). Paul Duncum[1] notes this shift in emphasis, from studying 'art of the institutionalised artworld' to what he sees as the more 'inclusive category of visual culture' (p. 101).

In a subject area which tends to be perceived as marginal, art and design educators are all too often in the business of justifying their allocation of time in the school curriculum. This is no bad thing and can ensure a dynamic and forward-looking profession. In order to progress, we need to re-appraise our past and challenge the present. Innovations and innovative ways of working come and go; some stay and evolve. Some new ways of working appear to be in contradiction to others; this appears to be the case with some fundamental rationales for the teaching of art. If we believe art education is concerned in the main with facilitating students' understanding of the nature of the visual environment rather than with self-expression, then it is axiomatic that our curriculum will reflect this. Similarly, if we believe that acquiring a range of studio art skills is more important than being able to understand the visual world, then this will surely be our focus in the classroom. However, a 'pluralistic' art curriculum should, I believe, be able to accommodate most approaches; the important thing in terms of justifying curriculum time is to be clear about why we adopt certain approaches and why we choose particular syllabus content.

Broadly speaking, those who might be seen as 'reconstructivistists' have adopted the visual culture approach to art education; this approach is seen not as an extension to existing practice but, as Duncum asserts, is seen as an entirely new paradigm.[2] This paradigm encompasses notions of empowerment and is overtly political (a trait which Eisner sees as 'a source of discomfort'[3]). The following quotations from Duncum reveal important elements which underpin the visual culture approach:

> Mainstream art education begins with the assumption that art is inherently valuable, whereas VCAE assumes that visual representations are sites of ideological struggle that can be deplorable as they are praiseworthy. The starting point is not the prescribed, inclusive canon of the institutionalised art world, but students' own cultural experience.[4]

Such assertions have been roundly criticized and are seen as evidence of 'a fundamental lack of understanding or appreciation regarding the distinctive nature or value of art'.[5] It is clear that VCAE is firmly based in a student-centred approach to teaching and learning, but goes further in terms of actively challenging orthodoxies: Duncum goes on to declare (p. 8):

> A major goal is empowerment in relation to the pressures and processes of contemporary image-makers, mostly those who work on behalf of corporate capitalism, not the cherishing of artistic traditions and the valuing of artistic experimentation. The basic orientation is to understand, not celebrate.

We can see therefore that an underlying rationale within VCAE is concerned with developing students' understanding of the visual world. This rationale is not new of course, and could be seen as having evolved from the concept of 'basic design', which tended to have a rather sterile emphasis upon the so-called 'visual elements'. However, VCAE offers more than this and has its roots in several earlier rationales put forward by art educators, such as those described by Barrett.[6]

Barrett described six 'rationales' for art education which he suggested were 'identifiable strategies supported by distinct rationales, all of which share common aims but attempt to achieve them in different ways'. Barrett's 'rationales' were (p. 61):

- The Conceptual or Art-based Rationale
- The Design Education Rationale
- The Visual Education Rationale
- The Graphicacy Rationale
- The Fine Art Rationale
- The Art and Craft Rationale

The Visual Culture approach to art education can claim to draw upon at least three of these 'rationales'. John Steers, General Secretary of the National Society for Education in Art and Design (NSEAD), referred to Barrett's list in a conference address[7], making the important distinction between published accounts of *approaches* to art education and *rationales* for art's inclusion in the curriculum; in this context, Barrett's 'rationales' do indeed appear to be a list of approaches or, as Barrett himself suggested, 'strategies'. It is clear that this distinction, between approaches to the art curriculum and rationales for art's inclusion in the general curriculum, must be made when reviewing Addison and Burgess's list in Table 2.1 (Chapter 2). This list of approaches outlines strategies which describe *how* curriculum aims can be realized; aims, such as the eight outlined below, indicate *what* is aspired toward. A rationale for art education however would be a rational exposition of principles, explaining the purpose underpinning the aims – *why* the aims are considered to be of value.

A further distinction can be made between presenting rationales and advocating. Presenting rationales is inherently concerned with justification from a philosophical standpoint, while advocacy is concerned with presenting arguments for (in this case) the inclusion of art in the curriculum, which may or may not be sound in themselves, but are useful within a particular social or political context.

In discussing the future of art education, lists of aims have limited value unless they are accompanied by sound justifications. Taking this further, we might want to consider, for example, the aim of 'facilitating creativity through developing lateral thinking skills': is facilitating creativity necessarily a 'good thing'? If so, why? I mention this particular aim as many people associate art with 'creativity' and it is taken for granted that 'creative behaviour' is a good thing. Educators from different parts of the world at different times have advocated creativity as an answer to various perceived shortcomings in the educational system. Schooling is a normative enterprise and one thing which does not sit comfortably with typical school culture is creative behaviour. Of course, creativity is not within the sole remit of art, or even the arts. It would seem that if we consider innovation, challenging the status quo and other aspects of creative behaviour, then creativity ought to be a desirable goal for all subjects.

The inclusion of art in the school curriculum is often seen as being 'a good thing' and is in some way worthy. Some basic rationales not often put forward by art teachers can be summarized as follows:

- Art is good for raising student self-esteem ('they are no good at anything else').
- Art is useful as student therapy ('to release their pent up feelings').
- Art provides leisure for students ('give them something to do … it keeps them off the streets').
- Art can be vocationally rewarding ('they learn a practical skill').

While all of these might be true, to a greater or lesser extent, or at least are commonly held beliefs, there are some loftier aims which can be gleaned from stated aims for art education around the world. I will give a condensed version of eight:

- To enhance students' understanding of their cultural heritage.
- To enhance students' understanding of the cultural heritage of 'others'.
- To develop students' perception of the visual world.
- To develop students' understanding of their inner world.

- To develop practical problem-solving skills through manipulation of materials.
- To facilitate creative behaviour and lateral thinking skills.
- To promote inventiveness and risk taking.
- To enhance students' ability to make informed judgements about the made environment.[8]

Although these aims might not be peculiar to art, art education can play a significant role in achieving them. In addition to these eight aims, we must not forget the pleasure, sense of purpose, and joy of making which can be associated with art. These aims are well within a broad remit for the arts in education, but do they fall within the 'visual culture' vision for art education? The answer to this is 'to some extent'. Certainly, advocates of VCAE have responded to criticism that the emphasis upon critique displaces working with materials (which includes image-making) by re-asserting the notion that making and critique are 'symbiotic'. However, Duncum notes that:

> image making in VCAE would tend to adopt more of a design procedure
> – such as discovering, planning, doing and assessing – than the open
> ended exploratory approach of some artists.[9]

So, while making is still seen as central, it is of a different kind to that advocated by those art teachers who claim to value expression and exploration of materials above all else in their teaching. There are two main issues here with regard to curriculum content: the balance between the practical and the theoretical and the nature of the theoretical content. There is also a tension between student-centred and discipline-centred approaches.

The so-called cognitive approach[10] tends to be tied up with the notion that understanding and knowing about art is a crucial and integral part of art education. This of course has implications for curriculum time – it might mean, for example, that art history, art criticism and aesthetics compete in some way with studio practice. Art educators need therefore to be clear about not only what they are putting before students, but why. In considering the cognitive aspect of engaging with art and art making, Eisner makes the crucial point that art production requires students to think in particular and singular ways; the processes which are vital to the making of visual art 'stimulate, develop, and refine among the highest and most sophisticated forms of human cognition'.[11]

Art education is part of general education and can make a substantial contribution to being 'an educated person'. The eight aims outlined above will have underlying rationales which can be related to the broad ideals exemplified in, for example, the theme of the International Society for Education through Art (InSEA) 38th World Congress in Brisbane:

Learning to Know,
Learning to Be,
Learning to Do,
Learning to Live Together.

I will discuss each of these briefly in relation to aims for art education.

LEARNING TO KNOW

Several commentators, such as Louis Arnaud Reid,[12] have put forward the view that art is, or promotes, a particular way of knowing. As noted above, the notion that art education has in itself a sound epistemological base has been promoted by Elliot Eisner. However, Eisner warns against using the 'Transference' argument (that general cognitive development is enhanced through learning in art) as a convincing rationale for art education. Eisner has suggested that there might be *some* truth in the assertion that learning in art facilitates learning in other areas of the curriculum, but suggests that we should rather be asking what other subjects can do for learning in art.[13] David Perkins, a co-director of Harvard Project Zero, has written that interacting with art can help develop a particular kind of intelligence, specifically reflective intelligence, described as 'a control system for experiential intelligence'.[14] We should note that Perkins refers only to *interacting* with art, not making it. To my mind there is a kind of aridity associated with it, but education ministers of countries which do not at present have art as a part of the secondary school curriculum might well respond favourably to this aspect of art advocacy. Art as a way of knowing has a certain appeal to many art teachers who, aptly, appear to understand intuitively the importance of intuition and feeling in coming to understand the world around us.

LEARNING TO DO

Much contemporary art is concerned less with 'making' and more with social commentary. In some quarters this has been promoted in schools and colleges, to the extent that we now see a 'swinging back of the pendulum' to cries for a return to traditional art skills. Stuart Richmond,[15] a Canadian writing in the *Journal of Aesthetic Education*, represents what some might see as a backlash against art as a branch of sociology, and the reconstructivist view of art education. He argues for the importance of making to be recognized, writing that:

> The practice of art in education involves students in skill development, use of materials, and creative process ... fusing feeling, imagination, perception and skill; qualities that, together with knowledge of tradition, form the genesis of style and originality in art bearing universal significance.

Few of us would be happy to go under the surgeon's knife or dentist's drill if we knew that they had received no practical skills training. Such training is always going to be a part of the curriculum, but although it is important, the development of a practical skill in itself has never been the be-all of an education in art.

In Japanese culture, great emphasis is put upon the acquisition of craft skills. Rachel Mason, in her chapter above on the meaning and value of craft, notes that the functional aspect, and the skills associated with it, which is often absent in Western studio ceramics, is considered to be of great importance. In Japan, as in many Asian countries, the development of particular artistic skills needs to be viewed within the context of promoting knowledge of cultural heritage.

LEARNING TO LIVE TOGETHER

Educators adopting a post-modern stance with regard to the art curriculum have stressed the need for a pluralistic approach which, amongst other things, promotes cross-cultural understanding. Art lessons have a lot of potential for both perpetuating and challenging racial and cultural stereotyping. Such stereotyping can be, for example, perpetuated in art lessons through caricature, in activities such as making a 'Red Indian' doll, and strip cartoons of 'African Natives', both of which I have seen in schools. I have noted elsewhere[16] that there can also be a more insidious form of mis-education if students are ill-prepared or ill-informed about the art and artefacts of cultures other than their own. It is self-evident that understanding and appreciating the art of different cultures enables people to become more aware of, and sensitive to, a wide range of philosophies and beliefs, but it is not simply a matter of exposure. In day-to-day terms in the school situation, many teachers promote co-operative working as part of their normal classroom activities. This is something to be promoted and is an approach which is actively pursued by many art teachers; the art project which necessitates group co-operation should be the norm. After all, it is certainly not unusual in the world of work.

The notion of learning to live together is intrinsically bound up with learning about one's own culture and that of others. While the emphasis in art education in many Western countries still appears to be on expression, other countries have tended to promote the idea of using art in schools for students to learn about their cultural heritage. In some developing and newly industrialized countries it is seen as vital that traditional art and its attendant culture and values do not disappear. In Botswana, for example, one project initiated by an art education lecturer was concerned with painting the round wattle and daub houses in their traditional colours, at a time when such a practice was in danger of dying out. The Malaysian Ministry of Education sees education as a vital tool in nation-building:

> Education in Malaysia [...] is designed to produce Malaysian citizens who are knowledgeable and competent, who possess high moral standards, and who are responsible and capable of achieving a high level of personal well-being as well as being able to contribute to the betterment of the family, the society and the nation at large.[17]

To achieve this, art has a specific role, in particular to 'enhance knowledge of related traditional and cultural crafts as well as visual art heritage or cultural inheritance' and to 'apply knowledge of art gained toward betterment of life and the development of the nation' (p. 4).

In contrast to the conservative idea of teaching about cultural inheritance, some countries, particularly South American countries, value art greatly as an agent of social change. This is in keeping with the notion of art as a tool for social change, rather than an end in itself. In a pluralistic society, when one speaks of 'our cultural heritage', it is important to ask '*whose* cultural heritage?' Educators need therefore to be careful when referring to the heritage of 'others'.

LEARNING TO BE

There is a need for us to experience 'awe and wonder' in our day-to-day lives. Art can act as a conduit to our inner selves and it can also be a pointer towards something greater than itself. James Hall, in his chapter above on art education and spirituality, notes that students studying art are also studying themselves, and so we can see art as a route to self-knowledge. Before people can co-operate effectively with other people they must understand themselves; the production of art brings about a greater understanding of the self through exploration of personal ideas and feelings. In societies where young people are feeling increasingly alienated, the need for aspects of art education such as these to be part of the curriculum becomes more urgent. On a more mundane level perhaps, one of the principal benefits of a broad education in art is the enhanced capacity for exercising the imagination. Would the world have people of vision if there were to be no room for the development of imagination in young people's education?

CONCLUDING REMARKS

The key to the future of art education lies with new teachers and teachers in training. I conducted a questionnaire survey in three institutions[18] to find out about beginning art teachers' perceptions of the aims of art education and what they feel is likely to be the way forward for the subject. Using the eight broad aims listed above, trainee teachers of art in their final term of training were asked to rate the aims in order of importance and to comment on them; they were also asked to identify which aims are likely to be the most and least important in the future.

Interestingly, there was no apparent consensus, either within each group or between the three cohorts. This is healthy, and reveals the dynamic and fluid nature of art and design in education. However, there remains a tension between those who favour a more cognitive approach and those who promote a more 'practical' approach with an attendant emphasis upon expression and imagination; the most significant differences in the responses related to the aim of 'enhancing students' understanding of their inner world, of feelings and imagination', with approximately equal numbers of respondents feeling that this was the most and the least important aim for art education. Interestingly, with regard to what the respondents felt would be more or less important in the *future*, this particular aim was seen as being the least important, while 'understanding the cultural heritage of others' was seen by the majority as likely to be the most important.

So, what does it mean to be educated in art? Perhaps we need to turn to earlier commentators for some direction; in the first chapter of this book, I drew heavily upon the work of Herbert Read, and as a kind of complement to this, I now refer to Lansing, writing some twenty-five years later about general educational aims and the role of art in education, for a largely American audience.[19] He outlined a number of features which may be considered to be characteristic of 'the educated person' and outlined the role which art could play in developing such characteristics. These included reference to the role of art in educating that most voracious of beasts, the American consumer. Lansing wrote that educated consumers develop standards for guiding their expenditure; because the production and appreciation of art requires aesthetic sensitivity, it equips people with aesthetic criteria. Further to this, he asserted that the educated person is an informed and skilful buyer; as producers and appreciators of art develop aesthetic standards, they therefore become more informed and skilful in their buying. Lansing also highlighted many other aspects of art which contribute to a fully rounded education, which include the notion that art fosters individuality and, consequently, causes its creator to appreciate and respect uniqueness in others. While worthwhile, it can be seen that these sentiments are decidedly Western in flavour. It is not surprising that VCAE, with its commitment to challenging the visual hegemony of corporate institutions, has found fertile ground in America.

There are many current and ongoing projects which exemplify the changing nature of visual education. Rachel Mason, whose chapter in this book gives an international dimension to the study of craft, has, for example, initiated a large research project which examines the day-to-day use of making skills in a range of environments. An additional area of interest here in terms of the nature of education in society is the focus on learning outside of schooling. However, schools remain the principal location for the acquisition of skills in art practice and understanding of visual forms. The development of 'virtual' learning institutions is likely to be associated with and parallel to actual institutions; we are already seeing evidence of this in art education. Tom Davies and colleagues at the University of Central England[20] exemplify the kind of innovative work in art education which might point a way forward for the subject. Their project *International Collaboration and ePedagogy: a strategy for course design* features two dimensions of current practice which reflect recent developments: the centrality of ICT in art and design education and the increasingly international character of the subject. At school level, such practice is not uncommon: for example, school students at Netherhall school in Cambridge regularly swap animated storyboards with counterparts at Korunovacni school in Prague.[21]

In a balanced curriculum, which is not beholden to any centrally imposed ideology, there is room for visual culture to be an intrinsic part of a student's education in addition to, and associated with, practical studio work. The problem lies with schools and schooling, not with art education. Ideally, we need appropriately trained teachers of visual culture as well as teachers who are experts in studio skills. We might need to adopt what Steers referred to as 'multiple visions of art education',[22] which could accommodate all views. However, if VCAE is indeed an entirely new paradigm, a completely new way of interacting with visual form, then there are major implications for training and for curriculum time and associated resources. What remains clear is that the area of human experience which for now we can call 'art education' remains a vital force in realising our humanity, through both studio practice and meaningful interaction with the visual world.

Notes

1. Duncum, P. (2001). 'Visual culture: developments, definitions, and directions for art education'. *Studies in Art Education*, **42**(2), 101–12.
2. Duncum, P. (2002) 'Clarifying visual culture art education'. *Art Education*, May 2002, p. 7.
3. Eisner, E. (2001) 'Should we create New Aims for Art Education?'. *Art Education*, September 2001, p. 8.
4. Duncum, P. *op. cit.*, p. 8
5. This quotation is from an online article by Khami, M.M. (2002) entitled 'Where's the art in today's education?'. See http://www.aristos.org/whatart/arted-1.htm. *What Art Is Online* is a supplement to *What Art Is: The Esthetic Theory of Ayn Rand* by L. Torres and M.M. Kamhi (2000). This article relates to the section 'Teaching the Arts to Children' in Chapter 15: 'Public Implications'.
6. Barrett, M. (1979) *Art Education: A Strategy for Course Design*. London: Heinemann.
7. This was an updated version of the original paper [Steers, J. (1997) 'Ten Questions about the Future of Art Education'. *Australian Art Education*, 21 (1 & 2), 9–20] delivered to the ACTA conference, Melbourne, Australia, 23 May 1998.
8. These were first proposed at the 38th World Congress of INSEA. See Hickman, R. (1999), 'Rationales for teaching art – an international perspective', in *Proceedings of the 38th World Congress of the International Society for Education through Art*. Brisbane (electronic publication).
9. Duncum, P. (2002) *op. cit.*, p. 7.
10. See, for example, Efland, A. (2002) *Art and Cognition – Integrating the Visual Arts in the Curriculum*. New York: Teachers College Press.
11. Eisner, E. (2001) *op. cit.*, p. 9.
12. Reid, L.A. (1986) *Ways of Understanding and Education*. London: University of London Institute of Education. See also Ross, M. (1983) *The Arts: A Way of Knowing*. London: Pergamon Press
13. Eisner. E. (1998) 'Does experience in the arts boost academic achievement?'. *Journal of Art and Design Education*, **17**(1), 51–60. See also Winner, E. and Cooper, M. (2000) 'Mute those claims: no evidence (yet) for a causal link between arts study and academic achievement'. *The Journal of Aesthetic Education*, **34**(3–4), 11–76.
14. Perkins, D. (1994) *The Intelligent Eye – Learning to Think by Looking at Art*. Santa Monica: Getty, p. 15
15. Richmond, S. (1998) 'In praise of practice: a defence of art making in education'. *Journal of Aesthetic Education*, **32**(2), 11–20, p. 11.
16. Hickman, R. (1999) 'Representational art and Islam – a case for further investigation', in Mason, R. and Boughton, D. (eds) *Beyond Multi-Cultural Art Education – International Perspectives*. New York: Waxmann.

17. Curriculum Development Centre (Malaysia) (2000) *Revised Curriculum for 2003*. Kuala Lumpur: Ministry of Education. The 'Philosophy of Education' can be found on the Ministry of Education web-site: http://www.ppk.kpm.my/nep1.htm

18. The three institutions were the University of Cambridge, University of Exeter and University of London Institute of Education; these institutions were selected on the basis of having consistently received the highest praise for their art education programmes from government inspectors. The total number of responses was 47.

19. Lansing, K. (1971) *Art Artists and Art Education*. New York: McGraw-Hill

20. Davies, T., Pimentel, L., Orava, J. and Worrall, P. (2003) *International Collaboration and ePedagogy: A Strategy for Course Design*. For information on course developments in this area, see http://www.arted.uiah.fi/

21. See the art department's 'Czech IT Out!' page on the Netherhall School's website: www.netherhall.cambs.sch.uk

22. Steers, J. (1997) 'Ten questions about the future of art education'. *Australian Art Education*, **21** (1 & 2), 9–20.

Index

Lightning Source UK Ltd.
Milton Keynes UK
UKOW06f0801190216

268716UK00007B/244/P